Longfellow

❧❦❧

Longfellow

A Rediscovered Life

CHARLES C. CALHOUN

BEACON
150

BEACON PRESS
Boston

Beacon Press
25 Beacon Street
Boston, Massachusetts 02108-2892
www.beacon.org

Beacon Press books
are published under the auspices of
the Unitarian Universalist Association of Congregations.

07 06 05 04 8 7 6 5 4 3 2 1

This book is printed on acid-free paper that meets the uncoated paper
ANSI/NISO specifications for permanence as revised in 1992.

Frontispiece: M. August Edouart, silhouette of Henry
Wadsworth Longfellow, 1841. Courtesy National Park
Service, Longfellow National Historic Site.

Composition by Wilsted & Taylor Publishing Services

Library of Congress Cataloging-in-Publication Data

Calhoun, Charles C.
Longfellow : a rediscovered life / Charles C. Calhoun.
p. cm.
Includes bibliographical references (p.) and index.
ISBN 0-8070-7026-2 (cloth : alk. paper)
1. Longfellow, Henry Wadsworth, 1807–1882.
2. Poets, American—19th century—Biography. I. Title.

PS2281.C25 2004
811'.3—dc22   2003025980

For Michael Horvath

✎ CONTENTS ✎

◊ INTRODUCTION ◊

I N SEPTEMBER OF 2002, the National Park Service rededicated the
Longfellow National Historic Site, the house at 105 Brattle Street
in Cambridge, Massachusetts, where Henry Wadsworth Longfellow
lived from 1837 until his death in 1882. The event marked not only
the thirtieth anniversary of public ownership of the property, but the
completion of four years of badly needed restoration made possible by
the Save America's Treasures Act of 1997. Under a large tent on the
lawn where Longfellow's children had often played, some three hundred guests heard writers, politicians, federal officials, musicians, and
schoolchildren pay tribute to a man whose name most Americans still
recognize, but whose work scarcely anybody reads.

For a moment that afternoon, something else seemed restored: the
Longfellow house's centrality in our culture—that intermingling of
poetry and politics, of architecture and music, of cultural power and
sense of public duty that the Craigie House had represented for about
forty years in the middle of the nineteenth century.

The senior senator from Massachusetts recalled how his mother
encouraged all the Kennedy children to learn "The Midnight Ride
of Paul Revere" by heart. The junior senator from New York, Hilary
Clinton, said that lines from "A Psalm of Life"—"but to act, that each
tomorrow/Find us farther than to-day . . ."—had sustained her in her
legislative career. Senator Clinton confirmed that Edward Kennedy
had indeed recited "Paul Revere" from memory before Senator
Robert Byrd, chair of the Appropriations Committee—who had recited it back to him, during the hearings on the funding bill.

Historian David McCullough evoked the ghosts of an earlier
period—the dark winter of 1775–76 when General Washington lived
in the house and pondered the fate of American independence. Former U.S. Poet Laureate Robert Pinsky said that Longfellow's poetic

project had been to "make it new"—"it" being the sense of national identity that Americans of his day were still struggling, violently in 1861–65, to define. Members of the Boston Pops played the Largo from Dvořák's Ninth (with its echoes of *Hiawatha*), and a soprano sang Charles Ives's haunting setting of "The Children's Hour."

And then it was over. Like the Arabs in "The Day Is Done," someone eventually folded the tent and silently stole away.

Was this celebration an anomaly, or does Longfellow still live, even on the margins of our culture? If he does survive, whether as a diffuse poetical influence or as some broader cultural force, why do most people (literary historians included) know so little about him? There has long been a need for a comprehensive account of his life and career, written for the general public but drawing on a generation of new scholarship in history, literature, and the study of national identity.

The problem, of course, is that Longfellow was so very nice a man. He did not sleep with his sister, grow addicted to opium, have to flee college because of his gambling debts, cruise the waterfront, sire an illegitimate child abroad, or drink himself into dementia. He did not, in other words, behave the way the public has come to hope great poets will behave. While his life had an uncommon share of personal triumph and personal tragedy, his days in general were so placid, his livelihood so secure, his contemporary fame so universal, that in time he came to be seen as a symbol of everything that a writer should not be.

And that is where we find him today. To the extent that nineteenth-century poetry survives only in the classroom, Longfellow has dropped off the charts. He has never recovered from the battering he received at the hands of the Modernists, and he rarely caught the attention of the new, politically engaged scholarly communities of the 1980s and '90s (when he did, it was usually as a reminder of the complacencies, moral and aesthetic, of the successful white male Eurocentric poet-craftsman). Not that he ever really disappeared. He still has the respect of some practicing poets—read, for example, the enthusiastic essay by Dana Gioia in the *Columbia History of American*

Poetry (1993) or Pinsky's tributes to him as a Dante translator—and his words are ineradicably lodged in the mind of every American of a certain age who had to memorize "The Wreck of the Hesperus" or "The Village Blacksmith" in school. Others, innocent of Victorian poetry, nonetheless say they have "shot an arrow into the air" or passed "like ships in the night" or seen "footprints on the sands of time" or unwittingly echo the dozen or so other Longfellow quotes that have become part of the language. In a more general cultural sense, anyone outside of southern Louisiana who bites into some pan-blackened Cajun catfish or listens to zydeco is paying tribute, at only a slight remove, to Longfellow's role in rescuing the Acadians from historical oblivion.

Longfellow is not only a more admirable poet than his twentieth-century detractors would have admitted; his most enduring cultural achievement is to have created and disseminated much of what we think of as Victorian American culture. That we still have conflicted feelings about this culture seems evident, especially in the field of sexual and religious politics. Yet we need to recognize over how large a field Longfellow operated. He played a central role in establishing New England's cultural hegemony—in the sense that Americans were persuaded that "America" was New England writ large. He served as a major conduit into this country for European culture, from the radical German romanticism of the 1830s through his Dante studies in the 1860s and '70s. In turn, he represented the best of the new American culture to sympathetic Europeans. He did much to inspire Colonial Revivalism in architecture and the decorative arts in the 1870s, just as he had helped to popularize Medieval Revivalism in the 1830s and 1840s. He virtually invented the Evangeline story, the foundational myth of modern Acadian culture in Canada, Maine, and Louisiana. He supplied his fellow citizens with such emblematic literary characters as Hiawatha, Paul Revere, Priscilla Alden, and Miles Standish. He expressed in his work, and represented in his life, a style of masculinity in bold contrast to the Social Darwinists and muscular Christians of the next generation. However genteel and unthreatening his verse seems to us, he did produce over a long career an alternative vision to the America of the relentless market economy.

My interest in writing this book goes back to the time, ten years ago, when I was researching a history of Bowdoin College. In trying to determine to what extent the college could be said to have "produced" some of its most famous graduates, I was surprised to find that, while Hawthorne's life had been minutely examined, there was no competent modern biography of his classmate Longfellow. I had not realized quite how precipitously so famous a man had fallen out of academic regard. Newton Arvin's *Longfellow: His Life and Work* had appeared in 1962 and been reprinted in 1977, but it was more a critical study (the best to date) of the poetry than a biography drawing on primary sources. It showed the strain of Arvin's own struggle to balance his genuine affection for the poet with his intellectual allegiance to the New Criticism and its virtues of irony, ambiguity, and the stiff upper lip. Edward Wagenknecht's 1955 biography was old-fashioned, stately, and short. Earlier twentieth-century biographies—with the exception of Lawrance Thompson's somewhat overwrought *Young Longfellow* in 1938—were rewritings of the Reverend Samuel Longfellow's three-volume memorial (1886), which had served to embalm his brother as the "good gray poet" of the Craigie House fireside. The absence of a reliable biography, asking the questions a modern biographer is expected to ask, seemed an astonishing empty spot in the otherwise busy field of nineteenth-century American literary scholarship. The closest thing to it was the excellent information provided in the notes in Andrew Hilen's six-volume edition of Longfellow's letters, published between 1967 and 1982, but only a specialist would have read such a work in whole, and only about a third of Longfellow's vast correspondence had survived.

The notion that such a biography was worth writing found many small encouragements—not least, the number of visitors I saw each summer lining up to visit the poet's boyhood home in downtown Portland, Maine. In visiting other historic houses, while working on a cultural guide to Maine, I was struck by the frequency with which busts of Dante appeared in these otherwise solidly Anglo-American interiors. This image began jumping out at me everywhere—antiques shops, country auctions, small-town libraries. Why, among these Protestants, these often nativist Yankees, all the beak-nosed, hooded Dantes, brooding in plaster or marble or bronze? Meanwhile, I had begun reading about the Dante Club that met in Longfellow's study in the 1860s and the immense cultural authority of his translation of the *Divine Comedy*, and it became clearer how cultural influences could survive even the decline of the reputation that had set them in motion. Late-nineteenth-century Boston's identification of itself with that other mercantile republic, Florence, was no coincidence. A line of descent could be traced from Longfellow's Dante studies through Charles Eliot Norton's lectures on Florentine art, to Isabella Stewart Gardner, to Bernard Berenson, to the great American museums of the early twentieth century.

Nor were the cultural reverberations all that antiquarian. In 1996, for example, I attended the Maine Humanities Council's "premiere" of the newly restored print of the 1929 silent film *Evangeline*, starring Dolores Del Rio. The music was spirited (improvised for the occasion), even if the acting seemed stiff and mawkish. Then, suddenly, we saw the British soldiers on the beach (many of them, in historical reality, New Englanders) forcing the frightened Acadian women and children into the boats that would carry them into exile and poverty. There was a brief but palpable moment of tension in the room. A vintage film had become a real movie. The papers and television screens that week had been filled with images from Bosnia—of refugees torn from their homes, of families with all their surviving goods on a cart, of soldiers terrorizing women and children.

In the intervening years, many other small discoveries have confirmed those two experiences—namely, that Longfellow, almost two hundred years after his birth, exerts a cultural force that goes far beyond his poetry and that he was a master storyteller whose narratives can still resonate for a modern audience. His poetic oeuvre itself will most likely survive, at least in fragments—for example, the short lyrics such as "Aftermath" and "The Tide Rises, the Tide Falls" that find their way into anthologies. But his real legacy—his claim to our attention—is surely extraliterary.

Let me give two examples of this. In 1994, Harvard University established its Longfellow Institute, named in tribute not to Longfellow's poetry but to his pioneering role in teaching comparative literature in this country. The institute is devoted to the study and republication of historically, aesthetically, and culturally significant works written in what is now the United States but published in languages other than English. It turns out that there is an astonishing variety of such work, in more than forty languages; a fifty-volume series is contemplated over the next decade. Longfellow himself would have been astonished that Americans can graduate from college and think themselves educated without being able to read one or more foreign languages. (He was fluent in French, Spanish, German, and Italian and could read at least half a dozen other modern languages and two ancient ones.) The linkage of his name and this ambitious modern project suggests a new way of looking at the poet—as a pioneer multiculturalist championing the "civil rights of language" of this country's neglected non-English writers and thinkers.

The other side of this twenty-first-century Longfellow is our new appreciation of his role as a nation builder. Benedict Anderson, among others, has helped us understand how important a role "invented" memory and mythopoetics play in those sometimes shaky constructs we call nations. Recently, the Maine Historical Society held the first major exhibition ever dedicated to the poet's career, titled "Longfellow: The Man Who Invented America"—a bit of a stretch, perhaps, but a useful corrective. In this light, it is significant that one of the major thrusts of activity today at the Longfellow National Historic Site (the Craigie House, named for its post–Revolutionary War era owner, but Longfellow's home for almost half a century) is the scholarly study of the poet's role in inspiring the Colonial Revival move-

ment in late-nineteenth- and early-twentieth-century America. An
amazing variety of cultural artifacts—from the much-reproduced
image of Priscilla at her Pilgrim Century spinning wheel to the replicas of the Craigie House itself that were built all over the country—
attest to the Longfellow influence on the ways in which Americans
continue to construct their national identity. Henry and Fanny
Longfellow's determination in the 1840s to maintain the house as a
shrine to George Washington—who had lived there for nine months
during the Siege of Boston and who had perfected his own notion of a
separate American republic in the very rooms in which the poet slept
and worked—was itself a powerful stimulant to the historic preservation movement. Historians once wrote off such efforts as the back-
ward-looking defense mechanisms of a threatened elite. Today, there
is a more nuanced appreciation of how importantly historic preservation is linked with environmentalism, urban civility, and a Ruskinian
sense of the moral implications of the visual.

This drift into art history suggests another way of revivifying
Longfellow. Recently, exhibitions of the work of the painters Eastman
Johnson (a Maine-born painter whose early career Longfellow supported) and Martin Johnson Heade (a painter whose love of the New
England salt marshes Longfellow shared) drew both critical attention
and good-sized crowds in Brooklyn and Boston, respectively. The
achievements of these two nineteenth-century American painters will
never rival those of Eakins and Homer, any more than we can read
Longfellow today with the sense of self-recognition that we bring to
Whitman and Dickinson. Yet at the same time we cannot ignore any
of this work if we want to understand the American nineteenth century. Art historians (encouraged, admittedly, by the art market) seem
to have grasped this fact more readily than their colleagues in the
English departments.

There is a note of apology, even of defensiveness, that still attaches
itself to any serious look at Longfellow's life and career. Let's try to
abandon it for the moment. His contemporaries saw him not just as a

world-famous poet and an admirable man but as a vitalizing force at the very center of their culture. We cannot put him back there. But we can seek to rediscover the sources of this enormous cultural power and the ways in which he stamped his imprint on three generations of Americans.

The Craigie House, January 30, 1882

IN THE HALF-LIGHT OF A MORNING BLIZZARD,
Cambridge would have been easy to miss. Its ice-filled tidal river
scraped against the backside of gardens and houses, stables and stores,
erasing any clear definition of what might be water, what might be
land. For an Oxford man, its collegiate buildings were of no special distinction. Passing through Harvard Square and turning into Brattle
Street, he could make out a row of frame dwellings that had survived
from colonial times. And then there it was: pale yellow, set well back
from the road, bracketed by bare elms, the grandest house of them all.
Amid the flying snow, it might have seemed, in its ample but provincial way, something far northern and neoclassical—Gustavian, even
tsarist—a frost-castle conjured up in a fairy tale.

It was in fact Castle Craigie, as its intimates liked to call it, a subtle
reminder that the house had been there longer than the United States
had been a republic. The young man was Oscar Wilde, come to bur-
nish his reputation in the New World. His cab pulled into the circular
drive to the west of the house, and passing through the Blue Entry
he soon faced the pleasure of a hot breakfast on a cold day. His host
was Henry Wadsworth Longfellow, the most widely read poet in the
English-speaking world.

The old house had been the scene of many odd and interesting encounters, but this was perhaps the most singular. One age was brush-
ing shoulders with another, as in a Max Beerbohm cartoon. It was a
generous move on Longfellow's part, for he was seriously ill—would
be dead before spring—and had extended the invitation simply because of the insistence of his old New York friend (and now enthusiastic Wildolator) Sam Ward. Longfellow had trouble saying no to

anyone, but particularly to a dear friend he had met on his own first voyage across the Atlantic, half a century earlier. Wilde's immediate task was to publicize Gilbert and Sullivan's American tour of *Patience* —an operetta that satirized the Aesthetic Movement of which he was so decorative a part—but he also wanted to try out Oscar Wilde, as it were, on a new and untested audience. In a few days he was to lecture at the Boston Music Hall—a notorious event, it was to prove, in the annals of Harvard philistinism, for the sixty undergraduates who paraded into the hall dressed as Oscar Wilde (velvet breeches, floppy hats, a sunflower in a limp hand) were chagrined to find their target dressed in the most elegant of evening clothes. (He had been warned of the prank in advance.)

Had Wilde had time to poke about a bit, he would have been surprised to discover that aestheticism had reached the Craigie House about ten years before him. Longfellow's otherwise conventional elder son, Charley, had decorated every surface of his rooms upstairs— ceiling included—with Japanese silks, woodcuts, porcelains, swords, screens, and bric-a-brac, possibly as a reminder of his Japanese mistress of a decade earlier. But the downstairs was in earnest: souvenirs of General Washington, society portraits of the previous generation, High Victorian clutter. Not a kimono in sight. Yet it was Longfellow himself—this American answer to Tennyson—whom Wilde had come to see. The poet was as much a local landmark as the Old North Church or Bunker Hill, a survival, a man who had known Dickens and Carlyle and Thackeray and Fanny Kemble.

Aside from Sam Ward, the two had at least one other thing in common: Longfellow had corresponded with Wilde's mother, Lady Wilde, herself a poet of repute back in Dublin. For her son, the Craigie House breakfast was a relatively quiet interlude in the social frenzy of his American tour. He was to be the last in a chain of distinguished British visitors who had enjoyed the legendary hospitality of the Craigie House since the 1840s. On his part, Longfellow surely remembered the kindness of the literary men who had welcomed him in 1826, when, at about Wilde's age, he had first set foot in Europe.

We do not really know much of what they talked about over that breakfast—Wilde's later anecdotes of the trip are not entirely to be trusted—but it would be fun to think that the subject of Salome had come up (Longfellow had depicted her in a religious drama of his own in 1872). Afterwards, Wilde was to repeat with glee his host's account of an audience with Queen Victoria at Windsor in 1869: When he had modestly expressed surprise at his own fame in England, Her Majesty had replied, "O, I assure you, Mr. Longfellow, you are very well known. All my servants read you."

"Sometimes," Longfellow confessed to Wilde, "I will wake up in the night and wonder if it was a deliberate slight." Wilde was certain it was "the rebuke of Majesty to the vanity of the poet." But was it? The late Prince Albert would not have thought so. A poet who could bring down from Parnassus uplifting words that even the working classes would cherish and memorize—now *there* was a Victorian.

And that was just the problem. To Wilde this high-mindedness was not poetry. To Longfellow, nothing else would do. But they seemed to have enjoyed their breakfast. Wilde—still twelve years away from the scandal that would destroy him—was genuinely touched by the old man: "Longfellow was himself a beautiful poem, more beautiful than anything he ever wrote." Longfellow—aware that his own fame was dimming—was far more tolerant of Wilde's performance than had been the sexually panicked young Henry James a week earlier in New York.

The wit who sought to provoke said good-bye to the poet who tried very hard to please. Meanwhile, the snow had turned into howling rain.

One

THE CITY BY THE SEA

Portland, in the District of Maine

A NOTHER HOUSE, a more distant place. The original settlement of Portland had been strung across a three-mile-long peninsula. Longfellow grew up in the house his grandfather had built along the ridge of that peninsula, roughly halfway between its fortified eastern tip at Mountjoy's Hill and steep, wooded Bramhall's Hill to the west. From the windows of the third story, where Henry and his older brother Stephen and their maiden aunt Lucia had their chambers, you could look south and east to the wharf-lined Fore River and Casco Bay, and out beyond to Portland Head Light, Cape Elizabeth, and the cold Atlantic; to the north and west, across the mussel beds of the Back Cove, were the meadows of Gorham, home of many of the Longfellows, and the distant hills that sheltered Hiram, where the Wadsworths had their farm. When the weather was clear in this land of frequent fog and damp, you could see Mount Washington, seventy miles away in the White Mountains of New Hampshire. The doubleness of this view—the running back and forth from one window to another to encompass it all—was to color the younger boy's poetry and his life. On the one side, the new American republic; on the other, the passage to Europe. Portland was a small place, and at night, when the wind had died down, you could hear the swift, incoming tide slapping at the harbor pilings, down one slope of the hill, and the gentler rhythm of the waves stroking the shoals in the broad cove out back.

Longfellow had not been born in this house. On February 27, 1807, the day of his birth, his parents, Stephen and Zilpah, were living with Stephen's sister, at the corner of Fore and Hancock streets, in a three-story frame house in the Federal style, separated by a small beach from the harbor. It was an easterly part of town, so distant that people called it "Jaffa," although a century earlier this had been the "court end" of Portland, full of large dwellings, and almost a century before that, it had been the site of the first European settlement on the Neck. The house belonged to Captain Samuel Stephenson, who had asked the young couple to keep his wife Abigail company during the winter while he was at sea. Like many coastal New Englanders who depended on maritime trade, Stephenson would, by the end of that year, find his livelihood threatened by Jefferson's embargo—indeed, he would face bankruptcy. About eight months after Henry was born, rather than return to their own house on Temple Street, the Longfellows moved to Zilpah's father's house, on Congress Street, a two-story red-brick Georgian house built in 1785–86 with a large store attached. It was at the heart of the town, a few steps from the marketplace, the First Parish Church, and the courthouse, where Stephen practiced as an attorney.

Zilpah's father, General Peleg Wadsworth, was one of those men who had done well in the Revolution. He had set himself up as a country squire by purchasing from a grateful commonwealth, at the good rate of 12.5¢ per acre, some 7,800 acres of land in the western hills, between the Ossipee and Saco Rivers, where he established the town of Hiram and built Wadsworth Hall. Although today only an hour's drive from Portland, Wadsworth Hall—still inhabited by his descendants—seems defended by its hilly fastness, very much the property of someone who wants to protect himself from a surprise raid from the sea. This rather martial air is even more pronounced when you enter the front door. The exterior looks very much like other big, white-clapboard farmhouses of Federal New England, but the floor plan is almost medieval: rooms open off a huge central hall, whose unpainted pine has darkened over two centuries to a rich tobacco hue. It served for militia drills, church services, family gatherings, country dances. There is nothing else quite like it in Maine.

But Wadsworth was shrewd enough to know that money came more quickly in a flourishing port than in rural Hiram; at the same time, he established himself as a merchant in town. In 1784, in what was then still a rural neighborhood, he built a barn and store on the well-traveled route leading to the town's hay scales. By January 1785, he had opened for business, advertising in the *Falmouth Gazette* "an assortment of goods" available on credit, in exchange for lumber, or for public securities of every kind. That was one vocation the Revolution had affirmed for New England: a gentleman lost no face by engaging in trade. Wadsworth was soon shipping pigs as well as flour and firewood to his Portland neighbors from the Hiram farm. In fact, his letters to his son Charles from Washington, while attending Congress, have less to do with politics than with advice on sending hogs into the woods for acorns and beechnuts, or luring pigeons with corn, or pickling beef, or which beans to plant. The general was closer to Jefferson's ideal agrarian republican than to a Yankee trader. Yet, as a staunch Federalist, there was no one he distrusted more than Jefferson, unless it was the French.

Our first glimpse of Henry is on his grandfather's knee. Writing to her husband in town while visiting her parents in Hiram, Zilpah reports that the seven-month-old boy "is very fond of Grandpa's singing and trotting on the knee." For a poet who would be known for his musicality and his galloping rhythms, it was an auspicious start.

The boy would also become a storyteller (and reteller) of mythic potency, and one of the best stories he ever heard concerned his own grandfather.

Peleg Wadsworth, born of Pilgrim ancestry in Duxbury, Massachusetts, had come of age in the years leading up to the American Revolution. A Harvard graduate of the class of 1769, with military tastes, he saw action at the Siege of Boston and played a central role in the ill-fated Penobscot Expedition of 1779, a debacle of such magnitude that it is scarcely mentioned in American history texts. The colonials' effort to dislodge the British from Bagaduce (modern Castine), at the mouth of the Penobscot River in Maine, and thereby reduce the threat to Massachusetts from the east, had led instead to the destruction of the American fleet, largely as a result of its commanders' incompetence. Thanks to his coolheadedness in the retreat, Wadsworth was, in the words of one historian, "the only American officer to emerge from the Penobscot disaster with an enhanced reputation." Paul Revere, among the other commanders, was disgraced and had to face a pro forma court martial.

A year later, the General Court (as the Massachusetts legislature was called) put the thirty-two-year-old Wadsworth in command of the District of Maine, to use the term applied until 1820 to the three easternmost counties of Massachusetts. Finding he had only some five hundred troops spread along a lengthy coastline in a region verging on civil war, Wadsworth resorted to a heavy-handed imposition of martial law and felt obligated to hang one feeble-minded man who had unwittingly guided a party of Loyalist raiders.

With the Royal Navy across the Gulf of Maine at Halifax, the British army firmly in control of the Penobscot valley, much of the population wavering in its loyalties, and Boston unable to supply or pay his forces, Wadsworth was about to resign his command, when, on a February night in 1781, a party of twenty-five British regulars, alerted by a Tory sympathizer, surrounded the house at Thomaston in which the Wadsworth family was sleeping. Easily chasing away the sentry, the raiding party shot its way into the house, where it met spirited resistance from the young general, wielding a pair of pistols, a blunderbuss, and a fusee. But a British bullet tore into Wadsworth's left arm, and he had to surrender. To the horror of his family, the raiders marched the severely wounded general away in the snow, and imprisoned him at Fort George (the site of which can still be seen at modern Castine).

What followed reads like an adventure story. His arm slowly healed, and he received from his captors the gentlemanly treatment accorded to prisoners of rank in the eighteenth century—even lending him books, inviting him to the officers' mess, and allowing his wife to visit. He was heartened to learn that his young son Charles, who had not been seen amid the confusion and violence and was feared dead, had slept through the entire raid. But it soon became clear to

Wadsworth that he was not going to be ransomed or exchanged, but rather shipped to Halifax and possibly to London for the duration of the war. In 1781, it was far from clear that the Americans would win their independence, and the general himself might very well have been hanged as a rebel. In any event, he feared a long separation from his family and the deprivations of a prison ship.

He and a fellow prisoner determined that they would escape, whatever the risk. They knew they had little time. They had carefully studied the plan of Fort George, the movements of the sentries, and the construction of the attic of the building in which they had been locked up. Borrowing a gimlet from an unsuspecting servant, they painstakingly sawed, night after night, through a section of plank in the ceiling of their chamber. To disguise their efforts, they filled the holes with chewed up bread, which happened to be the same color as the wood. One night, a heavy thunderstorm gave them the opportunity they thought might never again come. Protected by the noise of the pelting rain and the darkness, they climbed into the attic—Wadsworth with great difficulty, because of his injured arm—and crawled along the rafters, unnoticed by their guards in the room below. They were stealthy enough not even to alarm the chickens roosting in the rafters. They dropped through an opening in the ceiling, slipped out the door of their prison, scaled a slippery embankment, negotiated the dangerously sharp pickets and chevaux-de-frise of the fortifications, and crossed the mud flats to at least temporary safety. Wadsworth had become separated from his companion in the dark, but they found each other in the forest and, after several close calls and a slow and difficult journey overland, they reappeared before their astonished friends at Thomaston. The general's family meanwhile had returned to the safety of Plymouth.

The story, with all its subplots and digressions, must have been told again and again, as the family epic, in the "great room" of Wadsworth Hall, to the general's own ten children and eventually to a small army of grandchildren, nephews, nieces, and cousins. The most complete version that has come down to us is told by the Reverend Timothy

Dwight in the second volume of his widely read *Travels in New-England and New York* (1821). He heard the story from John Abbot, the librarian of Bowdoin College, who had heard it from Zilpah Longfellow, the general's daughter. Dwight retells it in cinematic detail—with some dramatic small touches, such as the near-betrayal of their escape by the chickens roosting under the eaves and by the melting of the butter in the chewed bread—and he turns their adventure into a Federalist parable. (An orthodox Congregationalist and president of Yale, Dwight also does not fail to point out that one of the locals who betrayed the general was a Methodist preacher.) However fictive some of the details may have been, Wadsworth emerges in Dwight's account not only as a man of physical daring and Yankee inventiveness but as a fervent republican, willing to risk his life rather than submit to a tyrannical power that tears him from his bed in the middle of the night and terrorizes his family. And Dwight does not fail to say a word for the ladies—Henry's grandmother and her companion, Miss Fenno—and for heroic republican motherhood. He describes the blood-soaked house the raiders left behind:

> To add to the sufferings of these unfortunate ladies, a number of the neighboring inhabitants, having heard of the disaster, flocked in, and filled the house. Here they did nothing but gaze about with an idle curiosity, or make useless, numerous, and very troublesome, inquiries. Scarcely any thing could be more wearisome, or more provoking. At length the ladies assumed resolution enough to reprove them with some severity; and thus restored them from the stupor, produced by these novel and disastrous events, to thought, feeling, and exertion. And as soon as they had fairly recovered themselves, they very cordially, and kindly, united their efforts to render the best offices in their power. The next morning they repaired the doors and windows; cleansed the floors; dressed [a] wounded man in the best manner in their power; and placed the family in as comfortable circumstances, as the case would admit.

The general's grandson was to go through much of his life not as Henry Longfellow but as Henry Wadsworth Longfellow, and his name encapsulates another exemplary tale for any young man growing up in the new republic. Henry Wadsworth, Zilpah's favorite brother, went to sea in 1804, at age nineteen, as a midshipman with the fleet commanded by their Portland neighbor, Commodore Edward Preble. After years of humiliation at sea by the British and the French in the Napoleonic Wars, the United States government sought to establish its navy's prestige by curbing the Barbary pirates of North Africa, whose demands for tribute from American merchants sailing the Mediterranean were a hindrance to commerce. Attempting to set fire to the pirate fleet that had taken refuge in Tripoli harbor, in what is now Libya, Preble sent in a small vessel, the *Intrepid*, under cover of darkness with a crew of volunteers, including Lieutenant Wadsworth. Since the pirates could not be lured into open sea, the plan was to sail the *Intrepid*, laden with gunpowder, close enough to the enemy fleet for the tide to carry it into the inner harbor, where it would explode. The crew of ten, led by young Wadsworth and another officer, would escape in a small boat. There is no reliable account of exactly what went wrong. Possibly the Americans met unexpected resistance, or underestimated the strength of the current, or miscalculated the timing of the fuse. Their mangled bodies washed ashore the next day. The official version was that the heroic young Wadsworth and the other Americans had sacrificed themselves—or, in the words of the family memorialist sixty-two years later: "'Preferring death to slavery,' he had voluntarily perished, with his companions, in the fire-ship *Intrepid*, which was blown up before Tripoli in the night of Sept. 4, 1804, to save it from falling into the enemy's hands."

Zilpah's desire to perpetuate her beloved brother's memory in her own second son reflects more than the family's sense of patriotic mission. She knew that she would probably never be called upon to duplicate the heroism her mother had shown on that snowy night in 1781—"the windows dashed, the Doors broken, the House torn to pieces and Blood and Slaughter all around," in Dwight's words. Yet she had a sense of republican motherhood that went beyond merely being a general's daughter. The most significant moment of her girlhood, for example, occurred on June 25, 1799, when a very nervous Zilpah stood at the door of the Congress Street house and presented to a possibly equally nervous young ensign at the head of the First Company of Federal Volunteers a silk banner, representing the arms of the United States joined with those of the Commonwealth, with the motto "Defend the Laws." It was the work of "the Young Ladies of Portland," or at least those genteel enough to be invited into General Wadsworth's house. "My dress was simple white muslin, white kid gloves, blue kid slippers, a high white muslin turban with white feathers," she wrote her cousin. "Plain as possible. Ensign Wiggins delivered an address of thanks to the 'Daughters of Columbia.'" Zilpah was mortified to find her name in the newspapers but enjoyed the ball that evening.

She was a gifted observer of the world immediately around her; her girlhood letters and journals are still a delight to read. She caught the sense of wonder at how one generation "passes" to another in a domestic idyll which she recorded in a letter from the parlor of the Portland house in 1797 to a friend:

> It is now evening. There sits Mama on her lolling chair by the fire. Betsy is playing on the Piano "Ye Tribes of Adam join." John and Lucia are singing at the back of her chair. George Alexander and Sam are singing in different parts of the room. Little Peleg is stepping about the floor surveying one and another. Charles is sitting at the table with me he was writing his pen dropt from his fingers, and he listens to the music. Harry is reading beside me, you know he is always self collected. I fancy however that he does not understand much what he reads. You know how my ladyship is employed. Excuse my being thus particular in describing the family, I have been singing while I wrote and could not write any thing that required reflection. Ten children! what a circle! I should like to know what are mamas thoughts as she looks around on us.

Their father was away at Congress, where he served seven terms as a Federalist representative from 1792 to 1806. The notion of public service and patient sacrifice, of the mother holding the family together, was to be a powerful one, and subject to some testing, in Zilpah's own marriage to Stephen Longfellow.

In their later lives, both Zilpah and Stephen were subject to such long periods of invalidism, it is difficult to imagine them young—dancing, singing, sleigh riding, exchanging glances during services in the meeting house, playing blind man's bluff, reading poetry aloud. Portland was a prosperous and growing city, but in the 1790s it did not offer the urban diversions of Boston or New York. The life of its leading families was intensely social, however, and based on extended family ties and genteel rituals of courtship. Dancing was a particular passion among the young—a warming activity in a cold climate. The image of Zilpah that survives in her many letters to her Boston cousin Nancy Doane is of a vividly social, unusually self-possessed young woman, not in the least hurry to find a husband. Young men—the "beaux"—had to be taken seriously, but they, too, could be judged on their physical merits; her letters are full of sharp observations on male beauty and with mocking names—"Adonis," "Narcissus," "Despairing Pyramus," "Beauty Boyd"—assigned to the eligible suitors, including the occasional "Boston buck" who came to town. Stephen was not one of Zilpah's beaux, although as a promising young Harvard-educated lawyer, he was becoming well known to the family. She was pleased to note, in the fall of 1800, that he was increasingly attentive to her older sister Betsy, visiting the house two or three times a day during her illnesses, and being one of the few young gentlemen allowed upstairs in her sickroom. Betsy's health fluctuated—at one point, she seemed near death, then quickly rallied—and the attachment deepened. Stephen became a regular. On the last day of the year 1801, Zilpah described the three of them sitting in the small back parlor overlooking the garden (the "rainy day room" of the present house museum)—"the room in which we used to read, to digress, to return but to digress again." The view is not so pleasant as in summer, she notes, but they make the room so by the company of their friends. Betsy has her honey for her cough, and her laudanum syrup for her pain; Stephen takes her pulse.

FIGURE 1: Stephen and Zilpah Longfellow, c. 1805.
Courtesy Maine Historical Society.

In September of 1802, Betsy, lying in the front room, with an affectionate smile "playing around the mouth [as] at the approach of a
friend," died of consumption. "I presume you know of which I room I
speak," Zilpah wrote Nancy. "It is the largest parlor, unfrequented by
the family, excepting such as retire for meditation. Hours and hours
have I walked here, frequently with Stephen. I have had a great deal of
conversation with him on serious subjects. Nancy he is very good, I
was convinced of it when Betsy approved him, but I knew it not so fully
until this severe trial; his purity of mind, his goodness, his resignation
and his fortitude are unequalled, excepting by that dear friend whose
death called these virtues into action . . . 'You will still be my sisters.'
He said to Lucia and me after the funeral. And is it strange that I love
him as a dear brother?"

For her sister Lucia, fraternal affection sufficed. She had no interest
in marriage, found comfort in the friendship of several other women,
knew she would be adequately provided for by her father, and spent

most of her long life managing the house and helping raise four nieces and four nephews. But Zilpah—who, at least in her letters to Nancy, had suggested that growing old unmarried among "the smiles & approbation of our friends" was not so deplorable a fate—began to feel differently. So did Stephen, and on New Year's Day 1804 they were married, before what one hopes was a roaring fire, in the same parlor in which Betsy had died. Their first son, the fifth Stephen in the line, was born in 1805. Henry in 1807 was followed by Elizabeth in 1808, Anne in 1810, Alexander Wadsworth in 1814, Mary in 1816, Ellen in 1818, and Samuel in 1819.

⚜

Compared to the Wadsworths, the Longfellows might have seemed a dull lot. They did have deeper roots in Maine. For three generations, Longfellows—all named Stephen—had been loyal servants of the commonwealth. Zilpah's husband was to continue this tradition and expected his eldest son to do likewise. The family was descended from William Longfellow, a Yorkshireman who had settled in Byfield Parish, Newbury, in the Massachusetts Bay Colony, in 1678, and who had married into the powerful Sewall clan. From early on, the family name had provoked mirth: Anne Sewall, after the death of William, married Henry Short; "and, as Savage says in his Genealogical Dictionary, 'had both Longfellows and Shorts'" (Shipton, *New England Life in the Eighteenth Century*, 1996). The first Stephen in the long line, a prosperous farmer and artisan and a lieutenant in the Indian wars, was almost illiterate but was to be memorialized by his great-great-grandson in 1839 in "The Village Blacksmith."

The second Stephen (1722/3–1790) was a member of the Harvard class of 1742, suggesting the respect for learning that permeated even the middling folk of the Massachusetts Bay Colony—and the clout of a Sewall connection. He became a schoolmaster in York, in the District of Maine, moving in 1744 to teach in Falmouth (modern Portland), at a time when its people still felt the danger of being so close to the French in Canada and their Indian allies. Men of learning were scarce on the Maine frontier, and Longfellow soon rose to serve as parish clerk, town clerk, notary public, clerk of courts, register of probate, and finally justice of the peace of the quorum (a job in which he did well, despite lack of any formal legal training). Among his many other public services (in the eyes of his compatriots), he helped finance a scalping expedition—expecting a profit from the bounties paid for dead Indians—and helped care for Maine's quota of Acadian exiles after their expulsion from Nova Scotia in 1755. He does not seem to have been an ardent patriot, however, and was even suspected of loyalist sentiments, but this did not prevent his house on Fore Street and other property from being burned by the British in the shelling of Portland in 1775. He took refuge at his farm at Gorham and stayed there. He was known for his good humor and for weighing 245 pounds. As Clifford Shipton dryly notes, "His interleaved almanacs for 1768–1790 ... are one of the most disappointing of historical documents. They are concerned almost entirely with the management of the farm, and dismiss the burning of Falmouth in five words."

The third Stephen (1750–1824) was the leading citizen of Gorham. In early life, like so many ambitious young men on the Maine frontier, he had perfected his skills as a surveyor, a valuable talent in a region where so many land titles were subject to dispute. He was elected nine times to represent Gorham in the General Court at Boston, was a founding Overseer of Bowdoin College, and served as Judge of the Court of Common Pleas from 1797 to 1811. His substantial two-story, yellow-clapboard farmhouse, with its center chimney and dog-leg staircase, still stands as Longfellow Farm, a few miles from Gorham village.

The fourth Stephen (1776–1849) followed the family pattern of a Harvard education, class of 1798 and Phi Beta Kappa. He was considered unusually mature for his age—or, as a classmate less charitably put it, his mind "was not rapid in its movement, nor brilliant in its course, but its conclusions were sound and correct." This impression of him as solid but slightly plodding—it comes through in the portrait he sat for during his one term as a Congressman—was to be confirmed

throughout his life. At the same time, he was considered "a born gentleman" (Phi Beta Kappa at that time being as much a social distinction as an intellectual one), well mannered, and good company. He
liked to point out that his classmates had included such luminaries
as the jurist Joseph Story and the liberal theologian William Ellery
Channing. He studied law with Salmon Chase and was admitted to
the Cumberland County Bar in 1801, the eighth lawyer in a town of
3,800.

Like many well-brought-up young men of his generation, he could
not depend on the degree of deference his father and grandfather had
taken as their due, yet he proved less successful than some of his peers
in adapting to the more democratic world of post-Revolutionary New
England. Like most others of his social class in Maine, he identified
with the Federalist Party and feared the excesses of democracy and its
tendency toward leveling. Like many others of his Harvard generation, his religious sympathies were Unitarian, though he came to this
stance gradually. The church of his youth had proudly traced its
Calvinism back to the founding generation of the Massachusetts Bay
Colony. But its theology had mellowed, under the influence of the
rationalism of eighteenth-century transatlantic thought, and his
Portland congregation had, in cautious steps, abandoned its Trinitarian doctrines and its conviction of the depravity of mankind. Stephen's
combination of political conservatism and theological liberalism may
strike a modern reader as incongruous, but it was at the very heart
of the worldview of the educated lawyers, ministers, and merchants
of eastern Massachusetts.

At the same time, Stephen could point to his childhood on the
Longfellow farm at Gorham as evidence of his solid roots in the
soil. As William Willis writes in his history of the law in Maine,
"Sometimes, in his addresses to the jury, he adroitly drew illustrations
from his farmer's apprenticeship, to point his argument or secure
their favorable attention." In the boomtown atmosphere of post-
Revolutionary Portland, there was money to be made, especially by
lawyers engaged in the fierce litigation over property claims in the

FIGURE 2: The house (now demolished) on the Portland, Maine,
waterfront in which Henry Longfellow was born, on February 27, 1807.
Courtesy Maine Historical Society.

poorly surveyed wilderness lands along Maine's great river valleys.
The rights of absentee proprietors, many of them Boston merchants
tracing their title to conflicting royal land grants, were angrily—even
violently—contested by the squatters, many of them Revolutionary
veterans who had actually settled and cleared the land. The legal work
was hard—it was necessary to travel on circuit with the judges, over
bad roads, often in miserable weather—but the District's small, mutu-
ally supportive community of lawyers and judges was not an unpleasant circle in which to build a career, at least until party politics began
to dominate the scene.

By the time of his second son Henry's birth in 1807, Stephen Longfellow was regarded as a rising star in the eastern skies. He was sent to
the General Court in Boston in 1814, served as a presidential elector
in 1816, served in the Eighteenth Congress in 1822–24, represented

Portland in the Maine legislature in 1826, was president of the Maine
Historical Society in 1834, and for nineteen years served on the governing boards of Bowdoin College. On the question of Maine's statehood, he took the Federalist position in favor of separation in the early
stages of the debate (when Maine's coastal elite of the 1790s sought
fiscal independence from distant Boston) and followed his party to the
other side, and to dignified defeat, in 1816–19, when the propertied
class sought to maintain its ties to Boston out of a justified fear that
the Jeffersonian Republicans—uneducated backcountry Baptists or
Methodists or worse—would dominate the new state. Yet for all the
esteem he enjoyed among his peers (and he had married up a degree or
two in linking himself with the Wadsworth clan), there is a shadow of
failure over his career. Most obviously, he never obtained a judgeship,
unlike his own father and his two older sons' fathers-in-law, Judges
Preble and Potter.

In particular, Stephen Longfellow's participation in the controversial Hartford Convention of 1814 darkened his public reputation.
Modern historians have concluded that the discussions among New
England Federalists at the convention were far more moderate than
their enemies claimed—were, indeed, an attempt by the more respon-
sible leaders to tone down separationist talk. Yet anger at the national
government and President Madison's war with Britain was so widespread in coastal New England that some adjustment in the nature of
the federal union was widely assumed to be overdue. A delegation
from Hartford was about to leave for Washington when news exploded throughout the country of Andrew Jackson's brilliant victory
over the British at New Orleans, some weeks after the otherwise em-
barrassing War of 1812 had been officially ended. For years to come,
deeply wounded Federalists protested that no political event in
American life had "ever been the theme of more gross representation,
or more constant reproach" than the Hartford Convention (in the
words of their apologist Theodore Dwight in 1833). But the Federalist Party never recovered, and soon disappeared, among lingering
charges that its delegates at Hartford had been disloyal to their coun-

try. Henry Wadsworth Longfellow's nationalist stance in his poetry of the 1840s and 1850s had many sources, his father's political misjudgment in 1814 perhaps among them.

Stephen Longfellow's problems were not simply political or professional; as we shall see, he suffered from debilitating ailments, including what were diagnosed as epileptic attacks, and in midcareer he seems to have suffered a major failure of confidence in himself. He remained well regarded among his peers, however, and was given the great honor in 1824 of officially welcoming the Marquis de Lafayette to Portland on the general's triumphal American tour. Stephen is not as immediately likable a person as Zilpah, but he was a conscientious father, and, once he recognized that his second son had exceptional gifts, he did everything possible, in his cautious way, to bring them to fruition.

Young Henry started with an enormous advantage: he did not have to be a Stephen. If anything, the challenge was to carve out an alternative mode of being a Longfellow. He seems to have begun by making a great deal of noise. "Do you not want to kiss Henry?" Zilpah wrote her husband from her parents' house in October of 1809. "A charming little fellow he is. Nothing will do for him but jumping and dancing He fatigues every one in the house with tending him." In one of her infrequent letters, his aunt Lucia reported in May of 1812, amid the excitements of war with Britain, that five-year-old "Henry is ready to march, he had his tin gun prepared and his head powdered a week ago." Writing amid his legislative duties in Boston in 1814, Stephen praised Henry for having composed a letter, and promised him "a very pretty drum with an eagle painted on it." He offered Stephen Jr. a gun and sword, but warned both boys not to expect the gifts soon. "You know the Embargo stops all the vessels from going from Boston to Portland." If this early lesson in the evils of the Madison administration was not clear enough, he added to Stephen, "And so you see, my Son, that the Embargo is troublesome to little boys as well as men."

The second war with Britain was more than a hindrance to New England commerce; it terrified the residents of coastal Maine who remembered the destruction of Portland in the previous war and who noted the ease with which the British had occupied the eastern half of the District, down to the Penobscot. Only southern Maine's relative military insignificance saved it from a similar fate; farther Down East (to travel north along the Maine coast was to sail with the prevailing winds "Down East" from Boston), many respectable citizens were so busy smuggling goods to and from Canada, they would not have cared which side prevailed. But for an imaginative young boy living within sight of Casco Bay, those were thrilling days. Talk of invasion of Canada was always in the air, if only as a diversion from the inactivity in the harbor. And there was the forty-five-minute battle off Monhegan Island in 1813 between the American brig *Enterprise* and the British brig *Boxer*. Both captains were killed and brought ashore for burial, but the *Enterprise* had prevailed and brought the *Boxer* into harbor. Longfellow was later to write, in his great Portland ode, "My Lost Youth," of hearing "the sea-fight far away" as it "thundered o'er the tide!"—poetic license, since the battle was well out of earshot— and seeing the young captains' graves. Elsewhere at sea, another of Zilpah's brothers, Alexander Scammell Wadsworth (1790–1851), won fame as second in command of the U.S.S. *Constitution* in the defeat of H.M.S. *Guerriere*.

The family's holidays in Gorham and Hiram during their father's frequent absences, on circuit or at the legislature, were intended as a healthful diversion, but Henry's closest brush with serious injury befell him at Wadsworth Hall in July of 1815, when an infected foot began to swell despite the alum curds his mother put upon it. He seemed to get better and on August 6 asked his father to send him "two or three little books of riddles if you can find any." Four days later, his heel worsened, bringing fever and great pain; his mother feared he would lose the use of his ankle, even his leg. She resorted to poultices (the verdigris salve the doctor had recommended had only inflamed the wound), and by late August he was on both feet again. Two years later, he had another painful accident: amusing himself after school by turning "heels over head," he severely wrenched his elbow. Bound up in a sling and dressed with wormwood and vinegar, his arm slowly healed, and he was able to write again.

Despite this evidence of physical exuberance, Henry was settling down. He had been sent to "Ma'am" Fellows's school at age three to learn the alphabet, and to the town-supported school at age five. According to his brother Samuel, writing more than eighty years later, Henry found the local roughs "distasteful" and moved to a private school run by a Mr. Wright. The next year, his education began in earnest with N. H. Carter at the estimable Portland Academy. By 1817, he was still earning good reports, with an occasional minor lapse: "This certifies," wrote Bezaleel Cushman, "that the bearer, Henry W. Longfellow, has, during this week, distinguished himself by his good deportment and close application to study; *monday morning's lesson & occasional levity excepted.*" The charge of "levity" supports the impression that one of his most distinctive qualities from early on was his sociability. When Longfellow was about to enter college in 1822, he thought some friendly gesture to his former teacher was in order. "I remember," he wrote later, "the Schoolmaster at the Academy; and the mingled odor that hovered about him of tobacco, india-rubber, and lead-pencil. A nervous, excitable man.... I went with a schoolmate to take leave of him and thank him for his patience with us. He thought we were in jest: and gave us a stern lecture on good behavior and the trials of a teacher's life."

His schoolmate Elijah Kellogg, later to be famous for his children's stories, recalled young Henry in these words in 1885: "He was a very handsome boy, retiring, without being reserved, there was a frankness about him that won you at once. He looked you square in the face. His eyes were full of expression, and it seemed as though you could look down into them as into a clear spring." Kellogg remembered him as thoughtful, but not melancholy, and totally lacking that tinge of sadness that his later years would bring.

Much of his real education, of course, took place in his father's library, which was small but well stocked in the classics of British literature, as filtered by eighteenth-century taste. Shakespeare, Milton,

Pope, Dryden, Thomson, Goldsmith, *The Spectator*, *The Rambler*, Plutarch's *Lives*; the histories of Hume, Gibbon, Gillies, and Robertson; Hannah More (to be read on Sundays)—these were the books that Samuel remembered seeing there. The Longfellow children also read aloud Cowper's poems, Moore's *Lalla Rookh*, *Robinson Crusoe*, *The Arabian Nights*, "and Henry took delight in *Don Quixote*, and Ossian, and would go about the house declaiming the windy and misty utterances of the latter." Below the Longfellows' house, on the western side of the Back Cove, was a tangle of trees, tidal estuaries, and overgrown ravines that separated the Deering estate from the town. This was the Deering's Woods of "My Lost Youth"—today's much tamer Deering Oaks Park—a place where Portland boys went to shoot birds and squirrels and escape the confines of home. Henry went along, but to sit under the trees and read and mediate the rough and resiny Maine forest into the greenwood of his British literary masters.

Then finally he found an American book that revealed to him how unpredictable the border between imagination and reality could be— or, rather, how seamlessly the imagination could transform everyday life into something deliciously sweet. He never quite got over it. In his own words, forty years later:

> Every reader has his first book; I mean to say, one book among all others which in early youth first fascinates his imagination, and at once excites and satisfies the desires of his mind. To me, this first book was the Sketch-Book of Washington Irving. I was a school-boy when it was published [in 1819], and read each succeeding number with ever increasing wonder and delight, spell-bound by its pleasant humor, its melancholy tenderness, its atmosphere of revery,—nay, even by its gray-brown covers, the shaded letters of its titles, and the fair clear type, which seemed an outward symbol of its style.... [W]henever I open its pages, I open also that mysterious door which leads back into the haunted chambers of youth.

By this point, Longfellow had already written a good deal of verse. But so had his brother and his older sisters; it was a social skill, like playing the piano or being able to sketch, and one which every genteel person was expected to attempt for personal or familial amusement. Henry wanted to see his in print. As a result, on November 17, 1820, readers of the Portland *Gazette*—a pro-Federalist weekly—found in its columns four stanzas entitled "The Battle of Lovell's Pond." It was a patriotic elegy for the colonists killed near Hiram in 1725 in a battle that had already achieved folkloric status in the Maine back country, as a kind of proto–Custer's Last Stand. The Massachusetts men had died at the hands of "howling savages," but civilization had marched on, as the myth had it. The poem was signed "HENRY." According to Samuel Longfellow's reverential biography of his older brother, Henry was visiting that evening in the house of his school friend Frederic Mellen (himself a future poet). Frederic's father, Judge Mellen, picked up the *Gazette* and asked if anyone had read the new poem. "Very stiff, remarkably stiff; moreover, it is all borrowed, every word of it." Henry was mortified but kept his mouth shut. The judge was not entirely wrong: a poem called "Lovellspond" by the future Bowdoin professor (and future Longfellow friend) Thomas C. Upham had appeared the previous year in his collection *American Sketches*. The theme is the same, as is some of the language. But Upham took five stanzas to do what the thirteen-year-old Longfellow did in four, and the boy managed to speed up and tighten the poem while giving it a patriotic flourish at the end. Neither poem is memorable, but judge which is worse—

> *In the earth's verdant bosom, still, crumbling, and cold,*
> *Sleep the soldiers who mingled in battle of old;*
> *They rushed to the slaughter, they struggled, and fell*
> *And the clarion of glory was heard in their knell . . .*

Or—

> *Cold, cold is the north wind and rude is the blast*
> *That sweeps like a hurricane loudly and fast,*
> *As it moans through the tall waving pines lone and drear,*
> *Sighs a requiem sad o'er the warrior's bier . . .*

In "Cold, cold is the north wind . . ." and what follows we catch the first hint of the familiar music and pulsating beat that was to make Longfellow, for more than a century, the most famous poet in the English-speaking world. What the thirteen-year-old boy had done was to write an imitation of Upham's work, in the best eighteenth-century sense of that word. (The grisly, racist subject of the two poems did prove atypical for both poets: Upham was to become a major force in the American peace movement of the 1840s; Longfellow was to conceive of his Indian hero Hiawatha as anything but a savage.)

What Henry had to do now was to learn how to be a nineteenth-century poet.

Two

A SMALL COLLEGE
IN MAINE

PORTLAND IN THE 1820s was not a bad place in which to learn
that lesson. Despite its apparent remoteness, it was a maritime
center, linked through its coasting trade with Boston and through its
lumber-based economy with an international market that stretched
from the West Indies to the Baltic. In a sense, Portland was not a distant appendage of Massachusetts at all; economically speaking, it was
part of a North Atlantic matrix of seafaring cities. Not only had a
Wadsworth died "on the shores of Tripoli" to protect this rapidly ex-
panding American commercial empire, but virtually every Portlander
had friends and relations in distant lands. Zilpah, who hated the northern winters, daydreamed of visiting her friend in Guadeloupe; when
her third son, Alexander, sailed with his uncle's squadron to the
Pacific, he discovered a familiar Portland family settled as merchants
in Peru; Zilpah's brothers traded in England, Russia, and France.
Maine had products much of the world wanted—every manner of
wood, from raw pine to skillfully shaved cedar shingles; every variety
of naval store, from ropes to tar; fish, smoked or dried; even ice, cut
from the frozen rivers, packed in sawdust in the holds of ships, and sent
as far as India. What Maine did not produce—cotton, for example—
was transported to Europe and beyond in Maine-built ships owned
and captained by Maine men, not infrequently accompanied by their
wives and families. By a nice coincidence, the oldest continually operated ship chandlery in the United States still does business, facing
Canada, on the waterfront of Eastport, Maine—S. L. Wadsworth &
Son, founded by the poet's uncle.

Portland unfortunately produced no Thomas Mann to chronicle

the rise and fall of its great merchant families; but as in that other northern Protestant seaport, Mann's Lübeck, the commercial activity on Casco Bay masked a good deal of human and economic upheaval. Stephen Longfellow had begun his law practice at the height of Maine's post-Revolutionary expansion, when almost overnight its population trebled and its merchants and lumber lords grew rich. When Henry was born in 1807, Jefferson's hated embargo was about to cripple the coastal New England economy and, in an image popular at that time, grass would grow on the wharves. This image of nature reclaiming what had so painstakingly been created by the backs and brains of New Englanders was a particularly chilling one. New England's mission was not simply to grow rich; it was to convert a wilderness into a civilized, Christianized land. In the 1790s it was considered a happy instance of God's blessings that the Maine lands that needed to be cleared before they could be settled and farmed were covered with trees whose lumber could be harvested. It would take another hundred years before the beauty of these forests *as* forests would be widely appreciated, and almost another hundred before there was any widespread understanding of environmentalism. But to an observer in Longfellow's youth, there was no necessary contradiction between "enjoying" nature as sublime and calculating the number of board feet of timber that same piece of nature might yield. Zilpah, for example, wrote from Hiram to her daughter Anne in June of 1825, after an excursion into the woods with her brother Peleg: "We remained there two or three hours, contemplating the grandeur and beauty of the scene, and observing the descent of the logs over the falls. The river drivers were at work ... and innumerable logs some of them very large, came thundering over the falls with the utmost rapidity, much to our amusement." By the time Longfellow was ready for college, the Maine frontier had been pushed far up the river valleys. Both residents and visitors assumed that in time the entire state would be covered with farms and villages and that even the climate would improve. (The theory was that removing the dense cover of trees would allow the soil to be more easily warmed.) Portland would serve as the great entrepot, shipping the produce of the hinterland and marketing the luxury goods imported by its far-ranging merchant fleet.

Despite the unpredictability of foreign commerce, by the 1820s Portland was again a prosperous and optimistic place, and a young man growing up there might easily have felt that he had broad horizons. Among the many objects that have survived in the Wadsworth-Longfellow House from the world of Longfellow's childhood —blue-and-white willowware china, hide-covered traveling chests, stacks of sheet music for piano and voice—perhaps none is so evocative as the brightly colored book of geography lessons painstakingly copied by Aunt Lucia as a child in 1794. Her nephews must have spent many hours poring over it, on that third floor of the house they shared with her. In vivid pinks and blues, and with exquisite penmanship, she had recreated the world: Lapland, Muscovy, Hindostan, Tartary, New Holland, Cochin China, the Mogul Empire. None of it was beyond a Portlander's reach.

But did trade bring culture? Could a poet survive in the counting rooms? The general pattern of American life—already so widely lamented, so rarely amended—was not encouraging: people were too busy. Nonetheless, the small city of Portland in the 1820s and early 1830s supported an exceptionally talented circle of writers and artists. The best known of these were a recent Bowdoin graduate, Seba Smith (whose journalistic creation "Major Jack Downing" made him the first in a long line of back-country political satirists and dialect humorists), and the more controversial John Neal, a novelist and pioneering art critic who had returned to Portland after a decade of travel. Still abroad but widely read at home was the Portland-born Nathaniel Parker Willis, who had shown how a smooth and charming American could conquer London (where Longfellow would meet him in 1835). Add to these the names of Elizabeth Oakes Smith (Seba's wife), Isaac McClellan, Ann Stephens, Joseph Holt Ingraham, Nathaniel Deering, Frederic and Prentice Mellen, and the young Longfellow, and you had the makings of what, by the standards of Jacksonian America, was a major literary center. In Lawrence Buell's words, "one could even

argue that the Portland contribution to antebellum New England letters came close to rivaling that of Cambridge or Concord."

The promise was never fulfilled, and by the end of the 1830s many
of these people had moved away or had failed to develop their careers.
The most obvious explanation is that Portland was too far from the
major publishing centers—at that time, Philadelphia and New York—
with their networks of editors, critics, booksellers, and distributors.
The ease with which American publishers pirated British writing also
made it more difficult for native writers to establish themselves in the
marketplace. Nonetheless, for a young man with literary interests,
Portland in the 1820s would have been a heady place in which to live
and write—a community in which the notion of a literary career
would have seemed neither inconceivable nor entirely quixotic.

Longfellow would gladly have gone off to Harvard—he had already
had an exhilarating taste of Boston life on a trip with Aunt Lucia—but
there were compelling reasons to go instead to the new college at
Brunswick, some thirty miles farther "Down East." His paternal
grandfather had been among its founders; his father took seriously his
duties as first an overseer, then a trustee of the promising "literary institution"; many of his family's closest associates had a large stake in
its success. Chartered in 1794, and in operation since 1802, Bowdoin
College was the physical embodiment of the cultural and civic aspirations of "the great and the good" of the District of Maine—an enterprise that would make the desert bloom (to use a phrase from Isaiah
often quoted by Bowdoin's founders), and the District a safe haven
for republican values and rational religion. And it was cheaper than
Harvard.

The family tradition handed on to biographers was that while
Stephen Longfellow had allowed the well-prepared Henry to matric-
ulate at Bowdoin in 1821, he kept the fourteen-year-old boy at home
that first year because he was too young to live in college. A more likely
explanation is that he was not sure sixteen-year-old Stephen Jr. was
ready to leave his supervision. It had long been clear that Stephen was
a difficult and exasperating child, though certainly not an unlovable

one—indeed, part of the pathos of Stephen's life was that he was so charming, so well meaning, so quick to acknowledge his shortcomings. Writing from Hiram in 1809, when Stephen was four, Zilpah noted: "Poor fellow. He always has something to bear. Something to prevent his enjoyment." Eight years later, when he balked at performing for a school prize in reading poetry aloud, she wrote: "This dear son wants peculiar management, he is so diffident of his powers so easily depressed, that he needs much encouragement from his friends." (Henry, on the other hand, was "in high spirits," eager to compete.) By midadolescence Stephen was drinking heavily, keeping dubious company, and causing his parents considerable anxiety. In 1824, for example, smallpox swept through Portland, reportedly spread on the waterfront by a Mrs. Brown "of dubious repute who caught it laundering a sailor's clothing." The males of Portland, Zilpah wrote to her husband attending Congress in Washington, dreaded being diagnosed with the disease, lest they were "found out as acquaintances of *Mrs. Brown . . .*" Young Stephen escaped that stigma, but his late-night roving and lack of self-control caused his mother much anguish.

"Your plan for the education of your sons was liberal and judicious," she wrote to Stephen Sr. in Washington, after seeing the eighteen-year-old Stephen Jr.'s list of college fines, "and as it respected one of them perfectly right. . . . But our sons are different, very different. I think they are so naturally, and it cannot, I think be imputed as a fault to one that he is not like the other." Following her father's advice, she urged Stephen Sr. to consult his son's own inclinations as to a career, suggesting the army or going to sea as an alternative to college and the law. "Indolence is his easily besotting sin, and only being subjected to the strictest discipline will rouse him from it." She even enrolled Henry in the effort to monitor the behavior of an older brother who rarely wrote letters home from college. "I should like to know the truth and the whole truth," she instructed him.

Henry was too much the peacemaker to oblige, and there is every indication that he deeply loved his brother, indeed was much closer to him than to the younger boys in the family, Alexander and Samuel.

Zilpah continued to "feel great anxiety on [Stephen's] account, he is so unsteady; and he appears to have no power to resist temptation. What shall we do with him? Or what will he do with himself?"

But she had other worries. "My dear husband," she wrote to Stephen in Congress in 1824, "I beg of you not to entertain the idea that your mind is at all impaired." She assured him that she had noticed no change in his behavior "excepting an increased diffidence." In a series of letters designed to bolster his confidence, she tried to coax him to go out more into the capital's society and, more important, to speak on some subject—preferably the tariff bill—on the floor of the House. His friends at home—that is, the Portland merchants and lawyers who had elected him—were beginning to wonder why they never saw his name in the records of debate. The congressman was suffering a depression that went beyond homesickness. It was to be his only term of national office. He would continue to play the role of Portland attorney and engaged citizen for another quarter century, but with an increasing feebleness of will and greatly reduced physical stamina.

The many letters exchanged between Stephen and Zilpah in those two Congressional years are supportive and affectionate—she refers to herself again and again as his "best friend"—and the only time she snaps back at him is when he criticizes her inability to control their eldest son. "You do well to preach patience, but you must practice too. I feel as if we have a severe trial to bear. But we must not cast off our son, though his errors were greater than they are; we must endeavor to reclaim him, for who will be his friend if his parents are not." These years took a toll on her. She wrote to her mother at Hiram in November of 1824:

> [I] frequently wish that I could enjoy a few hours in your society, in your quiet little room. I have no room here where worldly cares are shut out. The office is full of business, the parlor full of company and music, the back parlor is full of noisy children, the kitchen full of cares and domestics and very little time do I get to retire to the solitude of my own chamber, for reflextion or self-examination.

Henry, on the other hand, was a joy. "What can have made the difference between our two sons, educated together as they were together & alike," asked Zilpah in 1825, when Stephen had been rusticated by the college—that is, sent to live and study for a term with a clergyman in Kennebunk because of his chronic misbehavior. "Henry is beloved by all, his conduct is very correct, and he gives much pleasure to his friends...."

The college to which they had been sent was a stage for the enactment of this drama of the good brother and the disappointing one. Henry, as we shall see, was one of its stars even as an undergraduate. Stephen's passage through its halls left little trace, although he did graduate.

In writing in 1879 of the Longfellows' classmate Nathaniel Hawthorne, Henry James was to dismiss Bowdoin as "a highly honorable, but not very elaborately organized, nor a particularly impressive, seat of learning." He described it as "a homely, simple, frugal 'country college,' of the old-fashioned American stamp...." He allowed that it did exert "a civilizing influence" amid "the log-houses and the clearings" and sufficiently educated "the future lawyers, merchants, clergymen, politicians, and editors, of the very active and knowledge-loving community that supported it." And it "numbered poets and statesmen among its undergraduates, and on the roll-call of its sons it has several distinguished names." This was not an entirely accurate description of Bowdoin, but James was right in acknowledging the success of many of its early graduates.

In retrospect, the most distinguished among these was Hawthorne, although he never quite matched the contemporary fame of his friend Longfellow. In an early work that he later tried to suppress, Hawthorne described a country college that most critics, including James, took to be Bowdoin. Yet Harley College, the setting of Hawthorne's 1828 novel *Fanshawe*, suggests Bowdoin without actually depicting it. Bowdoin could not boast of "an existence of nearly a century," nor did it lack candidates for degrees. It was not situated in "a narrow vale" in almost inaccessible "hill-country" adjacent to a sparsely settled village of farmhouses. Among its students were no "young descendants of the aborigines," and its kindly head, Dr. Melmoth, in no way resembled Bowdoin's president in Hawthorne's day, the overbearing William Allen. Harley seems closer to hill-bound Dartmouth College, with its early tradition of educating the Indians. Where Harley does resemble Bowdoin is in the presence of a tavern next to campus (such inns were a common and not necessarily debilitating feature of every New England town, and served as public meeting places) and in something its author has to say about the students: "A few young men had found their way hither from the distant seaports; and these were the models of fashion to their rustic companions, over whom they asserted a superiority in exterior accomplishments, which the fresh though unpolished intellect of the sons of the forest denied them in their literary competitions." Hawthorne himself was from a not-too-distant seaport, Salem, though he had also spent an idyllic time as a son of the forest, or rather of the apple orchards, as a ward of his Manning uncles in rural Raymond, Maine. But it was Portland students like the brothers Longfellow who gave Brunswick much of its social tone in the 1820s. There were few rustics—save some divinity students on scholarship—but a good many well-positioned youths seeking to model themselves on the ideal of the republican New England gentleman. Each Maine town had its leading family—often the owners of the local lumber mill—and, well into the twentieth century, each generation of these families typically sent a son to Bowdoin. Stephen and Henry fit easily into this social world.

Henry's letters home, once he had settled into true collegiate life (after a sophomore year spent boarding with a clergyman on nearby Federal Street), reflect his jauntiness. In October of 1823, after moving with Stephen into third-floor rooms in what is now Maine Hall, he wrote his sister Elizabeth:

> The room we occupy at present, is situated in the North Eastern corner of the North College—but I forget myself! From such a description, you, who have never seen the colleges, can form no idea of its situation.... —the bed-room window looks toward the village and

Professor Cleaveland's,—the other two windows afford a delightful prospect,—no less so than the charm of an extensive woodland scenery of—pine trees,—groves, beautified by a great quantity of bushes cut during the Summer, and left, dry, withered, sere, to beauty and vary the Autumnal landscape—a fine view of the road to Harpswell and the College Wood Yard. But within! How shall I describe it! *Yellow* floor! *Green* fire-place. Mantel and window-seats, *blueish white,*—and three great doors, *mahogany color.* But jesting apart!—the room is a very good room, although more pleasant for Summer than Winter, as it is in back. . . .

Henry James had touched on the college's great strength. It did prepare lawyers, editors, statesmen for the great world. It did not prepare them for intensive scholarly pursuits or teach useful technological skills or encourage them to pursue commercial careers on a grand scale—no American college did any of that until after the Civil War—but it did not do a bad job of fulfilling its mission, which was to socialize a leadership class and polish those public skills—particularly in speaking and writing—with which they would pursue the common good. (Some graduates also proved entrepreneurial, especially in land speculation, but in truth a college education was a waste of time in the early nineteenth century for anyone who simply wanted to make money.) And Bowdoin was not quite as provincial as its landlocked fellow colleges. It shared with other small colleges such as Williams and Amherst and Middlebury an intensely local clientele (unlike Harvard, which was already attracting a national student body, despite its first loyalty to the Boston elite). But Bowdoin operated, at least in its early decades, on a larger scale than the other country colleges. Thanks to its new Medical School of Maine, it had the promise (never fulfilled) of becoming a small university. Thanks to bequests from its original benefactor, James Bowdoin III, it had one of the best libraries in the United States (especially rich in eighteenth-century French books), an interesting cabinet of natural curiosities (including an important mineral collection), and a collection of European art unmatched by any nineteenth-century American college or university (to the extent that this collection was open in Massachusetts Hall to any respectable person who wished to visit it, Bowdoin could be said to have had the first collegiate art museum in the country). The college did not have the cultural and social aura that flowed up the Charles with the tide from Boston to Cambridge, but in 1825 its faculty was enhanced by the presence of the pioneer mineralogist Parker Cleaveland—a good friend of the Longfellows—and the proximity of Portland across Casco Bay brought some small degree of worldliness to the sandy plains of Brunswick.

This moment of exceptional possibility was not going to last, and Bowdoin already had its problems. It was run by a very unpleasant (though gifted) man and by two governing bodies seething with animosity toward each other. (The bicameral system of governance, like much of the campus architecture, had been copied after Harvard's.) The president, the Reverend William Allen, was a learned man in the recitation room but a fire-breathing Calvinist in the pulpit, where the students heard him deliver daily prayers and Sunday sermons. Longfellow got out of the latter by means of a letter from his father allowing him to join a tiny Unitarian congregation in Brunswick. Hawthorne, who had grown up in Salem amid liberal clergy, was not so privileged, and President Allen may very well have been his introduction to the full brunt of the Puritan heritage and its doctrine of the depravity of man.

From its start, the college had been entangled in Maine politics and religion. The institution's very name suggested its political tone: James Bowdoin II, who was being memorialized by his son, was the conservative governor who, in the contentious years just after the Revolution, had put down Shays' Rebellion among the angry farmers of western Massachusetts. The college's early governing boards were, with a few exceptions, representative of the coastal elite. Many of these men had been religious liberals, but by the 1820s, the state's orthodox Congregationalists were on the verge of taking de facto control of the institution—which was never to have any official denominational affiliation—to the great alarm of a remnant of Unitarian and Episcopalian trustees. More perilously, Bowdoin's friends, including Stephen Longfellow, had put themselves on the wrong side in the final statehood debate in 1819, a generation-long struggle over whether to separate from Massachusetts. The leaders of Maine's new Republican (that is, Democratic) majority saw the college as a bastion of Federalism and oligarchy and, through the 1820s, plotted ways to do it harm.

In examining Longfellow's student days in this environment, the most interesting question is why he and Hawthorne did not become friends (as they famously did a decade later). It was a very small place—the class of 1825 had forty-five members, most of them living in two adjacent dormitories and dining in a common hall—and there would have been only a certain number of students keenly interested in literature. One explanation is social: for Longfellow, the son of a congressman and grandson of a Revolutionary general, the college was an extension of the world he had always known in Portland, and his passage from one to the other was relatively seamless; for Hawthorne, on the other hand, Bowdoin was a new, even foreign environment, and he quickly latched on to three amiable friends who eased his passage by giving him—perhaps for the first time in his life—a sense of camaraderie with other males. (Hawthorne's notorious reclusiveness seems to have been a postcollegiate shift in his dealings with the world.) This does not imply any degree of unworldliness on Hawthorne's part: his friend Franklin Pierce became fourteenth president of the United States, his friend Horatio Bridge was the son of Augusta's leading citizen, and his friend Jonathan Cilley became a Maine congressman who was killed in a famous duel in 1838.

The other explanation is political, in both undergraduate and partisan terms. The most intense part of student life did not take place amid the dull recitations or uninspired chapel services. It took place, at Bowdoin as in other antebellum American colleges, in the rivalry between two student societies. These societies had a literary and oratorical public face, but they were in essence fraternal organizations and tended to reflect the political views and social standing of the students' fathers. Henry Longfellow joined the older of the two, the Peucinian Society—more "establishment," a bit staid, properly Federalist (and later Whig) in its political leanings, both earnest and urbane in social tone—while Hawthorne chose the Athenaean— slightly more vulgar or at least boisterous, Democratic in its senti- ments, a little less predictable. (Stephen Longfellow Jr. became an Athenaean, too, perhaps to annoy his father, perhaps because they were just more fun to be with.) For all their undergraduate pomposity, these societies—whose meetings took place amid a colorful array of other extracurricular pursuits, ranging from cadet military reviews to brutal late-night pranks—fulfilled a serious purpose. For one thing, they had excellent lending libraries of contemporary books and jour- nals, conscientiously maintained and intelligently selected (Longfel- low was one of the Peucinian librarians in 1824–25 and helped compile its first catalogue). And the society debates were an important train- ing ground for ambitious young men seeking advancement in a post- collegiate culture that still depended so much on the spoken word—in the pulpit, before a jury, on the election stump. It would be anachro- nistic to label the Peucinian "conservative" and the Athenaean "lib- eral," as many commentators have done, for the modern labels do not exactly fit (Longfellow, for example, was far more progressive in his political views than Hawthorne or his fellow Athenaean Franklin Pierce). Perhaps it is more accurate to say they corresponded to certain ways of viewing the world, and on that the two young writers already diverged.

One other thing distinguished Longfellow from all his fellow stu- dents: he was becoming a well-known writer, at least among sub- scribers to the short-lived but respectable Boston monthly *The United States Literary Gazette*. Within the two years of its existence, the *Gazette* published twenty-four of his poems and short prose pieces, surely an unprecedented achievement for an American undergradu- ate. Fourteen of these poems were republished in *Miscellaneous Poems Selected from the United States Literary Gazette* in 1826—the first col- lected publication in book form of any of his work—and two of them,

"The Indian Hunter" and "Woods in Winter," appeared in 1830 in *Studies in Poetry*, an anthology compiled by his classmate, George Barrell Cheever. This exposure brought Longfellow his first public criticism: in the *North American Review* for April of 1826, the reviewer of *Miscellaneous Poems* noted "a good deal of poetical feeling and imagery in the pieces contributed by Mr. Longfellow.... He is generally flowing, manly, and correct; but he occasionally allows a feeble line, or negligent expression, to have place.... We could point to other occasional blemishes, but these weigh little in comparison with the author's prevailing merits."

As Henry wrote to his father in 1824, as they were considering what career he might follow: "I most eagerly aspire after future eminence in literature, my whole soul burns most ardently for it, and every earthly thought centers on it." But how could he escape the profession his father thought him most suited for, the law?

· *Three* ·

THE PASSIONATE PILGRIM

Le Havre de Grace, France

A T 4:00 P.M. ON JUNE 14, 1826, the ship *Cadmus* arrived safely at the mouth of the Seine after a thirty-day voyage from New York. Her passengers included a dozen or more Frenchmen and the nineteen-year-old Henry Longfellow. The extraordinarily smooth passage had been enlivened only by their chattering, "for Frenchmen you know talk incessantly," as Longfellow wrote to his mother. He had had his first jolt as a traveler: his schoolboy French, he had discovered, was not good enough for him to converse easily with a native. Nor was he prepared for European officialdom. He had thought he could hop immediately on the steamer for Rouen and did not realize the police and customs officers would detain him a day until his papers were determined to be in order. But the novelty of the scene at Le Havre—the seaport's quaint houses, the ancient fortifications, the laundry flapping from every upper window—diverted him, and he wrote to his brother Stephen that he had been "irresistably seized with divers fits of laughter" at the sight of fiercely whiskered "gens-d'armes," wooden-shoed women, and "the dames of Normandy with tall pyramidal caps." This was the giddiness of a youth who had been confined on shipboard for too many days and who could scarcely believe he had at last set foot in Europe. His deep-rooted need to pass all experience through the filter of literature did not fail him: the green highlands of Honfleur across the Seine reminded him that Washington Irving had set his tale "Annette Delarbre" there. And he was immediately struck by the French preoccupation with food: he wrote home with wonderment at the ten-course meal common in a "table d'hote." Having missed the steamer, he had to take the jostling diligence first to Rouen, where he

39

paid his respects at the tomb of Richard the Lion-Hearted and the site of Joan of Arc's martyrdom, and then to the "great Babylon" itself, Paris. Not wishing to appear too impressed, he told his sisters "Paris is a gloomy city—built all of yellow stone—streaked and defaced with smoke and dust—streets narrow and full of black mud . . . —no sidewalks—cabriolets—fiacres and carriages of all kinds driving close to the houses—and spattering or running down whole ranks of foot passengers—and noise and stench enough to drive a man mad."

Yet how thrilled he was to have come so far, so unexpectedly quickly. His last year at Bowdoin had found him worrying over what profession to pursue. He had no taste for medicine or the ministry and feared he lacked the oratorical skills required of a lawyer. The possibility of literary fame enticed him, but his father was adamant that no American could make a respectable living as a writer. A good Federalist in the cultural as well as political sense, Stephen Sr. saw literature as a useful, even important embellishment of a gentlemanly life, but hardly an end in itself. Then a door suddenly opened for his son.

According to the traditional accounts of Longfellow's life, he was offered the new professorship of modern languages at Bowdoin because an influential trustee of the college, Benjamin Orr, had been impressed by his smooth translation of an ode of Horace at a public examination; the college subsequently sent him abroad to perfect or acquire knowledge of the languages (French, Spanish, Italian) he was expected to teach. This is improbable on several grounds. Given the curricular war within the early-nineteenth-century colleges—between the traditionalists who championed Latin and Greek and the reformers who sought a more useful curriculum—skill at translating a classical poet would not have recommended anyone to the advocates of teaching modern languages. Nor was there an indication that Longfellow had any special abilities at modern languages beyond the veneer of French expected of every genteel young person. Nor was a college as financially insecure as Bowdoin likely to "send" anyone abroad, least of all a nineteen-year-old aspiring man of letters. The truth is that Longfellow found himself in Paris in the summer after his graduation as a sort of speculation on his father's part. It was a well-founded venture; a man as cautious as Stephen would not have risked wasting the money or exposing his son to the hazards of foreign travel had not a favorable outcome seemed very likely. But it was based on two premises: that the college was serious about funding such a professorship of languages and that Henry was clever enough to master French and Spanish and possibly Italian well enough to be able to teach them. There were, after all, very few Americans who could claim that degree of knowledge.

This solved several problems within the Longfellow family. It gave Henry a profession for which he was temperamentally suited and which would allow him some leisure for literary pursuits (his brother Stephen would, according to plan, follow his father into the law). It would enhance the reputation of the infant institution, since so few American colleges at that date taught modern languages. And it would strengthen the hand of those governing-board members at Bowdoin who were alarmed at the takeover of the college by the increasingly aggressive Maine Congregationalists. (A "takeover" in this context meant controlling the presidency, appointing the professors, and setting the religious and curricular tone of the institution.) In this view of things, every professorship held by a Unitarian (or even an Episcopalian) was a bulwark against the forces of Calvinist orthodoxy. As it turned out, this defense proved hopeless, for by the late 1830s the Congregationalists had "captured" the college, for all practical purposes, though never officially. But in 1826 there was still reason for Unitarians such as Stephen Longfellow to hope that Bowdoin might follow Harvard's lead in the direction of religious liberalism—indeed, that the new state of Maine might eventually be won over to rational religion.

The professorship for Henry was probably conceived by his father and his family friends Parker Cleaveland (the leading professor at the college), Benjamin Orr, and the Reverend Ichabod Nichols (the Unitarian minister at the Longfellows' First Parish Church in Portland). Nothing has survived to indicate that anything was promised in writing, but there must have been a clear understanding, at least among the more liberal trustees, that if the young man sufficiently prepared himself abroad—at his father's expense—he would be the leading candidate once the post was officially established. (The Board of Trustees had voted to establish such a professorship in 1825, but the Board of Overseers had not yet approved it.) There was no firm commitment on Henry's part; in the months before he sailed, he read law in his father's office, just in case he had to find another career. While abroad, he still hoped that a teaching job at Harvard might become available, and his father also hinted at the possibility of a diplomatic posting.

Stephen Sr. naively assumed that Henry would need about six months in France and three or four months in Spain to perfect his French and learn Spanish from scratch, after which he could devote whatever time remained to doing a brisk version of the Grand Tour in Italy, perhaps including Germany as well. He would be home again, in other words, in about a year and a half. As it turned out, Henry was to be away more than three years, and Bowdoin was to have second thoughts about the nature of the professorship. When it was all over, Stephen calculated that it had cost him $2,604.24—a huge sum in 1829—and he emphasized that this was an advance on Henry's share of his estate. The most remarkable thing of all, however, was that Henry surpassed anyone's reasonable expectations. When he returned, he had an excellent command of French, Spanish, and Italian, had begun to learn the far more difficult German, and seems to have been able at least to read Portuguese. The enthusiasm which this young pilgrim brought to the cultural shrines of Europe was combined with a rare ability to grasp the structure of a new language almost instantly, to memorize vast amounts of vocabulary, and to mimic the speech of the educated people among whom he traveled. Stephen's investment was to prove gilt-edged.

In the summer of 1826, Henry's first task was to acclimate himself to Paris, a city far larger and more confusing than any he had visited in America. Arriving on June 18, he hurried across the Seine, after another customs inspection, in search of his cousin Ebenezer Storer, who was studying medicine. Storer had booked him a room with his own landlady, the genial Madame Potet, at 49 rue Monsieur-le-Prince, in the Faubourg St. Germain, not far from the Odéon Theater and the Luxembourg Gardens. He made the seventh American lodged there, but, he assured his father, there was little danger of hearing too much English; anyone speaking it at dinner was fined one sou. Despite the city's filth, he was quick to assure his sisters that Paris was redeemed by the elegance of its public spaces. After a few weeks, he reported to Professor Cleaveland that he had done "little else than run from one quarter of the city to another, with eyes and mouth wide open—staring into print-shops—book-stores—gardens—palaces—and prisons." On Cleaveland's behalf, he called at the Jardin des Plantes, one of the premier scientific research institutions in the world, to see the mineralogist Alexandre Brongniart, who was also director of the famous porcelain manufactory at Sevres. (Brongniart's predecessor as professor of mineralogy had been Haüy, whose collection of crystal models James Bowdoin III had bought in 1806 as part of the geological cabinet for the new college in Maine.) It was Longfellow's first encounter abroad with the phenomenon of an international community of savants, scholars who greeted each other as colleagues across the barriers of space and political borders.

After five weeks in Paris, he wrote a jauntier letter to his brother Stephen.

> I have settled down in something half-way between a Frenchman and a New Englander:—within, all Jonathan—but outwardly a little of the Parlez-vous. That is to say, I have good home-feelings at heart—but have decorated my outward man with a long-waisted thin coat—claret-colored—and a pair of linen pantaloons:—and on Sundays and other fete days—I appear in all the glory of a little hard French hat—glossy—and brushed—and rolled up at the sides.... In this garb I jostle amongst the crowds in the Luxembourg, which is the favorite promenade in St. Germain.

It was the affirmation of a lifelong penchant for fine clothes.

His father read the letter with alarm. He was already worried by his son's everyday expenses in the great capital, his own notion of an adequate per diem having been acquired from frugal New England sea captains doing business in European ports. "It seems that you have changed your costume to that of a Parisian," he quickly wrote from Portland. "You will allow me to doubt the expediency of confirming your dress to the fashion of the country in which you may reside for a short term. You will find it expensive to you, as your french dress would be useless to you in Spain, or any other country; for an American in Spain, Italy, or Germany decked out in the dress of a frenchman will exhibit a very singular appearance. You should remember that you are an American, and as you are a visitor for a short time only in a place, you should retain your own national costume." Longfellow hastened to reply that he had been joking; "what clothes I have had made was all after the English model."

Nonetheless, his parents—faced, for the first time, with a child effectively beyond their supervision—expressed continual anxiety about his well-being, even his whereabouts. He was hardly out the door—on the stage for Boston, en route to New York and his ship—when his mother had written, "I will not say how much we miss your elastic step, your cheerful voice, your melodious flute. . . . I feel as if you were going into a thousand perils, you must be very watchful & guard against every temptation." She took up the theme of vigilance again in a letter to Paris in December 1826:

Your parents have great confidence in your uprightness, and in that purity of mind which will instantly take alarm, on coming in contact with any thing vicious or unworthy. We have confidence, but you must be careful, & watchful and always on your guard, that you may never be led to take one step—no not one step in forbidden paths. Virtue allows no deviation from duty. One cannot sin and return with an unsullied mind to the place they left, in every aberation they lose ground which can never be regained. But enough, I do not mistrust you, and here come the girls to change the subject.

Stephen Sr. added to these moral injunctions a note of practicality:

> Your tour is one for improvement rather than pleasure, and you
> must make every exertion to cultivate and improve your mind, consis-
> tent with the preservation of your health. . . . Be careful not to take any
> part in opposition to the religion or politics of the Countries through
> which you pass, or in which you reside. They are local concerns in
> which a stranger has no right to interfere.

That was not bad advice for an inexperienced young man entering
the territory of the reactionary regimes of Metternich's Europe. Later
in 1826, Stephen added:

> Your expenses are much more than I had been led to expect; and
> though I wish you to appear respectably you will recollect the necessity
> of observing as much economy as you can with propriety. And as your
> great object is to acquire a knowledge of the modern languages, the
> importance of great diligence will strongly impress your mind and
> influence your conduct. You are surrounded with temptations and al-
> lurements and it will be necessary for you to set a double guard upon
> yourself; and a close attention to your studies will be one of the most ef-
> fectual securities against dissipation—Go but little into Company, &
> be careful to associate with none but the wise & virtuous. Such is your
> youth & inexperience that I feel great solicitude for your safety. . . .

France, to a good Federalist, was the seat of iniquity. But to
nineteen-year-old Henry it was very like heaven. The boulevards—a
series of broad, tree-shaded, café-lined avenues across the northern
edge of the city—were the place to be on a warm summer's evening to
eat ice-creams, he told his brother.

> You cannot conceive what 'carryings on' there are there at all hours
> of the day and evening! Musicians singing and playing the harp—
> jugglers—fiddlers,—jewish cymbals and cat-calls—blind beggars and
> lame beggars,—and beggars without any qualifying term, except im-
> portunity,—men with monkeys—raree shows—venders of tooth-
> picks and cheap wares—Turks in the oriental costume—Frenchmen
> with curling whiskers, and round-plated straw hats—long skirted

coats and tight wrinkled trousers—real-nankeen-ers—coblers—book-sellers with their stalls—little boutiques where no article is sold for more than 15 sous....

The carnivalesque tone of all this probably alarmed his father more than the claret-colored coat. It was the world of *Les Enfants du Paradis*, and Henry, too, became enraptured with the stage. He wrote excitedly, for example, to his Portland friend Patrick Greenleaf of the ageless Mademoiselle Mars, a star at the Comédie Française, and of her half-dozen lovers ("for all French women are naughty women:—as a general rule"). He began a lifelong passion for the opera, particularly after hearing the sopranos Giuditta Pasta and Henrietta Sontag (the latter of whom he would meet years later in Boston).

Learning French was another matter. Like many Americans studying abroad, he found himself too easily falling into the habit of associating only with his compatriots, or with the thousands of Englishmen filling up "every chink and cranny." Since Paris more or less closed down for the month of August, with the help of one of the Frenchmen from the *Cadmus* he found lodgings in the village of Auteuil, in those days three miles out of town, on the edge of the Bois de Boulogne. The extraordinary quiet of the place owed something to its being a *maison de santé*, a sort of convalescent home, but one of its inmates tried too incessantly to practice his English. Longfellow was soon happy to find a totally French-speaking family back in the Faubourg St. Germain, at 5 rue Racine, who rented him winter quarters. Yet the month at Auteuil produced a pang of homesickness. The village's dark streets and unfriendly stone walls, he wrote his mother, reminded him too much of the city. He missed New England villages, "fresh and cheerful and breezy." In a reverse image of Henry James's famous catalogue of America's deficiencies, Longfellow lamented that in France there were "no corn-fields garnished with yellow pumpkins—no green trees, and orchards by the road side—no slab-fences—no well-poles—no painted cottages, with huge barns and outhouses,—ornamented in front with monstrous piles of wood for winter-firing:—nothing in fine to bring to the mind of an American a remembrance of the beautiful villages of his native land."

Before winter set in, he hiked—his flute in his knapsack—during the *vendange*, through the Loire Valley, which he found "one continued vineyard:—on each side of the road as far as the eye could reach—there was nothing but vines save here and there a glimpse of the Loire and the turrets of an old chateau or of a village church." He explored the deserted Château de Chambord, commemorating his visit "by breaking off the head of a little stone dragon"—one of François I's heraldic salamanders—"which I found amongst other ornaments upon the principal staircase—which I shall bring home as a trophy of my journey" (the one self-confessed crime in a long and blameless life). He got as far as Amboise and Tours and Savenièrres, a route filled for him with thoughts of Sir Walter Scott's recently published *Quentin Durward* and of Madame de Staël's exile during Napoleon's reign. The historical and literary significance of what he saw moved him deeply, but Gothic architecture itself was a taste he had yet to acquire—he passed through Chartres on his return to Paris without a comment.

"French comes on famously," he reported to his brother in November. He blamed his earlier difficulties on having been taught in Portland in 1825 by a Monsieur D'Eon, a Swiss or Alsatian whose pronunciation he now realized had been so incorrect that he found himself "speaking French with a German as well as an English accent." This embarrassment may explain why he did not call sooner on the Marquis de Lafayette—a friend of both his father and his grandfather Wadsworth—who in June had given him tickets to debates in the Chamber of Deputies and had invited him to his house at LaGrange. He eventually encountered the general on the street that fall. "He was alone—on foot—and nobody seemed to notice him particularly! What a difference from what it was in America! He gives a great dinner to all the Americans in Paris on the Anniversary of his return to France." With his surer command of French, Longfellow was beginning to feel at ease in Paris and looked forward to a productive winter. To his consternation, his father wanted him to move on to Spain, which Stephen Sr. had the notion could only be comfortably visited in winter.

Actually, Longfellow was not certain what his father wanted him to do. The transatlantic mails had proven slow and erratic. Around the first of October he received a letter that his father had written in August, the *first* letter he had received from home since arriving in France in June. His letters to Portland took nearly three months to reach his family. A dutiful son, Longfellow wanted to honor his father's intentions. But what were they? He also wanted to make sure that the funds he needed for his travels arrived in a timely fashion. His father had established a letter of credit with Dodge & Oxnard in Marseilles— Thomas Oxnard was a Portlander, further evidence of that city's long commercial reach. They in turn had set up an account for the Longfellows with the fashionable Paris banker Samuel Welles, who also received and forwarded Henry's mail.

The chief question was what to do about Germany. Stephen's original idea had been for his son to perfect his French—a language any civilized person should know—and to learn as much Spanish as possible, for more practical reasons. "Your ulterior objects cannot be accomplished unless you obtain an *accurate* knowledge of the *French & Spanish* languages," he wrote in December. "The *situation you have in view cannot be obtained unless you qualify yourself to teach both these languages correctly*. Such are the relations now existing between this country & South America that a knowledge of the Spanish is quite as important as the French." If travel to Spain seemed too hazardous, he told him, find a Spanish instructor in France or even Germany.

> Permit me however to say that I consider the knowledge of the *Spanish* of more importance to you than *German & Italian* both. These latter languages are very desirable, but are by no means so important to *you* as the *French & Spanish*. Indeed if you neglect *either* of *them* your whole object will be defeated, and *you may be sure of not obtaining the station which you have in view*. And I should never have consented to your visiting Europe, had it not been to secure that station.

The emphasis says it all: a tightening of the reins, across three thousand miles. Yet it was not an unfriendly letter. Stephen begged for more details of Henry's sightseeing, on behalf of those who could not visit such places themselves. And he admitted that his son would need two full years abroad.

Germany, however, had grown ever larger on Henry's intellectual horizon. Before leaving America back in the spring, he had consulted with George Ticknor in Boston—probably the most learned man in New England and a great champion of the new German scholarship—and with George Bancroft and Joseph G. Cogswell at their progressive Round Hill School in Northampton, Massachusetts. They urged him to go to the university town of Göttingen, where Ticknor and Bancroft had studied, even if it meant giving up Italy. In a long letter home in October, Longfellow argued for skipping Spain, passing the winter in Paris, and spending the following year in Germany. Even if he could not learn German perfectly in that time, he would be able to read it and understand the lectures on literature. Moreover, his Portland friend and neighbor Edward Preble was planning to be in Göttingen in the spring. This perplexed his parents. The new German critical scholarship—with its emphasis not on *belles lettres* or moral improvement but on the rigorous examination of texts, with the aid of increasingly sophisticated philological tools—had scarcely reached Boston, much less Brunswick. Indeed, his mother wondered why he needed to learn to speak German fluently, since there would be no one in New England to converse with him. She also feared that he would be drawn into the German student vice of dueling. His father saw the Bowdoin professorship slipping away. It was only after Stephen's Harvard classmate, the distinguished jurist Joseph Story, endorsed the idea of a term at Göttingen that the family began to come around.

Meanwhile, Henry had decided to go to Italy instead. To learn German in a year was impossible, after all. He had hinted darkly that it was dangerous to travel in a country so infested with bandits as Spain. So Italy it would be—"the sunny regions of the south." He had grown disgusted, he told his mother, with French manners and customs and would leave for Italy early in the new year, in time for carnival. Then, in February 1827, without a word of explanation, he announced that he was leaving for Spain after all. Stephen, meanwhile, had written him, suggesting he study Spanish in Paris or even Göttingen, rather than venture into a country so torn by civil strife. Henry's abrupt change of plans strengthened Stephen's regret that his son lacked "some judicious companion" to advise him. But what was to be done?

Henry traveled by way of Orléans to Bordeaux—"the most beautiful city I have seen in France." Yet thoughts of his native Maine were never far from mind. From the bridge over the Garonne, he saw on either side "a thick forest of masts—the best kind of forest that a commercial city can be surrounded with." The sandy scrub woods south of the city resembled "the pine plains which surround the village of Brunswick; which makes me wonder that the French do not place a college there—it would keep the students out of temptation!" He was soon at the "dirty little city of Bayonne," which was redeemed in his eyes by the beauty of the sunburnt Basque women—"nut-brown maids"—who conducted travelers by horseback over the border to Irun. He tried to sum up for his father his eight months in France. He did not regret leaving, although he had found the French "a hospitable kind-hearted people." Not particularly interested in politics, he had nonetheless noticed the tension caused by "a weak good-hearted king" and a repressive ministry—a situation that would lead in three years to another revolution and cost Charles X his throne. "I must say that I am well satisfied with the knowledge I have acquired of the french language. My friends all tell me that I have a good pronunciation. . . . I cannot imagine who told you that six months was enough for the French—he would have been more correct if he had said six years—that is—speaking of perfection in the language."

❧

Longfellow was to present Spain to his American readers as a land of romance, but one of the first things that struck a traveler from France, he wrote home, was "the poverty-stricken appearance of everything around him." The country had still not recovered from the Goyaesque horrors of the Peninsular War more than a decade earlier, and it continued to suffer from one of the worst kings in its history, Ferdinand VII, who had exiled everyone of liberal views, reinstituted the Inquisition, and surrounded himself with corrupt and incompetent advisers. Economic ruin had forced a good part of the rural population into brigandage. Writing from Madrid in March, Longfellow nonetheless assured his father that despite "the tales of all that is wild and wonderful in bloody murder and highway robbery" he had reached the capital without incident. It was important to be in Madrid, he went on, because:

> The metropolis of a country is always the great literary mart ... literary advantages are always greater—books always more numerous and accessible:—in this country, where the art of printing itself has nearly fallen into disuse from the rigorous censorship of the press—and consequently all the editions of works whose spirit is at all liberal and elevated,—are old editions—it is important that a student should resort to the Capital; for there he will find literary fountains unsealed and flowing. There are the provincial accents, too, which cannot be too assiduously avoided—and my expenses are much less here than at Paris.

He was delighted with the city and immediately attracted to the language. His sojourn was made more pleasant by the fact that the tiny circle of North Americans in Madrid welcomed him at once, Spain being a place few Americans visited for pleasure. This circle consisted of Alexander H. Everett, the United States minister to Spain (and later editor of the *North American Review*), and his wife, for whom Longfellow soon became a favorite; John Adams Smith, secretary of legation; the much admired Washington Irving, attaché; Irving's expatriate brother Peter; the bibliophile Obadiah Rich, consul and a major conduit for Hispanic culture into the United States; and a traveling naval officer on leave who was only four years older than Longfellow, Lieutenant Alexander Slidell (who later added the family name of Mackenzie to his own, in order to obtain the legacy of a childless uncle). Longfellow had met Peter Irving in Paris, and it is possible that the chance to befriend his literary hero is what persuaded him to venture into Spain. Washington Irving, he wrote home, was "one of those men who put you at ease with them in a moment. He makes no ceremony whatever with one ... —all mirth and good humor." A lawyer who had turned to literature, Irving had achieved international fame in his late thirties as author of *The Sketch Book* and its sequel, *Bracebridge Hall*, each a collection of genial, rambling essays and tales. Along with Bryant and Cooper, he offered evidence that an American might achieve fame, perhaps even a tolerable living, as an author. He was at work on what was to prove a highly successful life of Columbus and would go on to write perhaps the most famous of all accounts of the Alhambra (a site Longfellow actually visited before Irving did). None of this was lost on the young Longfellow, whose first book was to be inspired by Irving and who would draw heavily on the Spanish lore he began to acquire from his new friends in Madrid.

But, in the short run, it was Lieutenant Slidell who had the greater impact. He was a character out of a Patrick O'Brian novel: a daring young naval officer with strong literary interests and sharp powers of observation. He was exactly the sort of resourceful, energetic companion the bookish Longfellow needed in order to take on as hazardous a country as Spain. Longfellow was to stay in Spain from March through November of 1827, but the most vivid part of the visit was the trip through the mountains to Segovia, which he made with Slidell, who later wrote:

> Nor was I doomed on this occasion to travel without a companion. Fortune, in a happy moment, provided one in the person of a young countryman, who had come to Spain in search of instruction. He was just from college, full of all the ardent feeling excited by classical pursuits, with health unbroken, hope that was a stranger to disappointment, curiosity which had never yet been fed to satiety. Then he had sunny locks, a fresh complexion, and a clear blue eye, all indications of a joyous temperment. We had been thrown almost alone together in a strange and unknown land, our ages were not dissimilar, and, though

our previous occupations had been more so, we were, nevertheless, soon acquainted, first with each other, then with each other's views, and presently after we had agreed to be companions on the journey.

Longfellow spared his family many of the harsher details of his months in Spain, filling his long letters instead with local color, but Slidell left behind a graphic account of his own experiences, published anonymously in 1829 under the title *A Year in Spain, by a Young American*. It is a very readable book, attesting to his powers as a reporter: he is one of the first Anglo-American writers to appreciate the primitive. Slidell describes being robbed in a mountain pass by bandits, who tortured and almost killed his guides; he describes in sickening detail a public hanging in Madrid; he gives the first detailed account in American literature of a bullfight. (He does the bullfight so well that the more squeamish Longfellow, in *Outre-Mer*, could say that it had been done before and pass over it.) He loves Spain, but does not pretend to understand its abrupt juxtapositions of beauty and horror.

In one of his letters after they had parted company, Slidell teases Longfellow a bit about the wonderful Florencia, the daughter of the family in whose house they lived in Madrid, in the Calle de la Montera. She had married a Cuban, he had heard, which he hoped was true (so he could visit her by ship someday) and which was probably a good thing, for she would otherwise "run a great risque of becoming either a nun or a prostitute, two evils between which there is little choice." In *A Year in Spain* he elaborates on this theme, possibly even describing Florencia Gonzalez:

> The Spanish woman is, indeed, a most fascinating creature. Her complexion is usually a mellow olive, often russet, rarely rosy ... Her skin smooth and rich—face round, full, and well proportioned, with eyes large, black, brilliant ... when she moves, every gesture becomes a grace and every step a study. Her habitual expression is one of sadness and melancholy; but when she meets an acquaintance and makes an effort to please, opening her full-orbed and enkindling eyes, and parting

her rich lips to make room for the contrasting pearl of her teeth, or to give passage to some honied word, the heart must be more than adamant that can withstand her blandishments.

There is, however—let us show the whole truth—one female virtue, which, though it may belong to many in Spain, is yet not universal—and this is chastity.... I know not whence this decline of morals, if not from the poverty of the country; which, while it checks marriages and the creation of families, cannot check the passions enkindled by an ardent clime.

This may all be shipboard fantasy, but Slidell does describe a physical type of woman that appealed to Longfellow all his life, and it raises the question of whether Longfellow's own infatuation with Spain was linked with a sexual awakening. He was, after all, an attractive young man far from home with money in his pocket—in a country where people killed for bread. He lived an extraordinarily well documented life, but those documents were thoroughly sorted through in his own lifetime, and further edited by his heirs, and no hint of sexual adventure survives. He had grown up in a busy port that certainly had its demimonde, but it was a small place where everyone knew everyone else's business (to Stephen Jr.'s loss), and where he had gone to some effort to set himself apart from his rakish older brother. Bowdoin College had been built in a quiet country town to spare its students temptations. But when Longfellow arrived in Europe, there was nothing to restrain him other than his own inhibitions—and some anxiety about what rumors might reach home. Certainly every pleasure was procurable for a price in Restoration Paris; Madrid would have required a greater degree of circumspection, but even less money. All of this is speculative. Yet Longfellow was to prove in years to come a highly sensual man, addicted to the pleasures of wine, cigars, good food, music, and beautiful and luxurious objects, and with a well-documented eye for handsome, dark-haired women. There is no reason to assume that by 1828 he was sexually inexperienced.

What we do know that he found in Spain was a country virtually unknown to other North Americans, with a rich and unexplored literature, written in a language that was both beautiful to his ear and comparatively easy to learn and pronounce. He was reasonably fluent in Spanish by the time he left, an extraordinary accomplishment in nine months of travel. For reasons he never explained, he never returned there (Slidell, on the other hand, would reappear in his life, in tragic circumstances, some fifteen years later). But Longfellow's fascination with *Hispanidad*—Spanishness, both as a literary tradition and a worldview—enriched his work for the rest of his life. His very last poem, written a few weeks before he died in 1882, he entitled "The Bells of San Blas."

The Italian part of Longfellow's first European trip seems by comparison the most conventionally Grand Tour in character of all his travels. He had left Madrid in September of 1827 and by way of Seville and Cadiz reached Gibraltar, where he spent a month amid the British garrison, followed by visits to Malaga and Granada. He took ship for Marseilles in mid-December, and by Christmas Eve had reached Genoa. He spent January of 1828 in Florence, then proceeded south, reaching Rome in time for carnival and staying there for the rest of the year, with an excursion to Naples and the ruins of Pompeii in April and a summer retreat to L'Arricia, in the hills above Rome. A flirtation with his Roman landlord's daughter seems to have helped the days pass quickly. By Christmas of 1828, he was in Venice, en route via Trieste, Vienna, and Prague to Germany.

In retrospect, the Italian year had a deep influence on Longfellow's life and career; after all, he was to become the most famous translator of Dante in nineteenth-century America, and in his final years he was to become fascinated by the life and poetry of Michelangelo. More immediately, he formed a deep bond with another young American, whom he met while traveling from Toulon to Pisa. George Washington Greene was, like Longfellow, the grandson of a famous Revolutionary War general—in his case, Nathaniel Greene of Rhode Island—and he shared Longfellow's literary and historical interests. Having moved to Rome for his health, he also spoke fluent Italian and knew a great deal about both classical antiquities and contemporary art. He was, in other words, as perfect a companion in his own way as Slidell had been in Spain. Their friendship was to last for fifty-four years. In his old age, when Greene was to depend emotionally and financially on Longfellow's continuing good will, he frequently recalled for him "our fairy life at Naples, our moonlight strolls in the Forum, our morning excursions in the Campagna" and their Christmas together at Genoa—"her splendid Cathedral with the imposing midnight service of the Catholic Church, our little terrace with the 'tideless Mediterranean' spreading in majesty before us."

Longfellow picked up Italian quickly, finding its only complication being that so many words were only a letter or two different from the same words in Spanish. By the end of 1828, he could boast to his father that "all at the Hotel, where I lodge took me for an Italian, until I gave them my passport, and told them I was an American." He may have mistaken flattery for frankness, but his achievement was real. Yet somehow Italy did not move him as deeply as Spain had—possibly because its tourist routes had been so well traveled. He took his tourism seriously, though—sketching the ruins on the Appian Way, taking detailed notes on the Roman carnival for future use, managing to arrive at Venice by boat in the moonlight, even befriending Lord Byron's favorite gondolier (himself a poet who wrote a sonnet for Longfellow). For much of the summer, however, Longfellow felt ill, recovering only after a retreat to the hill town of L'Arricia. Perhaps it was "Roman fever" (malaria), perhaps it was simply fatigue after so many inns, so many irregular verbs.

Like most Protestant Americans visiting the south of Europe, he was both fascinated and repulsed by Catholicism. France, at least in Paris, had seemed a secular culture; Spain, so darkened by the Church that a first-time visitor could not begin to delve into its mysteries. But Italy—with its colorful feast days, its churches which seemed muse-

ums, and its citizens' apparent nonchalance about religious obser-
vance—offered an easier study. In September of 1828, for example,
Longfellow wrote to his sisters:

> You would be shocked at the misery of the people—especially in the
> Pope's dominions:—but their element seems to be in rags and misery—
> and with the mummery of their religion and the holidays of the
> church—which average nearly three a week, they are poor—and lazy,
> and happy—I mean happy in their way:—for the negro slaves within
> the precincts of the Southern States are their equals in liberty, and
> infinitely their superiors in every comfort:—so you may judge what
> happiness is among the poorer classes of Italians.

This was a stereotypical Anglo-American view of Italian peasants
(and Longfellow at this point knew little about the lives of Southern
slaves) but "the mummery of their religion" did make an impression
on him. He saw it as a stage of civilization that his own society had
long progressed beyond, yet he did not fear or despise it (as so many
New Englanders did) but rather identified it with a medievalism in
which he discovered much of value. In 1847, the Acadian peasant
Evangeline—Longfellow's greatest creation—arose from that "mummery" and found in it her deepest satisfaction. And in *The Golden
Legend* (1851) and many shorter works, the poet was to borrow again
from Catholicism's rich treasury of narratives.

⚜

News from his family began to catch up with him. In the spring of
1828, one of the people he heard from, surely to his surprise, was his
Aunt Lucia. She was not by nature a letter writer, preferring to add a
line at the end of Zilpah's letters, if at all, but she had played a large role
in Henry's childhood, as the aunt on whom much of the burden of running the busy Portland household had fallen. The few glimpses we get
of her from others reveal a woman who certainly knew her own mind.
Her letter to her nephew deserves to be quoted in full, for it is one of
the very few times we hear her actual voice:

Portland, April 26, 1828

Dear Henry,

I am unwilling to be the only member of the family who does not express, in form of a letter, the affection they feel for you, still I am aware that a letter from a maiden aunt cannot afford you much amusement, for to be written in character, it must contain sage maxims and advice, cautions against the temptations to which you are so constantly exposed, against dissipation of every kind, urgent entreaties to take special care of your health, recipes for colds, coughs, &c and tho' much age will entitle me to do all this, yet I am not so thoroughly initiated into the mysteries and privileges of a "state of single blessedness," as will induce me to undertake it, therefore I cannot pursue this course. all useful and necessary counsel you will receive from your parents, all domestic information from others, of the family, all accounts of matters and things in general, from your numerous correspondents, and from the mouth of Edward [Preble] himself. flights of imagination, sentiment and all that, you know I never attempt a letter on science and literature is altogether out of my line, so what remains for me, but to assure you that I love you as well as any of your friends do, that I feel as great an interest in your welfare and happiness, and shall rejoice as much, when the objects of your tour are attained, and you return again to your friends.

Your aunt
L W.

A sly note of satire on his parents' admonishing letters comes through.

A more alarming letter from Stephen Sr. reached him in Rome, apparently in the first week of December of 1828. The letter is lost, but it informed him that Bowdoin College would not offer him the professorship (at an annual salary of one thousand dollars) but only a tutorship in modern languages (salary: six hundred dollars). The rationale for this is uncertain—possibly some belt tightening on the college's part, but more likely the result of a squabble between the two boards,

perhaps encouraged by President Allen and exacerbated by Maine politics and religious factionalism (Stephen did not lack enemies). At any
rate, Longfellow was outraged. Having brooded for two weeks, he exploded in a letter from Venice on December 19:

> I assure you—my dear father—I am very indignant at this. They say
> I am too young! Were they not aware of this three years ago? If I am not
> capable of performing the duties of the office, they may be very sure of
> my not accepting it . . . [F]or my own part I do not in the least regard it
> as a favor conferred upon me. It is no sinecure: and if my services are an
> equivalent to my salary,—there is no favor done me:—if they be not, I
> do not desire the situation. If they think I would accept the place they
> offer me,—as I presume they do,—they are much mistaken in my char-
> acter. No Sir—I am not yet reduced to this. I am not a dog to eat the
> crumbs, that fall from such a table. . . .

Stephen, while regretting that his son had expressed himself "with
quite so much warmth," admitted that his own feelings were quite similar. But he counseled moderation. The tutorship could be seen as a
probationary year, he suggested, after which the college would surely
give him the professorship. They would discuss it when he returned. In
August of 1829, amid the debate over whether to spend the funds for
the professorship of modern languages on a new chapel instead, trustee
William Pitt Preble suggested a motive for Bowdoin's action in a letter
to his fellow trustee Reuel Williams: "There is a project on foot I am
assured from a source that cannot be mistaken," wrote Preble, "to defeat the appointment of Mr. Longfellow on account of his supposed
Unitarianism."

Henry meanwhile had reached Trieste, "so very melancholy and
down-hearted," uncertain whether to spend the winter in Dresden or
Göttingen. Washington Irving, who had been a great success at the
Saxon court a decade earlier, had given Longfellow letters of introduction that would have guaranteed him a brilliant social life in the capital. Dresden—with its glorious architecture, superb opera and
orchestras, royal collections, and great libraries—represented one of
the pinnacles of European civilization. Yet he spent a listless, homesick

month there. In February he decided he could wait no longer to see his old friend Preble and rushed off by way of Leipzig, through the Thuringian forests, and on to the famous Hanoverian university town. He arrived in Göttingen on February 22, five days short of his twenty-second birthday.

⚜

Göttingen was the first choice of the handful of Americans in the 1820s who had heard or intuited that something was going on in the German universities quite different from the experience offered by their French or British counterparts. Founded in 1737 by George II of England, in his role as Elector of Hanover, it had proven particularly hospitable to English-speaking students. It had also cultivated an aristocratic tone, with all that implied in the way of reckless behavior. As Henry's mother fretted in a letter in 1826, "In one account of the University in that place the students are represented as being very numerous, very licentious, unrestrained by the government; *extremely* addicted to duelling. Dear Henry such associates would be neither pleasant or profitable to you, and if they were unprincipled, they would not scruple to use any means, however unjustifiable, to entangle you in their schemes."

In truth, the enticements a young New Englander might face at Göttingen were more intellectual than sensual. The university had already produced, in the late eighteenth century, a circle of poets—the Göttinger Hain ("grove")—who prefigured German Romanticism. In Longfellow's own day, scholars at Göttingen were engaged in one of the great intellectual upheavals of the nineteenth century—the close, philological examination of Biblical texts, a line of inquiry that would eventually undermine many an intelligent Christian's belief in the literal truth of scripture. (In the early twentieth century, Göttingen was to produce another great intellectual thunderbolt: the discoveries in physics associated with Max Born and Werner Heisenberg.) It is unclear how much Longfellow, with his beginner's German, could understand of what was going on in the lecture halls, but, in contrast to

FIGURE 3: Longfellow's sketch *My Book and Friend*, Göttingen, 1829.
Edward Preble (right) reads *The Old Dominion Zeitung*. Courtesy
National Park Service, Longfellow National Historic Site.

the conventional education he had received at Bowdoin, he suddenly
found himself in one of the most intellectually advanced communities
in Europe. He was to sit in on lectures and study the language with a
distinguished Germanist, Hofrat Benecke.

His first instinct, though, was to find Ned Preble and catch up on
the news from home. He arrived by post chaise at 2:00 a.m., too late to
call, so he slept at "The Crown" and hurried in the morning to Juden-
gasse 462 (or, as Longfellow wrote, "Jew Alley"). Preble was out, but
Longfellow insisted on waiting inside.

In the antichamber stood a sofa with crimson plush covering: opposite hung a portrait of Napoleon, and in a corner a four-stringed guitar.
I entered Ned's room—his sitting room—study room. Splendidly
lodged—thought I. In one corner stood a writing table and book-case,
and in another the stove, in another a sofa, with a round table before
it—and in the fourth a clock ticked from a mahogany bureau. A check-

ered morning gown hung against the wall—here was a map of Germany, and there sundry long-stemmed porcelain pipes with a tobacco-pouch made of a bladder. . . .

I shall not attempt to describe my feelings when at length Ned came in. I had taken him completely by surprise. . . . What talk of old times! With three numbers of the Yankee before us—half an Eastern Argus— and an old Eastport [Maine] Sentinel!

Edward Deering Preble had grown up next door to the Longfellows in Portland. His father, who had died when Edward was one year old, was the Commodore Preble of Barbary war fame. Edward, an only child, had graduated in the Longfellow brothers' class at Bowdoin and had tried his hand at business. But literature appealed to him more, and by 1828 he had found his way to Göttingen. Urbane and cultivated, he was never to amount to anything, by the standards of his tribe, although for a few years he did read law in Portland. As his Bowdoin memorialist made certain to point out, upon his early death in 1846, "What many young persons consider a favorable circumstance in life was to Mr. Preble . . . its greatest evil. He was born to a fortune which, however, he did not live to possess; but the expectation of it, and the gratification of every desire, paralyzed exertion, rendered him versatile, morbid, and unhappy. With talents capable of high achievement . . . he failed of accomplishing anything useful by irresolution and want of a settled purpose of action." All this was in the future, but the example set by Preble's decision to turn his back on the Deering family's lucrative business connections in favor of travel and literature surely had given Stephen Longfellow Sr. some moments of anxiety.

Henry could not have been more delighted, on the other hand, and seems to have spent most of his time at Göttingen in Preble's company. The student cloak and cap, the broad swords, the deerskin dueling gloves to be seen on and about Preble suggest a rapid if superficial assimilation in the local culture. Neither young man had lived before in a society in which university students were so privileged and so visually distinctive, and the arcana of *Burschenschaft* life—the ceremonial duels, the heroic beer drinking, the "medieval" songs—enthralled them, at least from a distance. Longfellow found rooms in what is now the Rote Strasse, a few steps from the old Town Hall and the famous modern statue of "The Little Goose Girl." The house is much altered, but the roof line still looks sixteenth-century, and a small marble plaque indicates that Henry W. Longfellow lived there in 1829. (In the late nineteenth century, such markers were put up to commemorate the residences of several famous Americans who had studied at Göttingen.)

Somewhat cut off from everyday German student life, Longfellow and Preble diverted themselves by producing their own four-page, quarto-sized, handwritten newspaper, five issues of which (and part of a sixth) survive. Mildly ribald in tone and full of student jokes, it was intended not for their families but for a small circle of male Portland intimates. Longfellow did most of the writing and drew the many illustrations, and Preble added comments or filled in the blank spots. The "Prospectus" parodied both the political newspapers that Stephen Sr. spent so much time reading and the rather earnest American literary reviews:

> A Journal, that should be at once a vehicle of amusement and of Foreign Intelligence, has long been a desideratum in the literary world. It is to fill up this hiatus, that the Editors of the Old Dominion Zeitung have determined to issue this Journal. In making it worthy of themselves and of their subscribers, no time nor pains will be spared them —they are resolved to "go the whole hog."—.... Coming from the University Press we hope it may be an acceptable offering to the Public. There is a literary atmosphere about the walls of Gottingen which breathes new life into the nostrils that inhale it.... The Old Dominion Zeitung will be published once a week at Gottingen and forwarded to subscribers at the moderate rate of their kind remembrance—"payable in advance!!"

Their painstakingly produced *Zeitung*, or newspaper, had nothing to do with Virginia; the "Old Dominion" probably referred to the United States more generally, as suggested by Longfellow's large drawing of an American eagle dominating the globe in the fourth issue, which declared itself "Published every Saturday evening at the corner of Rothen and Weender Strasse—Gottingen." Much of the text —snippets from their reading in several languages, allusions to politics back home, odds and ends of student lore—has lost its bite, but the illustrations reveal Longfellow's unsuspected gift for caricature. Many of them are visual souvenirs of German student life: elaborately carved pipes ("Ned says he never feels so philosophical, as when he has a pipe in his mouth"), dueling gear, the interior of Preble's room, and a complicated tableau depicting the "burial" of a *Bursch* (or student) by way of illustrating a local tale. But a surprising amount of space is devoted to an extended lampoon of Bowdoin College, and particularly of its militantly orthodox president, the Reverend William Allen. The first issue has over the masthead a tag from Thompson—"A little round, fat, oily man of God" and a drawing from the rear of just such a personage, with Bowdoin College in the distance. The second depicts an ass labeled "B. Coll." ridden backwards by a large man holding on to its tail in a sexually suggestive fashion. A figure labeled "Public Opinion" snaps a whip; in the distance, the sun—a symbol of the college—rises in the east (Maine). A line from Wordsworth completes the caricature: "The long-drawn see-saw of his horrible bray!" The fifth issue depicts one of the Gadarene swine (Matthew 8:28) racing down into the sea, with a little man with an umbrella sticking out of its rump. A gloss in Preble's hand explains: "The Devil (Gul.)[= Gulielmus, or William, as in Allen] entered in to the swine (B Col) and straightaway they ran violently down a steep place (public opinion) in to the sea (where they ought to have been ten years ago) and were drowned." The sixth issue includes a very graphic cartoon ("Public Opinion in the East") of a butcher slaughtering hogs ("Professors of the *Dead* languages").

Finally, an undated page—perhaps all that survives of the third issue—includes a cartoon labeled "Bowdoin College" and "The March of the Mind in the East!" It depicts an ass bearing baskets on each side, Spanish style, one of which is labeled "Northern Darkness." The beast tramples on a copy of Locke's *Essay Concerning Human*

Understanding, Paine's *Rights of Man,* and the *Laws of Bowdoin College,* while kicking over a tub out of which spills the "Professorship of Modern Languages." Lawrence Sterne provides the caption: "—a poor ass—who had just turned in with a couple of panniers upon his back to collect eleemosynary turnip-tops, and cabbage leaves." A further drawing depicts a view of the college, with a road sign pointing to it with the words "Road To Ruin."

"We have been creditably informed," the *Old Dominion Zeitung* goes on to say, "that a professorship being offered to a young man by the government of Bowd. Coll. on condition of his passing two years in Europe—at his own expense—at the expiration of that time the situation of Tutor was offered him, with little more than half a professor's salary!—we are happy to add—that such a proposition has been treated with all the contempt it deserved!" These verses in Longfellow's hand followed:

> *Said the old Professor to the young professor,*
> *Thou shalt be Tutor now!—*
> *Said the young professor to the old professor—*
> *I can teach as well as thou!*
> *Said the Old Trustee to the young professor,*
> *Will make a cheap bargain with you—*
> *Said the young professor to the Old Trustee—*
> *No—I'll be _____ if you do.*

The satire is coarse, the humor sophomoric, the anger real. The *Old Dominion Zeitung* could have cost Longfellow any opportunity to be employed at Bowdoin, had it fallen into the wrong hands. Yet it enabled him to vent his aggressions, doubtless with the encouragement of Preble, who had nothing to lose, and the zestiness of the whole production suggests that his Dresden depression had lifted.

It is unlikely that even Longfellow, as quick a study as he was, had learned much German in two and a half months at Göttingen, or comprehended very much of the lectures he attended there. But the seed was planted. Meanwhile, spring vacation stirred him to see more. He spent a month traveling down the Rhine ("a noble river: but not so fine as the Hudson") and via Brussels and Calais to England, where he spent a week in London (which seemed to make little impression on him), returning by way of Rotterdam, Amsterdam, and Utrecht. His father was willing to finance several more months of study in Germany (as long as his son sailed home before the seas turned rough), but Longfellow was ready by the first week of June to begin his journey back to America. There were alarming reports of his sister Elizabeth's health, and he had been away from his family far longer than anyone had anticipated. Still trying to sort through the personal and cultural experiences of three years abroad, he was nonetheless ready for a confrontation with the president and governing boards of Bowdoin.

Four

BUNGONUCK DAYS

THE EXCITEMENT OF HENRY'S RETURN to Portland after more than three years abroad was tempered by the tragedy that had struck his family in May of 1829. After nine months of illness, the last three of them marked by great suffering and depression, Henry's favorite sister, Elizabeth, aged twenty, had died of tuberculosis. The long and affectionate letter he had written her from Göttingen in March reached Portland three weeks too late. Her cough had worsened in the spring, and her family and fiancé, the promising young lawyer William Pitt Fessenden, drew near to bid her farewell. Her mother, her younger sister Ann, and her Aunt Lucia nursed her as best they could. Like many young people dying of consumption in the nineteenth century, she had a sudden flush of strength, physical and mental, at almost the last moment. Thought nearly dead on a Sunday, on the following Tuesday she pulled herself together, and in her father's words, "with the firmness & composure of a true christian, she took an affectionate leave of all her friends, not forgetting her dear absent brother. She had often expressed a wish to see you once more." Fessenden—known to the family as Pitt—arrived the night before she died. According to Zilpah, "she told him she had looked forward and anticipated enjoying a great deal of happiness with him in life, but that was past, God saw fit to take her home and he must not try to win her back to this world, for she was ready and willing to resign everything here, she wished him all happiness and trusted they should meet in a better world." In her parents' accounts of her final days, the horrors of the sickroom resolve themselves into the calm, loving passage of an innocent child trusting in a God as benevolent as he is inscrutable. It is the good death that was to play so large a role in the Victorian imagination. "To see a timid feeble girl meeting without dread the messenger who so often appals the stoutest heart was indeed a most consoling sight," wrote Zilpah. "When you left us," his father wrote Henry, "I did not expect we should all meet again in this world, but I expected myself to be the first victim. . . . Poor Ann, whose attentions to her sister have been constant, watchful and most affectionate, to the last moment of her existence, is almost disconsolate." The family circle had been broken, and the mother and father were never quite to recover. Fessenden recovered, married Ellen Deering in 1832, and went on to a distinguished legal and political career. As Lincoln's secretary of the treasury, he financed the Union war effort, and he is best remembered today as one of John F. Kennedy's "profiles in courage," the senator from Maine whose single vote saved the impeached Andrew Johnson from losing the presidency. The frail Elizabeth Longfellow had perhaps taught him his first lesson in personal courage.

Henry's return voyage was made in the shadow of this tragedy; his father's letter had reached him in Paris, where he had finally called on Lafayette, although his mother's letter to Liverpool had been delayed and eventually found its way back to Portland. By late August he was home. Despite his brave words of the previous year, there was no confrontation with the college; his father had successfully mediated between the officers of Bowdoin and his proud son. After conferring with Dr. Nichols at First Parish Church, Stephen had concluded that Henry ought to get his foot in the door. At the end of the first year, they could renegotiate. He assured Henry that, despite earlier rumors, "the guardians of the Institution" were well disposed toward him and did not think him too young to teach. The professors "seem to be kind & cordial, and I have no doubt but they would be happy to receive you into their fraternaty. It is very important that you should have some employment on your return, and this is better than any thing that occurs to me at present." Henry's proposal for a series of winter lectures drawn from his travels would be welcomed in Portland, he added, "but as we are not a literary people, I doubt whether any reliance could be placed on it as an employment, and the same objection exists with respect [to] other literary labors in this place, unconnected with some literary Institution." Teaching at Bowdoin would enable Henry to pursue his studies; "the compensation is not great but will answer for one year, and in that time you will be able to look round and mature your plans."

On August 27, however, Henry wrote to the president of Bowdoin, turning down the offer made a year earlier to be instructor in modern languages, at a salary of six hundred dollars: "having at great expense, devoted four years to the acquisition of the French, Spanish, Italian, and German, languages, I cannot accept a subordinate station with a salary so disproportionate to the duties required." This was an exaggeration of his command of German (and of his time in Europe), but the objection was well founded. Since the new term was soon to begin, the college faced some embarrassment (everyone he had seen in Boston, he told his father, assumed he had the professorship). The trustees persuaded the overseers to compromise. On September 2, he accepted the professorship, at a salary of eight hundred dollars, with an additional hundred for serving as college librarian (a post that required one hour of work a day in term), "with the understanding that my salary shall at some future day be made equal to that of the other professors." It was a nice piece of work, offering all parties a chance to save face. It also revealed an independent streak in Henry that put his father on notice that the terms of their relationship had changed.

Earlier that year, while still at Göttingen, Longfellow had allowed himself, in a letter to his father, to envision an ideal university. The traditional New England model of the country college, with its classical curriculum and its theological tone, was clearly out of date in a land that enjoyed both freedom of thought and "the matter-of-fact way of thinking"; it would soon be swept away, he predicted, by democratic public opinion. Germany and France had shown the way by making higher education available to everyone who deserved it. But what was the idea of an American university? "Two or three large brick buildings with a chapel, and a President to pray in it." Even Jefferson—"Mr. Jef-

ferson," he calls him—failed at his attempt to create a modern university because he began "where everybody else in *our* country would have
begun,—by building college halls and then trying to stock them with
Students." European universities had not shared this architectural
fixation—"one might live in Göttingen from one year's end to the
other without having the slightest idea of its being the seat of a
University." Rather, they had originated as gatherings of professors
renowned enough to draw students to them and "capable of teaching
them something they did not know before."

By this point in his prospectus, Longfellow had really got going—
one can see the fluttering student lamp on his table, smell the pipe
tobacco—and he rhapsodized: "instead of seeing a new College ushered into existence every winter by a petition to the Legislature for
funds to put up a parcel of Woolen-Factory buildings for students—we
should see capital better employed in enriching the libraries of the
country and making them *public*!—and instead of seeing the youth of
our country chained together like galley slaves and 'scouraged to the
dungeons'—as it were—our eyes would be cheered by the grateful
spectacle of mind throwing its fetters off—and education freed from
its chains and shackles."

It is not known what Stephen Longfellow, a very conventional man
and trustee of the local college, made of this. Possibly he took the
woolen-factory buildings as a reference to Waterville College (today,
Colby), Bowdoin's new rival in Maine; the Fichtean tone of "mind
throwing its fetters off" must have sounded like the worst excesses of
the new German romanticism. But his son was just warming up. The
University of Paris, with its free lectures, would be his model—"We
think in America, that there is nothing but frivolity in France—would
God we had a little *such* frivolity in our country." Or take German universities as models:

> Let two or three Professors—begin the work—let them deliver lec-
> tures in some town—(Portland seems to me better adapted for it than
> any other place in our part of the country)—not in a village—not in the

woods if their lectures be worth anything—they will have hearers and disciples enough—and a nucleus will thus be formed around which is to grow an University. In the outset, lectures could be gratis—no, the profits arising therefrom should be the Professor's support. Every one should rely upon his own talents for support—and his pay would in consequence be in proportion to his ability.

What followed must have caused Stephen some alarm. Henry reaffirmed that he wanted nothing to do with Bowdoin, whose "system is too limited and superficial." He would sow the seeds of university reform on the European model back in Maine. "Portland is just the spot for an University—(not a College)—it is neither too large nor too small." Upon returning home, he would put his shoulder to this particular wheel. He reminded his father that even he had once proposed giving up practice and offering lectures in the law instead (possibly on the model of Tapping Reeve's famous law school in Litchfield, Connecticut). The two of them would join forces and welcome others. "Let not a word be said about an University but let lectures upon different subjects be read—and students will collect. Thus we may steal silently upon the world with these innovations—and without Legislative grants, or College buildings, our State will see an University spring into existence in its very bosom—without its having even an intimation of its origin."

Longfellow was a generation ahead of his time in calling for universities on the European research model—he would live to see a version of this emerge in President Eliot's Harvard after the Civil War—and he romanticized the air of academic freedom and intellectual laissez-faire that he detected in his continental models; in truth, the German universities were all under close government oversight, as some liberal Göttingen professors were to discover to their peril in the 1830s. But he was strikingly progressive in calling for free higher education, free public libraries, merit pay for teaching, and something like a lyceum for the general intelligent public, and he was prescient in criticizing American educators for caring more for bricks and mortar than for ideas. (And he was right in implying that Bowdoin would have been a stronger, freer institution had it been situated in Portland.)

What Longfellow found when he started teaching in Brunswick in September of 1829 was a college even more deeply mired in politics than when he had left. The struggle between Trinitarian Congregationalists and liberal Unitarians for the "soul" of the institution seemed an intramural affair compared to the public controversy that had erupted over the right claimed by the Maine legislature to pack the college's governing boards with political appointees. In earlier days, this might have been an advantage in terms of the college's financial stability, but statehood in 1820 had changed all that. Bowdoin College was identified in the minds of many voters in the new state as a citadel of reaction, a cultural bastion of the antidemocratic views of its Federalist and later Whig supporters. The new Maine majority was Democratic and backcountry, suspicious of the older coastal elite, and decidedly evangelical in its religion, which tended to be Baptist or Methodist rather than Congregational, much less Unitarian. The new state's constitution placed Bowdoin firmly under the legislature's control, and it was not until 1833 (and the dramatic dismissal, then return—after a law suit—of President Allen) that the college was able to assert its contractual right to existence as a private institution. (At that point, the state subsidies stopped, and the Congregationalists—who were able to raise funds—tightened their grip for half a century on what was still, strictly speaking, a secular college.)

These quarrels would have seemed somewhat remote to the young professor, who in 1829 was more or less inventing his discipline as he went along (but not totally remote: it was Stephen Longfellow Sr. who represented the college, unsuccessfully, in the crucial suit *McKean v. Allen*). If American students were in fact galley slaves, it was now Henry who had to take his turn with the whip. New curricular arrangements at the end of fall term required Longfellow to hear the junior class recite French every afternoon, the seniors recite both French and Spanish three times a week (at noon), and the sophomores recite French every morning—in other words, three recitations a day,

Saturday afternoon excepted, in addition to a private lesson in German and the hour each day spent running the library. ("Recitation" in this context meant calling on each student, without warning, to repeat from memory an assigned lesson or to read and translate some lines of a foreign text on the spot. The instructor gave a numerical mark for each such performance; at the end of term, these were added up, and rank in class determined—often to the students' surprise, since they had not been told their marks.) "The prospect before me seems thick-sown with occupations," Henry soon complained to his father, "promising me little leisure for my private studies, which on account of my busy life this last term, already begin to assume a retrograde march."

Longfellow's most immediate challenge was the lack of adequate, up-to-date textbooks, so he set out to write his own, tailored for his students, and had them set in type by Brunswick's ambitious printer and bookdealer, Joseph Griffin. In 1830, for example, Longfellow edited (anonymously) a 156-page volume called *Manuel de Proverbes Dramatiques* for the benefit of his French students. As he explained in a letter to Alexander Slidell, "It is a collection of [seven] small comedies in french, such as are performed in the Soirees of Paris ... [F]rom necessity I shall be obliged to publish the work in parts, wanting it for immediate use in one of my classes." His next work that year had a more personal touch: a translation of Lhomond's *Elements of French Grammar ... with Notes, and Such Illustrations as Were Thought Necessary for the American Pupil*—an elementary textbook, much used in France, and especially adapted by its editor for his Bowdoin students. *French Exercises*, keyed to Lhomond, followed. The same year, Griffin printed Longfellow's edition of *Novelas Espanola. El Serrano de las Alpujarras; y el Cuadro Misterioso*. These were Spanish versions of Washington Irving's "Rip Van Winkle" and "The Young Italian." None of this was scholarly work in the modern sense, but it was a remarkable harvest for one year—and from a small provincial printing shop—and one that showed a real spirit of pedagogical enterprise. Longfellow was not the only Bowdoin professor whose textbooks found a national market— Parker Cleaveland on mineralogy, Samuel Newman on rhetoric, and

Thomas Upham's protopsychological treatise on the will were widely used in American colleges—but his rapidity of publication stands out. He personally paid Griffin for printing these works (the five hundred copies of the first Lhomond edition cost him seventy-two dollars) and had them published under the name of the Portland bookseller Samuel Colman; he recovered his costs as students purchased the books. The second edition of the French grammar in 1831 included the first title page to carry his name, a sign of confidence in his increasing skill, and was published in Boston by Gray and Bowen, a sign of his growing marketability. The same firm published his classroom edition of *Le Ministre de Wakefield*, translated by a Frenchman from Goldsmith, in 1831, and the next year a *Syllabus de la Grammaire Italienne. Par H. W. Longfellow, Professeur de Langues Modernes a Bowdoin-College. A l'Usage de Ceux Qui Possedent la Langue Francaise*—a subject so new to American collegians, it had to be presented in French. This was followed that year by a reader, *Saggi de' Novellieri Italiani d'Ogni Secolo: Tratti da Piu Celebri Scritorri, con Brevi Notizie intorno all Vita di Ciascheduno. Da H. L. Longfellow*—from Boston's "Presso Gray e Bowen."

These textbooks were more than an entrepreneurial venture, in either the monetary or careerist sense. As he explained to his father, he had been delighted to discover in the Bowdoin library some French tales—the *proverbes dramatiques*—that he knew would delight his students. He made a selection from them, designed for those who were advanced enough in the language to want "a manual of polite conversation on familiar topics." He was surprised no one had thought to do something along those lines earlier. "The more I see of the life of an instructer the more I wonder at the course generally pursued by teachers. They seem to forget, that the youthful mind is to be interested in order to be instructed: or at least they overlook the means, by which they may best lead on the mental faculties, at an age when amusement is a more powerful incentive than improvement." Instead, texts reproduced the works of the most polished writers, "fruit that hangs beyond the reach of children, and those whom ignorance of a foreign language puts on the same footing with children." Hence the appeal of his little collec-

tion of dramas, conversational in tone and full of the humor of everyday life.

The playfulness of this approach does not disguise the fact that
Longfellow was deeply unhappy in these first years back in Brunswick.
This was more than simply the deflation anyone might suffer if, after
years of wandering through the capitals of Europe and sampling a wide
range of pleasures, he found himself back where he had started, on the
edge of the pine woods and sandy plains of a small Maine town. It had
to do with his feeling of stasis. In June of 1830, in a letter full of nostalgia for Italy, he described for George Washington Greene his daily life
at college:

> My window looks out upon a balm-of-Gillead tree and the college
> Chapel—and by way of back-ground, I have a fine view of the presi-
> dent's barn and the great road to Portland. I rise at six in the morning
> and hear a french recitation immediately. At seven I breakfast and am
> then master of my time until eleven—when I hear a Spanish lesson.
> After recitation I take a lunch—and at 12 o'clock go into the Library
> where I remain till one. I am then at leisure for the afternoon until five
> when I have another french recitation—at six I take coffee—walk and
> visit friends until nine—study till twelve, and then sleep until six—
> when I begin the same round again. Such is the outline of my life. The
> intervals of college duty, I fill up with my own studies. Last term I was
> publishing books for the use of my pupils, in whom I take a very deep
> interest. This term I am writing a course of lectures on Modern
> Literature—or rather on French, Spanish, and Italian Literature—
> which I am to deliver in Portland next winter.... You see I lead a very
> sober, jog-trot kind of life. My circle of acquaintances in town is
> very limited, and I have taken great pains that it should be so—I am
> on very intimate terms in three families, and that is quite enough. I
> dont care for general society. I like intimate footings.

He took his revenge on Brunswick in a brief work called "The
Wondrous Tale of a Little Man in Gosling Green," which was published in Horace Greeley's *The New-Yorker* in November of 1834, after
winning fifty dollars for its author in that magazine's story contest.

Writing under the name George F. Brown, Longfellow invented a whimsical yet somehow disturbing story about a mysterious stranger who comes to town. Drawing on both the German *Märchen* tradition and the sly "Down East" humor popularized by Seba Smith, the tale takes place in "Bungonuck," which (like the real Brunswick) sits "upon the margin of one of the blue rivers that pour their tributary waters into the broad lap of Merry-meeting Bay." It is "a drowsy land, where the rush of a waterfall lulls the inhabitants into a dreamy state of existence, leaving them neither quite asleep, nor quite awake." The wide and sandy main street "yawns to receive the weary traveller"; the only daily event that breaks the calm is the arrival at noon of the mail coach, which stops briefly "and then wheels away again for the shadowy regions of Down East; for Down East recedes from you as you advance." Aside from the occasional circus, the only interruptions in the village routine arise from disputes at town meeting or schisms in the church, "of as great importance to the elders of the village as was the Arian or Socinian controversy to the early Christian Fathers." As for the inhabitants, "Having very little business of their own, they have ample leisure to devote to the affairs of their neighbors; and, it is said, that even to this day, if a Bungonucker wishes to find out what is going on in his own family, the surest and most expeditious way is to ask the person who lives next door."

Into this sleepy world arrives one summer day a stranger, "gentlemanly-looking," wearing a long surtout gosling green in color, accompanied by a large nail-bound trunk. He speaks English well but with a foreign accent. He eats his dinner at the inn, lights a cigar, and rides off again in the stage, as mysteriously as he had arrived. The mild stir this caused is soon forgotten, until he appears again in the fall, at the same hour and in the same clothes. Where had he been? He evades answering the townspeople directly.

> They pressed upon him close, and succeeded in tracking him as far as Owl's Head and Clam Cove. Then he dodged them, though they contrived to get another peep at him near Cape Split, and Haycock Harbor, and fairly came up with him again among the Passamaquoddy

Indians and the Blue Noses. They finally lost sight of him altogether, and gave up the pursuit. All they could gather from his evasive answers was, that though he found the place where they eat plum-cake for breakfast yet he did not get far enough to see the sun rise in the west. As for Down East, he said he could not find it. The farther he went, the farther that went; it was like trying to tread upon your own shadow.

To the puzzlement of the Bungonuckers, he settles in the town, opening a variety store "which, like a tailor's drawer, contained a little of everything," and drinking brandy, smoking his pipe, evading questions as to his true identity—"a very quiet, unoffending, urbane man, [who] had evidently seen better days; but where and when was an impenetrable mystery." Wild rumors circulate—that he is an exiled general, that he is a Jesuit. As the years pass, he falls into an irreversible decline, selling his worldly goods one by one and shutting himself away in his room over the shop. His health rapidly fails, and one day the deacon calls to determine once and for all if the rumors are true that he is an atheist. Satisfying himself that the Little Man in Gosling Green does at least believe in the Devil, the deacon reports back, and a flood of village charity sweeps down upon the starving, much misunderstood stranger. "Now he had more dinners sent to him in one week than he could eat in three. But alas! these blessings came too late." All the local samaritans can do is to provide him an extra blanket and a feather bed, to die on. "There are some places in the world where it is easier to die than to live." Even the mysterious trunk, when prised open, is "found to contain nothing but a Day-book and Ledger, a file of old musty accounts, and a razor, wrapped up in part of a cotton shirt." The Little Man in Gosling Green takes his secret with him to the grave.

Now this, for all its light satirical touches, is a very sad story—and one that refuses to offer any narrative satisfaction in the end. Is the reclusive little man, with his foreign ways and (to the locals) worthless trunkload of papery "rubbish," Longfellow himself? Had his pent-up anger at the college, at the townspeople, at the waste of his talents and experience turned inward in this little exercise in self-effacement? It would be interesting to know how many people in Brunswick read the story. Among his friends, he certainly made no secret of his feelings. Writing to James Berdan in New York, he called Maine "this land of Barbarians—this miserable Down East. I feel as if I were living in exile here."

Whatever his frustrations, personal or professional, he had one immediate outlet: a search for another job, which, as we have seen in his Harvard inquiries while abroad, had begun long before he took up his duties at Bowdoin. He kept feelers out in Boston and Cambridge. Word that New York University was about to appoint a professor of modern languages sparked his lively interest—and Stephen Sr.'s discouragement—as did hints of a job in 1834 at the University of Virginia. While it is not difficult to image Longfellow as a New Yorker, seeing him in slave-holding Charlottesville is another matter; how long would he have lasted? Jefferson's splendid experiment had fizzled, other than architecturally, in the face of Southern anti-intellectualism and Presbyterian suspicion of Jeffersonian free thought. It is an indication of Longfellow's desperation to leave Maine that he even considered establishing a "Female School in the city of New York, where I understand great things may be done in that way." More seriously, in July of 1833, the morning he read of the death of the secretary of the U.S. Legation in Madrid, he began lobbying for the post, even asking his Democratic brother-in-law (and Bowdoin classmate) George Washington Pierce for a good word in Washington. Longfellow's lack of enthusiasm for the Jacksonians was a liability, of course, in that age of ruthless patronage, however accurate his claim that his knowledge of Spain and its language could be matched by few Americans. In 1834, the possibility of taking over the progressive Round Hill School in Northampton, Massachusetts, was also seriously considered, and the prospect of some post editing a literary journal held perennial, if somewhat quixotic, appeal. Meanwhile, Longfellow was trying to find a job for his friend Greene, who had repatriated himself from Rome and was living in his natal Rhode Island, with his very young Roman bride.

Waterville College was one possibility; even better was the notion of Greene's succeeding Longfellow at Bowdoin.

The most puzzling aspect of Longfellow's five-year "exile" back in Maine is why he wrote so little poetry. He had, after all, while still an undergraduate, published more respectable work than many American writers twice his age. His Bowdoin classmate (and future social reformer) George Barrell Cheever had included several Longfellow poems in his *American Common-Place Book of Poetry* (Boston, 1831), adding this generous note:

> Most of Mr. Longfellow's poetry,—indeed, we believe nearly all that has been published,—appeared, during his college life, in the United States Literary Gazette. It displays a very refined taste, and a very pure vein of poetical feeling. It possesses what has been a rare quality in the American poets,—simplicity of expression, without any attempt to startle the reader, or to produce an effect by far-sought epithets. There is much sweetness in his imagery and language; and sometimes he is hardly excelled by any one for the quiet accuracy exhibited in his pictures of natural objects. His poetry will not easily be forgotten; some of it will be remembered with that of Dana and Bryant.

Yet even Cheever's praise has a note of valediction. The bone-aching labor of teaching grammar in four languages to adolescents—while searching for a better job and writing and lecturing on a wide range of literary subjects—is part of the explanation; Longfellow was too exhausted to summon up the concentration required to write poetry. Moreover, his years in Europe had exposed him more directly to the powerful currents of Romanticism, a force growing stronger in his mind as his German improved and he caught some inkling of the power of poets like Novalis and Jean Paul. This was a new idiom in which his ear had not been trained, and whose rejection of self-restraint and rationalism may have thoroughly frightened him. Was there an American audience for such things? The poets anthologized by the pious Cheever would suggest not. Tellingly, the notice of Cheever's book in the *North American Review* (October, 1831) speaks of

Longfellow as "one of the most promising scholars in the country." It was this side of his multifaceted talents that his admirers in the early 1830s found easiest to praise.

Thanks to his Madrid friend Alexander H. Everett, the pages of the prestigious *North American Review*—the intellectual voice of Unitarian Boston and a national forum for literary discussion—were opened to Longfellow's essays. In April of 1831, his "Origin and Progress of the French Language" appeared, a sketch of the progress of that language from its rustic roots to its age of refinement. "Its chief characteristics," Longfellow told his readers, "are ease, vivacity, precision, perspicuity and directness. It is superior to all the other languages in colloquial elegance." Visitors to the theater in France "must have been struck with the vast superiority of the French language to the English in its adaptation to the purposes of conversation and the refinement of its familiar dialogue ... But in the higher walks of tragic and epic poetry it but feebly seconds the high-aspiring mind."

The October issue introduced readers to "Anglo-Saxon Language and Literature." ("To Englishmen, and their offspring in every land, the Anglo-Saxon is precisely what the Latin is to the Italians, Spaniards, and Portuguese, or the Icelandic to the modern inhabitants of Denmark, Norway and Sweden.") It told them, in words that would echo through English Ph.D. programs in the century to come, that the study of Anglo-Saxon was "essential to a complete knowledge of modern English," and it at least introduced many American readers to the possibility that *Beowulf* was a very great poem. In April of 1832, Longfellow turned to a subject close to his heart, "Spanish Devotional and Moral Poetry"—a genre "strongly marked with the peculiarities of national character." He made this point even more strongly in the October issue, in tracing the "History of the Italian Languages and Dialects," for "the language of a nation is the external symbol of its character and its mind."

Longfellow admitted that these were merely general surveys of the literatures in question, not scholarly essays, even by the undemanding standards of his time and place, since much of his commentary con-

sisted of translations or paraphrases of European sources. But it would
be unfair to underestimate his accomplishment. In the early 1830s,
Longfellow more or less invented the discipline of comparative literature in the American college. (Ticknor had attempted something
similar at Harvard, but his range was narrower.) His vision of foreign
languages not as something "given" but as complex organisms that
have grown out of earlier tongues (and, by implication, will continue
to develop) may be a pale reflection of German philology, but it was
news to most of his American readers. His view that poetry in particular had served as a refining force in this development would have long-
range influence on his own work. The continuing link between
national character and national language—the idea that the word
shapes the action, and the action the word—introduced a note of his-
toricism that would not be thoroughly examined by scholars until
much later in the century. He summed up this new mode of knowledge
near the start of his encyclopedic essay on the seventeen most important Italian dialects:

> To learn, then, how other nations have thought, and felt, and spoken;
> —to observe how the language of a people is influenced by its character,
> customs and government; and to trace it in its gradual development, as
> it spreads and unfolds itself, like a broad banner, above the march of civ-
> ilization . . . this is a study worthy the best and noblest mind.

Longfellow's most important *North American Review* essay, however, dealt with a subject linguistically closer to home. In January of
1832 he reviewed a new edition of Sir Philip Sidney's sixteenth-
century *The Defence of Poesy*. He pays quick tribute to Sidney's achievements and then launches an energetic appeal of his own. Longfellow
has a poetics before he has a poetry. He sets out the program that his
own best work in the 1840s and 1850s will seek to fulfill. He begins on
a note of jeremiad, a ritualistic appeal to the fallen to mend their ways:

> With us, the spirit of the age is clamorous for utility,—for visible,
> tangible utility,—for bare, brawny, muscular utility. We would be
> roused to action by the voice of the populace, and the sounds of the

crowded mart, and not "lulled asleep in shady idleness with poet's pastimes." We are swallowed up in schemes for gain, and engrossed with contrivances for bodily enjoyments, as if this particle of dust were immortal,—as if the soul needed no aliment, and the mind no raiment. We glory in the extent of our territory, in our rapidly increasing population, in our agricultural privileges, and our commercial advantages. We boast of the magnificence and beauty of our natural scenery. . . . We boast of the increase and extent of our physical strength, the sound of populous cities, breaking the silence and solitude of our Western territories,—plantations conquered from the forest, and gardens springing up in the wilderness. Yet the true glory of a nation consists not in the extent of its territory, the pomp of its forests, the majesty of its rivers, the height of its mountains, and the beauty of its sky; but in the extent of its mental power,—the majesty of its intellect,—the height and depth and purity of its moral nature. . . . True greatness is the greatness of the mind; —the true glory of a nation is moral and intellectual preeminence.

He warns that we are led astray by this word "utility"—"We are too apt to think that nothing can be useful, but what is done with a noise, at noonday, and at the corners of the streets." Yet in a commercial-minded democracy, too many associate the name of scholar and man of letters with "effeminacy and inefficiency." Poetry in particular is singled out for contempt and denounced because, it is said, "it unfits for the common duties of life, and the intercourse of this matter-of-fact world." But none of this is necessary. "On the contrary, it may be made, and should be made, an instrument for improving the condition of society, and advancing the great purpose of human happiness. Man must have his hours of meditation as well as of action." Poetry has moral force because "the natural tendency of poetry is to give us correct moral impressions, and thereby advance the cause of truth and the improvement of society."

Back in his role of championing comparative literature, Longfellow points out that "a great and various literature is . . . the most valuable possession of which any nation can boast," and he cites the *Nibelungenlied*, the *Poema del mio Cid*, and the *Songs of the Troubadours* to prove his point. Great poetry often has this intensely national tone, he assures his readers, but "to effect this, it is not necessary that the war-whoop should ring in every line, and every page be rife with scalps, toma-hawks and wampum." It should be national in that it bears "the stamp of national character." In writing of nature in particular, let it be an American nature. "Let us have no more sky-larks and nightingales. For us they only warble in books. A painter might as well introduce an elephant or a rhinoceros into a New England landscape." In creating an American imagery, we even might look, he notes, at the language of our North American Indians.

Why, then, did his public have to wait twenty-three more years for *The Song of Hiawatha*? There is a clue in an almost parenthetical remark Longfellow makes toward the end of his long essay: "Another circum-stance which tends to give an effeminate and unmanly character of our literature, is the precocity of our writers. Premature exhibitions of talent are an unstable foundation to build a national literature upon." The concept of the "unmanly" was to be so coarsened later in the nine-teenth century and throughout the twentieth, that we need to try to figure out what Longfellow meant by it in 1832. "Irresponsible" and "self-indulgent" perhaps come closer to the connotation of that word for his generation, with "effeminacy" evoking a world in which mas-culine duty is neglected. Precocious he had been, but he was trying to make up for it.

As for his own life, there appeared two unmistakable indices of his new sense of maturity. He produced a substantial prose work that earned him an international audience, and he got married.

❧

The success in 1833 of Longfellow's first extensive work in prose, *Outre-Mer, A Pilgrimage Beyond the Sea*, is a reminder that his career as a writer might have taken a very different turn—for example, into the field of memoir, travel narrative, and literary journalism that was being industriously tilled in the 1830s by his fellow Portlander Nathaniel Parker Willis. The success of the book may perplex a modern reader, however, because *Outre-Mer* seems so lacking in immediate "felt" response to the landscapes and cultures its narrator is discovering, it could almost have been written by someone who had never been to Europe at all, but who had the run of a very good library. Yet Longfellow's contemporaries relished the work. It was even reprinted in Britain, where people notoriously asked, "Who reads an American book?" There are two possible explanations for this reception, at least among American readers. The first can be found in his father's reply in May of 1827 to Henry's letter written from Bordeaux three months earlier:

> You can have no idea how much pleasure your descriptions afford us. Being extremely happy in the manner in which you paint these scenes, they are presented to the mind's eye in vivid colours, & leave a lasting & pleasing impression. And, to us who have not an opportunity of visiting them personally, it affords a pleasure which I cannot describe—You must therefore recollect that you gaze on these wonders, not merely for your own gratification, but for the pleasure & instruction of others who are far distant.

There is a note of parental pride here—perhaps also an attempt to maximize the return, so to speak, on his hefty investment in his son's travels—but other book-buying Americans were also eager for descriptions of lands beyond the sea. The increasing "refinement" of America in the 1830s, which Richard Bushman and others have chronicled, involved more than domestic comforts and stylish furnishings; it implied a familiarity with the European cultures that still largely supplied the model for such improvements. Unable to visit such places themselves with much security or ease until the arrival of the transatlantic steamers in the 1850s, middle-class American readers had to rely on the personal narratives of naval officers and merchants, or on the historical and literary work of such writers as Willis and Irving.

Washington Irving is the key figure; *Outre-Mer* is an obvious attempt to emulate the success in 1819 of *The Sketch Book of Geoffrey Crayon, Gent.*, with which Irving had proved that an American could attract even a British audience if he mastered the cool, urbane, slightly bemused voice of the Augustan essayists. This was a successful career move away from the earthier, more burlesque "Dutch" style of Irving's *Salmagundi* days. *The Sketch Book* contained two classic stories—"Rip Van Winkle" and "The Legend of Sleepy Hollow"—and a nostalgic account of the traditional British Christmas that was to be a powerful influence on how that holiday was perceived in the English-speaking world (not least by Charles Dickens when he came to write "A Christmas Carol" in 1843). These were mixed with miscellaneous essays, in Irving's smooth conversational tone, offering a traveler's thoughts on Westminster Abbey, Stratford-on-Avon, British inns, and John Bull's character, among other odds and ends from his travel notebooks. (An embryonic tourist industry was taking shape before the reader's eyes.) The book was a hit—in England as well as at home—and Irving quickly cloned it in *Bracebridge Hall* (1821) and the less successful *Tales of a Traveller by Geoffrey Crayon, Gent.* (1824).

Longfellow extends Irving's geographic range. "Beyond the sea" meant for Longfellow the Mediterranean South, even though his book starts in northern France, lingers there for some seventy pages, and ends with its narrator en route to German-speaking lands. The Bowdoin professor took a step backward as well, by publishing *Outre-Mer* anonymously (most readers would have known who "Geoffrey Crayon" was)—a demurral more typical of the eighteenth century than of the nineteenth in its implied assumption that a gentleman did not write for a living, and most especially did not indulge in fiction and travel writing, if he wished to be taken seriously as a college professor. Both Irving's and Longfellow's books owe much to Goldsmith's moralizing poem *The Traveller* (1765), but Longfellow adds a Byronic note—a faint one, for he is Childe Harold with a Puritan conscience. And *Outre-Mer* is genuinely a travel book, sticking to an itinerary that matched Longfellow's own in 1826–29, rather than a miscellany of essays in the Irving manner. A very odd travel book, to be sure. With Slidell's *A Year in Spain* in hand, you might be able to find your way across the country even today. With Longfellow's, you would soon be lost in a thicket of anecdotes and tales, entangled with surveys of medieval literature.

Some of these tales are entertaining. The best is "Martin Franc and the Monk of Saint Anthony," a mildly racy story about a leering, red-faced, comic friar who attempts, in a dimly-lit chapel, to buy the favors of the beautiful wife of Martin Franc, a merchant who has fallen on hard times. She decides to teach the old reprobate a lesson and restore her worthy husband's fortunes with the friar's purse, by luring him to her house while her husband is said to be away. Franc of course beats the lecherous friar over the head and shoulders—a little too soundly, for he kills him. The pleasure of the tale arises from the efforts to dispose of the friar's body by a succession of innocent parties, each of whom accidentally comes into possession of the corpse and thinks he is the one who killed him. (With its quick, nocturnal movement, it would make a good one-act opera, in the *Gianni Schicchi* manner.) The narrator of *Outre-Mer* distances himself from this cheerfully amoral tale by saying he heard it from another guest at the Golden Lion at Rouen, and he makes it even more acceptable to his Protestant readers by confirming their suspicions about the corruption of the Church.

But its author had a price to pay. After its original appearance in an American newspaper, Longfellow was accused in the *New York Atlas and Constellation* of plagiarizing the story from a recent poem on a similar theme, "The Knight and the Friar," by George Colman. As he patiently explained in reply, he had based his tale on a thirteenth-century Norman fabliau, *Le Segretain Moine*, which probably went back to *The Arabian Nights*. It had been widely imitated through the centuries, "passing through as many hands as did the body of Friar Gui." It was a minor annoyance, having to respond to such an unfounded charge, but it was not to be the only occasion in his career when he was to be charged, unfairly, with plagiarism. Otherwise, the reviews were friendly. The *Boston Mercantile Journal* quickly determined that the anonymous author was "no other than a Brunswick professor, well known long since among the poets and scholars of the North." The

Eastern Argus in Portland praised *Outre-Mer's* moral tone: "It is a book which may be read in the domestic circle without creating a false excitement in young minds, or reconciling them to crime by gilding it with splendor." A review in the *Literary Journal* of Providence, Rhode Island—probably written by his friend George Washington Greene—praised the author's classic style. "It has none of the mysticism that disfigures so large a portion of the works of the day: none of those labored efforts at the description of feelings, whose indistinct expression shows that they have not their source in the heart." The author, in other words, was not to be mistaken for a Transcendentalist. Reviewing the second number, the Philadelphia *Saturday Evening Gazette* wished the author had chosen a "more euphonious title" but admired his "unaffected" prose and praised the quality of the printing ("the handsomest letter-press we have ever seen issued from any establishment in this country").

His father had also urged him to use something straightforward and English for a title, but Longfellow explained his choice in his preface: the Pays d'Outre-Mer, or Land Beyond the Sea, was what crusaders and pilgrims had called the Holy Land. "I, too, in a certain sense, have been a pilgrim of Outre-Mer; for to my youthful imagination the Old World was a kind of Holy Land, lying afar off beyond the blue horizon of the ocean; and when its shores first rose upon my sight, looming through the hazy atmosphere of the sea, my heart swelled with the deep emotions of the pilgrim, when he sees afar the spire which rises above the shrine of his devotion." This suggestion of seeing the objects of his pilgrimage through a kind of scrim, like the gauze used to suggest fog or haze on the nineteenth-century stage, idealizes his journey, despite all his attempts at picaresque detail. ("I have traversed France from Normandy to Navarre; smoked my pipe in a Flemish inn; floated through Holland in a Trekschuit; trimmed my midnight lamp in a German university; wandered and mused amid the classic scenes of Italy; and listened to the gay guitar and merry castanet on the borders of the blue Guadalquivir.") Although the work is styled as a pilgrimage, the actual nature of *Outre-Mer* is better expressed in the chapter title "A Tailor's Drawer"—"a title which the Spaniards give to a desultory discourse, wherein various and discordant themes are touched upon, and which is crammed full of little shreds and patches of erudition."

The stitched-together nature of the book owes much to Longfellow's method of prose composition at this stage of his career. He had told his father in a letter from Göttingen in 1829 that he was writing a book—"a kind of Sketch-Book of scenes in France, Spain, and Italy," presumably based on his travel journals. In 1831, when Joseph T. Buckingham asked him to contribute to the *New England Magazine*, Longfellow sent him some sketches that he had written abroad, under the general title of *The Schoolmaster*. The narrator lives and teaches in a New England village, but his restlessness as a youth, he confesses, had sent him wandering abroad. The second sketch includes the account of travel in a Norman diligence that reappears at the start of *Outre-Mer*, and the third draws on Longfellow's sojourn at the *maison de santé* at Auteuil. Three final sketches take "the schoolmaster" through Paris. At this point Longfellow dropped the project, telling Greene in March of 1833 that he was writing a book based on his travels, "composed of descriptions, sketches of character, tales illustrating manners and customs, and tales illustrating nothing in particular." The persona of the village schoolmaster reminiscing about his *Wanderjahre* in Europe had allowed the writer to test the market. He was encouraged by the result, although he told Greene, "I find it requires little courage to publish grammars and school books; but in the department of fine writing . . . it requires vastly more." The first number of *Outre-Mer*, incorporating much of *The Schoolmaster*, was printed in an edition of five hundred copies by Joseph Griffin in Brunswick and published by Hilliard, Gray & Co. in Boston in 1833. Longfellow assured a friend that future numbers would "*appear incessantly*"—he projected ten. A second number followed in 1834 from Lilly, Wait, and Co. in Boston, but publication in parts was abandoned, and in 1835 Harper & Brothers in New York published a two-volume edition containing much new material, including several of his *North American Review* essays on foreign literatures. A second edition was published in 1846 (with some deletions) in response to Longfellow's growing international reputation as a poet.

Longfellow's devastating experience on his second trip to Europe in 1835–36 made further sketches in the innocent, easygoing manner of *Outre-Mer* impossible, and the record of that journey would take a more diffuse form. Nonetheless, in publishing his first original book, he had shown a professional writer's skill in recycling material, and he had demonstrated the possibility of combining the scholarly and the experiential: the life of the study and the life of the road. How many of his fellow authors had risked passage through bandit-infested mountains or tracked down Lord Byron's gondolier? At the same time, *Outre-Mer* is a fashionably melancholy book—how many other young travelers spent so much time in cemeteries?—given Longfellow's penchant for meditations among the ruins. It is never as confessional as we would wish, yet it is a book of self-discovery—for the most part intellectual discovery, but occasionally something else. The heart of it is a chapter midway through called "The Village of El Pardillo." It tells of a short stay among humble Castilian peasants, on the slope of the Guadarrama Mountains, near a ruined Moorish castle, "in that delicious season when the coy and capricious maidenhood of spring is swelling into the warmer, riper, and more voluptuous womanhood of summer." The narrator travels there with his Madrid landlord Don Valentin and the landlord's beautiful daughter. He paints a genre scene of village life, including an unexpectedly sympathetic account of rural Catholicism, and he is enchanted by a culture in which Sunday morning Mass can be followed by sports in the afternoon and dancing and singing at night—how far he was from old New England! In a letter home from Spain in 1827, Longfellow had told of joining in one of these dances and swinging his arms and legs so vigorously, he had knocked off one man's hat and accidentally kicked another. The narrator of *Outre-Mer* skips over that lively detail, which might suggest tipsiness, and merely exclaims: "I love these rural dances,—from my heart I love them." He was beyond the sea indeed.

This toning down of his experience abroad, these idealizing glosses, may have reflected not only a professional writer's calculation of his audience's expectations, but Longfellow's own new sense of himself as a married man of stature in the community. Whatever his disappointment with Brunswick, his time as a professor there would always be associated in his mind with his first marriage—which may explain why he so rarely returned to the college during his annual visits in later life to Portland. The details of his marriage to Mary Storer Potter are even mistier than his *Outre-Mer*. They had met as children when they both attended Portland Academy (she was five years younger); her father was Barrett Potter, the long-term judge of probate for Cumberland County and a close associate of Longfellow's father. It must have pleased Stephen enormously to have both his older sons marry into the small circle of local lawyers and judges, and begin careers that would keep them within the extended family circle—in 1831, Stephen Jr. had married Marianne Preble after serving in the Netherlands as private secretary to her father, Judge William Pitt Preble, when he was U.S. Minister at The Hague.

Whether Henry and Mary corresponded during his 1826–29 trip we do not know; after her death, he burned all of her papers in his possession. At any rate, he must have seemed a very eligible young man upon his return to Maine—travel in Europe being a source of much prestige back home—and their courtship proceeded rapidly, even given the well-known protectiveness shown by Judge Potter, a widower, toward his three daughters. The couple was engaged by September of 1830 and married on September 14, 1831, in Portland, then immediately moved to Brunswick. What we know of Mary comes from a poorly painted portrait—a copy of a lost original—a handful of letters to her family, a friend's diary, and an occasional reference to her in other people's correspondence. In a letter to Judge Potter thanking him for his daughter's hand, Longfellow praised her "pure heart and guileless disposition." He added: "I have never seen a woman in whom every look, and word, and action seemed to proceed from so gentle and innocent a spirit. Indeed, how much she possesses of all we most admire in the female character!" (It is one of the rare references to her in any of his surviving correspondence.) On her part, Mary wrote to one of his sisters in June of 1831 that she bore being separated from him for three weeks "with the spirit of a martyr, always having in view the time when I shall never be separated from him. The high opinion I had of him before I knew him so well has been increased, and every time we meet I see some new point in his character, for which I love him better, if possible, than before. I certainly never imagined that I could find in this world so good and affectionate a person, and one who would love me so much. He answers much better to a being of my imagination than one of real life." Zilpah wrote to a friend that she was "much pleased with this engagement also, far more, so, than if Henry had introduced us to a city lady of fortune, with her airs & graces & expensive habits, as our future daughter in law." The marriage seemed to her a success—Stephen and Marianne already having shown signs of strain in theirs—and in 1835, after the couple had sailed for Europe, she described Mary as "a very lovely woman, very affectionate and amiable."

The young professor and "little Mary," as he often referred to her, set up housekeeping in a "cape" (a one-and-a-half-story New England house) on what is now Potter Street in Brunswick, a few minutes' walk from the Bowdoin campus. The house still exists, remarkably transmogrified: it forms the second story of the General Joshua L. Chamberlain House, the medieval-revival landmark on Maine Street where the Civil War hero (and sometime professor of modern languages) spent much of his adult life, including his time as governor of Maine and president of Bowdoin. The Longfellows' front door can still be recognized above the portico of Chamberlain's house. (It was a common practice in New England to move wooden-framed houses, with the aid of teams of oxen, and an occasional practice to raise them and build a new floor underneath.) Visiting the young couple's house in

July of 1833, Zilpah described it as so "surrounded by shrubbery, you would almost think they lived in a garden—it is a charming quiet place."

Mary had the same problem that many of her other married friends faced—finding a suitable servant. Zilpah reported that a "black girl" had been engaged (like many coastal New England towns, both Portland and Brunswick had small communities of African Americans, most of them descendants of sailors or locally owned eighteenth-century slaves). "I should not think Mary would care for the color of her skin if her conduct was *fair*," she added. Zilpah did wonder if the young woman would be allowed to ride to Brunswick in the public stage. There had just been a public debate in Portland, which some of the Longfellow family had attended, between colonizationists and abolitionists. The colonizationists—who favored returning the slaves, and possibly all people of African descent, to Africa—overwhelmingly prevailed. Attempts to debate slavery publicly in Brunswick throughout the early 1830s had been discouraged for fear of riot; as in other small ship-building and ship-owning towns on the Maine coast, many of the leading citizens had a vested interest in the cotton trade between the Southern ports and Europe. The Bowdoin faculty itself was split between fervent abolitionists and people who just wished the problem would go away.

An awareness of the problem of slavery on Longfellow's part is documented as early as 1834. In an incomplete journal, he sketches out an idea for "a wild drama, a tale of this world and of Fairyland," specifically of the malicious fairy Robin Goodfellow of old English romance. "The subject of the drama will be some of the evil deeds done in the world by the supposed agency of these fairy personages." There would be three parts:

> Part 1. The Elixir of Life.—Paracelsus searching for this elixir discovers alcohol. The effects, which ensue, are the subject of this portion of the tale.
>
> Part 2. Witchcraft. The fairy troop sail over the sea to New England.

The Salem Tragedy; and all the scenes of persecution which arose from a belief in witchcraft.

Part 3. The Slave. The idea of slavery supposed to have been a suggestion of the spirits of evil. Scenes of slavery portrayed.

There is some anachronism here. No matter. I will arrange that in the detail of the piece.

Longfellow was to return to some of this subject matter—to the plight of the slave in a group of poems in 1843 and to the Salem witch scare in his *New England Tragedies* of the 1860s. In another 1834 journal, he contemplated a tragedy on the life of Toussaint L'Ouverture, the Haitian revolutionary. "As soon as I can find or make leisure, I intend to write one upon that topic; thereby doing what my feeble talent enables me in the cause of slave-emancipation." Meanwhile he pondered material closer at hand. "Fate seems to decree that my next book after Outre-Mer shall be the Schoolmaster of Bungonuck." In his journal, he sketched its contents, which drew on a great deal of material he already had in his tailor's drawer:

1. The Table Book—being sundry sentences and sketches, and scraps of erudition, such as creep into my mind unawares, or are noted down from my reading. Critical remarks on Modern Literature etc.
2. Down East—a history of that land of shadows—more pleasant than authentic.
3. The Wondrous Tale of the Little Man in Gosling Green.
4. Essays on various topics.
   The Defense of Poetry.

Mary was aware from the start of her husband's overwhelming desire to quit "that land of shadows." Her own opinions on the subject are sketchy (she was definitely not keen on his taking the school mastership in Northampton), but when the opportunity arose for Longfellow to travel again to Europe, to prepare himself to succeed the great scholar George Ticknor as Smith Professor of Modern Languages and of Belles Lettres at Harvard University, she proved a good sport—and a better sailor than her frequently seasick husband. She could easily have stayed with her family in Portland (as did the wives of many shipmasters) for the year or more he needed to spend abroad, but she determined to go with him (as some shipmasters' wives did, too). She was considered frail, and Longfellow thought the long sea voyage might strengthen her health, a common nineteenth-century notion. She had already suffered at least one miscarriage. Longfellow's ever-anxious father thought the trip an unnecessary extravagance, not to mention a peril, and Mary may have shared some of his doubts, but the young professor's urge to taste again the cultural riches of Europe after his five years of "exile" in Brunswick overrode any objections. This time it would be not a Mediterranean journey, but rather a venture into the North—not just through Germany, but into the Nordic cultures of Scandinavia, a part of Europe known to very few Americans.

· Five ·

THE JOURNEY NORTH

LONGFELLOW'S PREVIOUS TRIP to Europe had had a dreamlike quality: he was an imaginative young man with ample resources, a flexible (indeed ever-changing) schedule, and an urgent desire to master languages and survey whole cultures, in whatever circumstances best suited him. His second trip found him laden with more baggage. He knew that his success at Harvard depended on his mastering German—by 1835, *the* language of scholarship in almost every field—and in buying the most useful books for its library. Unlikely ever to surpass Ticknor as a student of Spanish history and literature, he knew he could create a scholarly presence of his own if he returned to America with some familiarity with Danish, Swedish, and possibly Icelandic—languages virtually unknown in the United States. What little he knew of their literatures, especially the early medieval Norse sagas, struck a deep romantic chord in him. More practically, he was not traveling alone. In addition to his twenty-three-year-old wife, who had never ventured beyond the circle of her Portland and Boston family and friends, Longfellow had agreed to escort (at their own expense) two of Mary's friends, Mary Goddard and Clara Crowninshield. A few months after their arrival in Europe, a writer they had met in Stockholm summed up the party:

> [Longfellow] was an exceedingly agreeable man.... He had ... a couple of young ladies with him, of whom one was a pleasant little thing, not exactly beautiful but with an expression of kindness that was very pleasing. The other [Mary Goddard], who owned half a million dollars, was a large, Juno-like figure with a beautiful face and a fine skin. Her complexion was as white as a slice of fresh, boiled ham. Neither

95

could speak a word of anything but English until they obtained a
French teacher here. Mrs. Longfellow ... was the most beautiful and
the most agreeable of all three of Longfellow's ladies.

It is thanks to the "pleasant little thing" that we know so many details of the Longfellow party's everyday experience in Europe. Clara
Crowninshield kept a lengthy and very readable record of their travels
(and of her own recurrent self-doubts). Longfellow's own journals by
contrast are less personal but of interest as a record of his intellectual
growth, and only fragments of his wife's correspondence home survive. Crowninshield's sharp eye and modest demeanor owe a great deal
to her anomalous position in the upper ranks of New England society.
She was the illegitimate daughter of Salem's legendary George
Crowninshield, a successful privateer in the War of 1812 and a pioneer
yachtsman afterwards. (Some trace of his opulence survives in the
stateroom of his 191-ton hermaphroditic brig *Cleopatra's Barge*, preserved at the Peabody-Essex Museum in Salem.) When he died pre-
maturely in 1817, Salem was shocked to discover that he not only had a
"love child" but had provided for her in his will, which his family unsuccessfully challenged. Clarissa, or as she preferred, Clara, was raised
by her court-appointed guardian, the Salem attorney Benjamin Ropes
Nichols, who skillfully managed her inheritance (so skillfully, she lived
on it for the rest of her long life). She had befriended Mary Potter at
Miss Cushing's female seminary at Hingham and had frequently visited Portland, where her guardian's brother Ichabod Nichols was the
Longfellows' minister. After Henry and Mary's marriage, she stayed
with them in Brunswick. In other words, she was accepted in polite
society in spite of the circumstances of her birth and the powerful
Crowninshield family's hostility toward her. Mary begged her to
accompany them to Europe. Clara expressed reservations—about the
trip and about Mary—in a letter to a friend early in 1835:

> Shall I go? Mr. Longfellow goes to perfect himself in the German
> language and its different dialects—so that we shall be located for some
> time in each place and I shall be forced to study the language to drive off
> "ennui." But Mrs. Longfellow is not the sort of person who would feel

the least interest in acquiring the language. She is satisfied to have her husband do all the studying and her happiness consists in being by his side. . . . Now I have a great desire to accompany the Longfellows, but it would be very essential to my enjoyment to have another female companion of a different sort from Mrs. Longfellow. She is very sweet and amiable, but she is so absorbed in her husband that she only lives in him. She has not much physical energy and if her husband only goes about and sees what is worth seeing, she is satisfied to have it second-hand thro' him. Now I want to have somebody go who will excite instead of check any desire I may have to go about and improve myself.

Mary Goddard, by no means as rich as the Swedish thought, but with a father who promised to reimburse Longfellow for her expenses, proved the acceptable companion. She and Clara would divert Mary, while Longfellow devoted his days to wandering through the bookshops and libraries and seeking out the local literati.

On April 10, 1835, the party sailed from New York on the packet *Philadelphia*, Elisha Morgan captain, for the month-long voyage. The women were uncomfortable; Longfellow was miserable with seasickness for much of the time. It was a great relief to reach Portsmouth on May 8. After a quick excursion to the Isle of Wight—where Longfellow would return thirty-three years later to visit Tennyson—they reached London and the first major stage of their tragic journey.

❧

The size of London overwhelmed the travelers. "It is astonishing how little can be accomplished here in a day!" Longfellow wrote his father. "You can do nothing before 10 o'clock in the morning, and then the distances from point to point are so great—London is on so vast and magnificent a scale, that it is impossible to kill many *lions* [that is, visit celebrated people] in the course of a day, and at night you are so thoroughly tired, that you sleep late into the next morning." His party spent their first week in lodgings in "thronged and fashionable" Regent Street, then moved to 8 Princes Street, off Cavendish Square (the building, much altered, survives). In the afternoons, Longfellow frequented the vendors of rare and curious books, while the three women saw the sights and shopped. Eager to meet the leading writers and scholars of the capital, Longfellow at first did not quite know what to make of the cool offhandedness of the English, notably the English custom of not conversing at breakfast. Invited to breakfast by an important man of letters, John Bowring, he sat down to tea and toast and what he assumed would be a lively conversation, only to find his host ignoring him completely and opening and reading a large packet of letters. Another guest was buried in his newspaper. Reminding himself of the German proverb *ländlich, sittlich*—every country has its customs—Longfellow "reached back to a side table, and seized upon a book, in which I forthwith began to read, thereby conveying a gentle hint to mine hosts, though they heeded it not." Bowring proved chatty afterwards, when he invited Longfellow into his library to watch his portrait bust being modeled in clay. In his journal, Longfellow pronounced Bowring "overrated."

An even sharper humiliation awaited when he presented a letter from the Philadelphia publisher Willis Gaylord Clark to one of the most fashionable British writers of the day, the young Edward Bulwer, later Lord Lytton, who had recently published the highly successful historical novel *The Last Days of Pompeii*. Longfellow called but found him on his way out, "a true dandy," with a lisping accent and a thoroughly condescending manner to an American visitor. Bulwer twirled Clark's letter between his fingertips and issued a vague invitation for Longfellow to come back some other morning.

N. P. Willis, a Portlander who had had a glittering journalistic career abroad, came to his rescue with invitations to meet more welcoming company. At 10:00 p.m. on May 23, Longfellow went to a soiree at the house of William Babbage, the famous mathematician. There he found, reclining upon an ottoman, Ada Byron, the poet's daughter ("a countenance like her father's, though rather too red to be handsome"). Babbage himself was "a very plain and unostentatious man, with more the air of a recluse student than a man of the world." His guests were quite otherwise, and Longfellow was introduced to a series of fashionable, even beautiful women, including Lady Dudley Stuart, as well as to her father, Lucien Bonaparte, Prince de Canino. He admired the belles of the salon—"Mrs. Blackwood and Lady Seymour—sisters of the fashionable and celebrated Hon. Mrs. Norton. Glossy black hair, and clear, brilliant complexions." By 2:00 a.m., he was ready to leave, though not without noticing on a small table one of Babbage's famous calculating machines. "His son—a young and rather raw lad, who is said to be like his father a good mathematician, showed us the operation of the machine, which I cannot describe, for I do not understand it." Longfellow had unwittingly stumbled upon the future—Babbage's machine was a prototype of what would someday be known as the computer.

There were further reminders that he was no longer in New England. At Lady Dudley Stuart's house a few nights later, he encountered "the Marchioness of ——— naked almost to the waist; in appearance a magnificent whore [the word is almost effaced in his journal]; in character, if report be true, no less so; and taken all in all, a superb animal." The singers Grisi and Rubini "executed some glorious passages from Rossini." His other sightseeing, in the company of his wife and her friends, was more conventional: Poets' Corner in Westminster Abbey (where he caught glimpses "of a curate reading prayers and bobbing his head to and fro like Punch in the puppet-show"), a choral service at St. Paul's, the National Gallery, the celebrations for William IV's seventieth birthday, and an excursion upriver to Richmond and Hampton Court on a dreamy English summer afternoon. Willis's patron Mary Skinner invited them to her country house, Shirley Park, where they discovered her to be "a furious admirer" of that now largely forgotten writer; "she thinks him superior to Irving." Willis was in fact licking his wounds; his newspaper articles on British high society (published that year in America as *Pencillings by the Way*) had repeated private conversations he had heard in various stately dining rooms, to the outrage of his hosts. Back in London, only a night visit across the Thames to Vauxhall Gardens—the famous pleasure grounds of the previous century—proved a disappointment; the ladies pronounced it vulgar, and Longfellow agreed.

As the sojourn ended, Longfellow expressed regret that he had not met more of the literati. (He did dine with Jeremy Bentham's nephew and also met Sir Walter Scott's daughter, who had married J. G. Lockhart, Scott's biographer.) In fact, probably without fully appreciating it at the time, he had won the friendship of two of the most interesting British writers of the nineteenth century, Jane and Thomas Carlyle. Ralph Waldo Emerson had given him an introduction. It is not known how Emerson knew of Longfellow, but he had just returned from Europe himself and would have been well placed to advise the new Harvard professor on his itinerary. The Carlyles adored Emerson, who had visited them in 1833 at their house at Craigenputtock in a remote part of Scotland, and who was to serve for many years as Carlyle's unofficial agent and publicist in America. On May 21, after leaving the Bowrings, Longfellow had traveled to Chelsea, then a riverside village of market gardens well outside of London, to present his letter at what is now 24 Cheyne Row, where the Carlyles had been living just less than a year. (The house, remarkably little changed, is today a National Trust museum.) Carlyle was out, but his wife welcomed him—"a sweet, simple, lovely woman, with long black tresses, and a downcast, timid look," he wrote of her that night in his journal. She told him they strongly desired to see America (they were so chronically short of funds, Carlyle was considering a lecture tour), and spoke movingly of how much Emerson's visit had meant to them. Longfellow would not have been aware of how terribly she had suffered in the solitude of Craigenputtock, which she endured because her husband thought he could work best there. "It was like the visit of an angel," Longfellow quoted her as saying of Emerson, "and though he staid with us hardly 24 hours, yet when he left us I cried.—I could not help it."

Gradually Longfellow recognized that he was in the presence of a remarkable woman. Speaking with her of Hayward, who had just published a prose translation of *Faust* that neither of them liked, Longfellow pointed out Hayward's own harsh words about other translators. "O yes indeed," Jane Carlyle responded, "detraction is the element in which he moves and breathes and has his being!" She told Longfellow of the crushing accident that had befallen her husband some two months earlier—"one of the greatest calamities that could happen to an author." He had lent the only manuscript of the first volume of his *French Revolution*—the work that soon would make him world famous—to his friend John Stuart Mill, "who carelessly left it a week or two upon his study table; when to his great dismay he found it had been torn to pieces and consumed by the servants, who had made use of it to light the fire and lamps!"

Back in town, Longfellow bought a copy of Carlyle's *Life of Schiller* (1825)—the only clue that Clara Crowninshield had, a few days later, when an ungainly figure turned up at their lodgings in her chaperone's absence and presented a card: Mr. Carlyle of Craigenputtock.

> He was tall and awkward in his appearance and his countenance did not betray inward cultivation, but as soon as he began to converse his original mind beamed forth. He conversed a good deal and was often poetical in many of his expressions. I felt my enthusiasm kindle and I hung upon every word he let fall.

He invited them to tea at his house that evening at six. If the Longfellows were not back in time, he explained, the Carlyles would simply wait until they arrived. Longfellow recorded the occasion:

> He is a tall man—with coal-black hair—brown complexion—and a face that reminds you of Burns. His dress, an old blue coat—brown trousers—and carpet socks upon his feet. His manners awkward— almost clownish. but his conversation is glorious—so natural—and bearing the stamp of so free and original a mind. Spoke of Napoleon —thinks he would have made an excellent author, had his genius been directed that way. "His bulletins are perfect in their kind. They are characteristic of the man. He spoke pistol bullets. His brothers are authors. One has written tales—another, an Epic poem, the reading of which I have never had the audacity to undertake!
>
> "Bourienne's Memoirs is one of the most entertaining books I ever

read. It afforded me the greatest gratification. I read it on a hot summer's day in the country. It seemed as if a gorgeous pageant was passing
through my mind. It is more like an Epic poem, than anything I have
read of late." (What a vile memory I have—that I cannot recal [*sic*]
more definitely the conversation of the evening I have just passed; not
even the striking and peculiar expressions which I most wish to record,
as a memento of an original thinker.)

Mrs. Carlyle as modest, quiet, and lovely as ever. A sweet little
woman—a wild-flower from the Highlands of Scotland. . . .

The evening had worn Longfellow out. He underestimated Jane
Carlyle's gifts—in more recent times, thanks to her extraordinary letters, she has become more widely read than her husband. But she was
something new to the twenty-eight-year-old American: an attractive,
"womanly" woman, socially a step or two above her husband, willing to
help him in a self-effacing way in his strenuous intellectual work, and
quite capable of holding her own in a wide-ranging conversation.
Some memory of the possibilities she suggested would not leave him.

Settling himself in front of a coal fire, Longfellow spent much of the
next day reading *The Life of Schiller*—"a work of rare merit—written by
one who entered *con amore* into his subject"—and finished it at nearly
2:00 a.m. "I shall lie down to sleep with my soul quickened, and my
good resolutions and aspirations strengthened. God grant that the
light of morning may not dissipate them all." The biography was probably Carlyle's most lucid work—his prose was to grow louder and more
exaggerated with age—and it handily summarized for the Anglo-
American reader the full impact of *Sturm und Drang* romanticism and
Kantian idealism on German literature. On June 2, the Americans
went with Mrs. Carlyle to visit the studio of the sculptor Sir Francis
Chantrey (whom she pegged as "too mercenary" to "satisfy his ideal")
and were invited back to Chelsea the next day for breakfast. Mary
Longfellow had been suffering "from the ague" all the time they had
been in London, Clara had a dressmaker's appointment, and the other
Mary would not go without them, so Longfellow went alone.

Breakfasted at Mr. Carlyle's—in a quiet, friendly way. He spoke of the interesting spots in the old city of London—the surprise with which in threading some of the bye-lanes he came out upon little green squares—"and saw great trees growing in the heart of a brick and mortar wilderness."

He thinks bodily indisposition an inevitable consequence of great mental exertion. Exercise and diet will not relieve him—he gives himself up to toil for a month or so at a time—and is quite run down—at the end of that time—so that "he would die in it," if he did not desist. He then throws his books aside—and takes to relaxation and the free air.

He stepped out of the room for a few minutes and I asked his wife if he considered Gothe the greatest man that ever lived. She replied:

"Oh, yes. I believe he does indeed. He thinks him the greatest man that ever lived; excepting only Jesus Christ."

Mrs. Carlyle is also a German scholar. She told me her husband was much pleased with what she said of her own impressions of Schiller and Gothe: "What I read of Schiller makes me shed tears; but what I read of Gothe, I read a second time."—Her husband wrote this to Gothe, who expressed himself much gratified; as his aim was to make people think, and not to move their sympathies.—Gothe she thinks the greater man;—Schiller the most loveable.

After breakfast Carlyle took his guest a few doors up Cheyne Row to meet the elderly Leigh Hunt, popularly remembered today for "Abou Ben Adhem" (1834) but in his youth an early champion of Shelley and Keats and a writer who had suffered much for his political radicalism. Longfellow found "a thin man of medium stature, with a mop head of iron-gray hair, parted carelessly over his forehead like a girls—and a lively, intelligent countenance furrowed deeply with the mark of thought or sorrow. His manners are rather nervous, though open and friendly." Longfellow summed up this final visit with Carlyle in his journal:

Our conversation glanced from topic to topic—America—Willis's letters—the propriety of "showing up" people in print—which was advocated both by Hunt and Carlyle—and sundry other topics. Left him after half an hour's interview, with very favorable impressions—thinking that he may be a man as much—to say the least—as much sinned against as sinning. At the door Carlyle shook me by the hand cordially and said

"God bless you! A pleasant journey to you; and when you return to London do not forget to inquire us out!"

Longfellow and Carlyle make a very odd pair, but the visits were long and cordial, and in the American's presence Carlyle seems to have restrained himself from the biting social criticism and literary tirades that were to make him so feared and whose blustering tone would eventually make him so easy to dismiss. The unexpected appearance of a well-read and impressionable young New Englander in a city in which the Carlyles themselves did not feel at home surely renewed happy memories of Emerson's pilgrimage to Craigenputtock. It also reassured Carlyle that he had an American audience. Longfellow was a passionate pilgrim indeed when it came to the new German literature, and Carlyle had succeeded Coleridge as the chief conduit of that stream of idealism into New England, where it was to help shape transcendentalism. In Carlyle and Leigh Hunt, Longfellow also encountered a phenomenon he had not known in America: writers of the first importance who had not compromised their staunchly held artistic and political beliefs and who were paying for it, each in his own way. Longfellow himself avoided such confrontations, but he was to experience vicariously, in the life of his closest male friend, Charles Sumner, a similar firmness when it came to standing up for principle. For all their obvious differences, Carlyle and Longfellow did have one thing in common: in a literary world dominated by London, they were from the periphery—the one a Highland Scot, the other a North American.

Fortunately for Longfellow, this did not prevent English publishers from showing an interest in *Outre-Mer*. The editor of The Family Library, for example, offered to publish it in his series. When Longfellow told him he expected at least one hundred pounds sterling, "he opened his great goggle eyes in apparent astonishment, and said 'Oh, no! impossible! Why in three weeks I can get it for nothing'." Obadiah

Rich in Madrid had sent a copy to the well-known publisher Richard Bentley; Longfellow, fearing his work would be pirated if he did not act at once, quickly reached terms with him in 1835. Bentley promised he would "have it out in a week." They would divide the profits (as it turned out, there were none). The title page said that *Outre-Mer* was "By an American." One English reviewer guessed at the author—a Mr. Longbody.

The month in England had passed quickly, and Longfellow was determined to savor his final moments of "London the magnificent." On the deck of the steam packet *William Joliffe*, on June 9, the eve of their departure for Hamburg, Longfellow watched the sun set over the Thames.

> Lamps gleaming along the shore—and on the bridges—a full moon rising over the borough of Southwark, and silvering the scene with a ghostly light.... Barges and wherries move to and fro; and heavy-laden luggers are sweeping up stream with the rising tide, swinging sideways, with loose-flapping sails. Either side of the river is crowded with various sea-craft, whose black hulks lie in shadow, and whose tapering and mingling spars rise up into the moon-light like the leafless branches of a grove in winter. The distant sound of music floats on the air—a harp and a flute and a horn—It has an unearthly sound; and lo! like a shooting-star a light comes gliding on. It's the signal-lamp at the mast-head of a steam-vessel, that flits by like a spectre; unseen, save as a cloud, above which glides a silver star;—unheard, save by the beating paddles, and the fairy music on its deck. And from all this scene goes up a sound of human voices, curses, laughter and singing—mingled with the monotonous roar of the city—as its living tides ebb at evening through their paved channels—slowly settling like the ocean-currents to their bed.
>
> Gradually all sound and motion cease; the river tide is silent at its flood; and from the slumbering city comes only now and then a voice—a feeble murmur.

He listens as the church bells strike the hours—first from some distant suburb, then closer, then "a heavy, solemn sound" from St. Paul's, answered by the cathedral across the river in Southwark, picked up by a more distant church—"and then all around you the various and in-termingling clang, like a chime of bells—the clocks from thirty towers strike the hour—One—two! One—two!"

The moon is already sinking.—large and fiery through the vapors of the morning. It is just in the range of the chimneys and house-tops, and seems to follow us with great speed, as we float down the river. Day is dawning in the east—not with a pale streak in the horizon—but with a faint silver light spread through the eastern-sky almost to the zenith. It is the mingling of moonlight and daylight. The water is tinged with a green hue melting into purple and gold, like the brilliant scales of a fish. The air grows cool. It comes fresh from the eastern sea, towards which we are swiftly gliding.

By June 12 they had reached the mouth of the Elbe, and that evening they settled into the Hotel de Russie in Hamburg.

What little Longfellow knew of Sweden had come from the young poet Karl August Nicander, a lively and attractive figure in the circle of Swedish artists and writers whom he had met in Rome in 1828. Nicander had portrayed Stockholm as an Athens of the North, and Longfellow was eager to immerse himself for the summer in what for him would be virtually a new world of Nordic history and literature. The three young women could amuse themselves, as they easily had done in London, while he made the rounds of the bookshops, libraries, universities, museums, and literary salons. The first hint that the sum-mer might turn out differently came as the travelers approached Den-mark. They had ridden on the notoriously bad road from Hamburg to Lübeck and the next day had sailed out of Travemunde on a not very clean-smelling steamer for their first glimpse of Scandinavia. Copen-hagen proved an immediate disappointment. The grass growing between the paving stones of the harbor produced in Longfellow "a feeling of gloom and loneliness." To Clara, "it looked like a city of the dead." Even the fruit-and-wine soup they tried at their hotel proved too much like New England sago porridge and stuck to the roof of their mouths. They had not prepared themselves for the fact that they had left the wealth and energy of London behind and were now in one of the quietest corners of Europe.

After some perfunctory sightseeing, they boarded the steamer *Prinds Carl* for Sweden—only to run into a storm in the Kattegat so threatening that the boat had to take shelter off Elsinore. As a result they reached Gothenburg an hour after the connecting steamer to Stockholm had left—and there would not be another for two weeks. Gothenburg seemed pleasant enough, but not worth that long a delay. So Longfellow bought a Russian-made carriage—big, heavy, comfortable—and hired the Danish servant boy who had accompanied them to help drive it. ("He is a most good-natured fellow and nearly prostrates himself before you when you speak to him," noted Clara.) Longfellow was alert to every new sight—and smell. The Swedes strewed their tavern floors with little sprigs of pine ("a sweet flavor" but "a singular look"), for example, while their coach, he soon discovered, had "a classical smell—an odor of *Ancient Grease*." In the crowded innyards, he found "the sounds of an unknown tongue ringing in my ears, which at times so much resembles English, that I am in doubt whether an English sentence has not been imperfectly spoken." He saw the St. John's Day festivities at Trollhättan, where the villagers were dancing in the wet grass around the Maypole, and one of the *skeppssättningar* at Munksten—the medieval stone cenotaphs laid out in the shape of a Viking ship. But what truly astonished him was the far-northern summer light. "There is no night. I stood in the public square at midnight [in Lidköping], and read with perfect ease a written paper." Sweden in 1835 was a poorer country than Longfellow had expected, but he found "the peasantry exceedingly civil. Nearly all take off their hats as we pass." Clara amused herself on the road "watching the half-naked children run to open the gates for us." They would catch a penny if you threw it to them, she added, but never asked for one. On the other hand, the inns were primitive, and often it was raining, and the horses had great trouble on the muddy hills. It had taken them five days to travel three hundred miles. They were relieved to be in the capital at last and settled in at the Hotel Garni, but the four of them felt travel-worn.

The visit did not begin auspiciously. Longfellow had not written ahead to his friend, the writer Nicander, innocently assuming that the Swedish "season" took place, like the London one, in summer. On the contrary, the frugal Swedish nobility and professional classes spent their summers living cheaply in the country. Nicander had just left for his patron's distant estate. Longfellow had counted on the poet's help in meeting the Stockholm literati, who could guide his reading and brief him on their country's culture. Nicander's absence was a heavy blow. Longfellow did have a letter of introduction from Parker Cleaveland at Bowdoin to Jons Jakob Berzelius, the country's most famous chemist. He called, was cordially received, and learned that his host was leaving for Paris in two days. "So, here are two persons gone from town, upon whom I most relied for information and entertainment here. The town seems empty." In a cold drizzle, they changed lodgings to 22 Drottninggatan, which they immediately disliked, but could find nothing better. "So we go on," wrote a depressed Longfellow, "always disappointed—and still hoping; searching and never finding, and yet not tired with searching." Mary was still suffering from "the ague," and her companions from pangs of homesickness.

Longfellow was later to complain that his summer in Sweden had been a great mistake, but in fact he accomplished more there than perhaps he realized. Once again, in a remarkably short time, he learned enough of a new language to be able to read it with facility, and he began a lifelong exploration of Swedish literature, the high point of which was his discovery of the work of Bishop Tegnér, the country's leading poet and a writer whose work Longfellow was to introduce in translation to American readers. He also began to study Finnish, an interest that was to influence the way in which he would compose *The Song of Hiawatha* a decade later. He was struck by the similarities of the Swedish landscape and that of Maine—"wild scenery of rocks and pines"—and by the fact that a visitor was so quickly in the woods: "The moment you leave the northern gate of Stockholm the scene changes as if by magic.—There is not a house in sight. Nothing but pine forest. You would imagine yourself hundreds of miles from the capital."

His female companions were quickly bored with the city, but their social life did improve as Longfellow ventured into the diplomatic community and met several Swedish notables who had lived in America. The artist Maria Christina Rohl drew their portraits. They did what sightseeing they could, given the wet, cold weather. At Uppsala, Longfellow explored the university library, and they saw the Viking funeral mounds mentioned in *Beowulf*. The summer palace at Drottningholm pleased them. Just outside of the city, they walked through the woods of Count Horn's estate, Hufvudsta, the scene of the conspiracy that led to the assassination of Gustavus III. (Many years later, Longfellow—a passionate opera-goer—heard Verdi's *Un Ballo in Maschera*, which was based on this incident but, to evade French censorship, relocated to colonial Boston, Massachusetts!) They missed seeing in person the contemporary Swedish monarch, the former Napoleonic general Bernadotte, but caught a glimpse of the queen, the famous Desirée, as her carriage passed on the street. They indulged in the romantic fascination with caverns and mines and were bold enough to descend in a large bucket the famous Dannemora Grufvor. Mary Longfellow refused to go with them, remaining above, "leaning over the railing [Crowninshield reports] with her veil drawn over her face, looking the picture of distress." Longfellow himself looked pale and nervous as the bucket slowly lurched downward into the depths of the pit where the previous winter's ice and snow had not yet melted, and the air smelled of gunpowder. They got out, walked through the chilly tunnels, and collected some ore for Professor Cleaveland back in Brunswick.

Daily life, in other words, had its diversions. Tongue possibly in cheek, Longfellow described to George Washington Greene his amazement at the amount the Swedes drank. "Everybody takes a dram [of rum] before sitting down to dinner; and again after dinner. The *clergy* frequent confectioners shops—drink punch in public coffee rooms—play cards on Sunday—and smoke cigars in the street . . . quite scandalous." The Swedes, he added, were free-and-easy and politically liberal, but "in everything else, they are a century behind most parts of Christendom. They are all half-asleep." The lower classes in particular he found "dull and lumpish." As he noted in his journal, "Among the peasantry 'la stupidite est d'uniforme.' It is a national costume." He admitted to himself that he was peevish and discontented.

> I shall beware in future how I establish myself near a stable yard. Horns blowing—hammers klinking—stable boys swearing—dogs barking—in a word the very devil to pay. Now, here is a great lazy raskal amusing himself just beneath my window, with cracking a long, heavy coach-whip.

Even the clergy were noisy. At the cathedral, Longfellow heard "a preacher who screamed in one long scream a sermon of no inconsiderable length."

There was one moment of unexpected excitement. Lightning struck the steeple of the Riddarholmskyrkan, the most historic church in Stockholm, and set it afire. The flames moved slowly enough through the rafters for its treasures—historic battle flags and the like—to be saved, and to provide Longfellow the occasion for the best piece of reportage he ever wrote. In a long journal passage, he described the steeple "blazing from its open mouth, like the chimney of a Manchester factory" and the moment when the copper sheath of the roof "parted below, and slid downward, like the skin of a ripe fig." As alarm bells rang throughout the city, the church burned for two days, the flames at times disappearing only to burst forth elsewhere. Fortunately, the vaulting of the roof protected the tombs of the Swedish kings below.

In the last week of August they left Stockholm, taking the steamer *Amiral von Platen* on a leisurely—and this time smooth—trip through scenic lakes and canals, with their seventy-two locks, back to Gothenburg. At some point in July or August, Mary Longfellow had announced that she was pregnant. The shivering and feverishness that she had experienced in June, which she had assumed was "the ague," may have been early signs of her condition, suggesting that the child had been conceived during the month-long Atlantic crossing. After four years of marriage and at least one miscarriage, Mary was not uninformed about such things, but Clara and the other Mary were probably of no help, and it is possible that the Longfellows were ignorant of the pregnancy until they reached Stockholm. It is difficult to believe that they would have made the rough overland journey by carriage, rather than waiting patiently for the boat at Gothenburg, had Henry known of his wife's condition. Once confirmed, this news added enormously to the complexities of the whole European trip. A nurse would have to be hired, an English-speaking one if possible, adding to the expense. There surely would have to be changes of itinerary and all the unexpected delays associated with traveling with an infant. Never an enthusiastic traveler, Mary would now be even less company for the two young women. Longfellow had much to consider during those slow days of travel south.

They reached Gothenburg comfortably in six days, only to discover that cabins on the steamer back to Denmark were fully booked (because of the ladies, Longfellow refused to travel overnight on deck) and that they would have to wait a week for the next boat. In other circumstances, he wrote, he would not have minded the wait: "If I were not in such a hurry to get to the Rhine, I should not care a fig. But as it is, every hour is precious." Biographers have taken this as evidence of concern for his wife's fragile health. A more practical explanation is that he had promised to show his ladies the poetic spectacle of the grape harvest on the Rhine and was fretting that it would be over before they— and he—could enjoy it. When they finally did return to Copenhagen on September 10, the place had an unexpected charm. As Longfellow noted, "How different this city looks on coming from Sweden, than it did when we came from England!"

Settling into the Hotel Royal, he began improving his Danish. "This language has an unpleasant sound to my ear," he confided in his journal. "For softness and beauty it cannot be compared with the beautiful Swedish. The Danes speak with a *burr* in their throats." At the local athenaeum, he was pleased to read "a long and loud puff" for the British edition of *Outre-Mer* in the London *Atlas*. His immersion in medieval Nordic culture deepened as he began studying Icelandic ("a harsh, sharp and disagreeable sound") and saw the Viking artifacts in the new Museum of Northern Antiquities: "Funeral urns, with mouldering bones therein—swords—bracelets—gold and silver ornaments from days, when iron was as yet unknown—altar-pieces and church reliques from the early days of Christianity in the North—and shields and swords and helmets from the age of chivalry." Some of this would reappear in "The Skeleton in Armor" in 1841. But news from America had already broken this idyll.

Clara Crowninshield's diary tells the story best. Letters from home were rare and much treasured, and it was the custom among the three young women to read and reread them aloud to each other. Clara did so, innocently enough, on September 12. A mutual friend had written that Mary Goddard's brother, who was supposed to meet her in Germany, had suddenly returned to Boston.

> I began to read it aloud and stopped, of course, when I found there was something unpleasant for Mary to hear. She insisted upon my continuing. I read it aloud so far and then continued to myself. "His father was taken sick suddenly and died yesterday of apoplexy." Mary saw by my countenance that there was something more. She insisted on my telling her what it was. I was agitated and could hardly believe my own eyes as I read the words. I told her I could not read it and asked her to call Mary Longfellow. She obeyed me without knowing what she did. Mary Longfellow turned pale and read aloud till I told her to stop. Mary Goddard grew impatient and said, "I will see it, girls." I thought it could do no good to keep it from her and I gave her the letter. She burst into an agony of grief and called Henry immediately. . . .

PLATE 2. John G. Brown, *Bowdoin College Campus*, 1823. Longfellow and Hawthorne attended recitations in Massachusetts Hall (far left) and heard morning prayers in the Chapel, the wooden structure whose second floor housed the library. In the foreground is "Old Tench," who sold birch beer and gingerbread to the students. (Oil on canvas. Bowdoin College Museum of Art, Brunswick, Maine, Gift of Harold L. Berry, class of 1901.)

PLATE 3. Thomas Badger, *Longfellow*, c. 1829. Oil on canvas. Courtesy Maine Historical Society.

PLATE 4. Unknown artist, *Mary Storer Potter Longfellow*, c. 1830. Twentieth-century copy of lost original. Courtesy of Maine Historical Society.

PLATE 5. Eastman Johnson, *Henry W. Longfellow*, 1846. Crayon and chalk on paper. Courtesy National Park Service, Longfellow National Historic Site.

PLATE 6. Eastman Johnson, *Charles Sumner*, 1846. Crayon and chalk on paper. Courtesy National Park Service, Longfellow National Historic Site.

PLATE 7. Eastman Johnson, *Nathaniel Hawthorne*, 1846. Crayon and chalk on paper. Courtesy National Park Service, Longfellow National Historic Site.

PLATE 8. Eastman Johnson, *Ralph Waldo Emerson*, 1846. Crayon and chalk on paper. Courtesy National Park Service, Longfellow National Historic Site.

PLATE 9. *Longfellow*. Daguerreotype by Southworth and Hawes, Boston, c. 1848. The Metropolitan Museum of Art, gift of I. N. Phelps Stokes, Edward S. Hawes, Alice Mary Hawes, Marion Augusta Hawes.

PLATE 10. G. P. A. Healy, *Frances Elizabeth Appleton*, 1834. Oil on canvas. Courtesy National Park Service, Longfellow National Historic Site.

PLATE 11. *Craigie House*, early 1850s. Watercolor and ink on paper, attributed to Henry W. Longfellow. Longfellow amused his children with his sketches of domestic life. In this view, he and Fanny stand on the east piazza, while Charley, Erny, and possibly Alice peer through a window. Courtesy National Park Service, Longfellow National Historic Site.

PLATE 12. *The Longfellow Family*. Daguerreotype attributed to Southworth and Hawes, Boston, 1849. Five-year-old Charley (center) has trouble sitting still—his mother grasps his neck from behind—while four-year-old Erny glares at the camera. Courtesy National Park Service, Longfellow National Historic Site.

PLATE 13. *Longfellow*. Southworth and Hawes, daguerreotype, Boston, 1850. Courtesy National Park Service, Longfellow National Historic Site.

Plans were quickly made to send Mary Goddard to London, where she could find passage back to Boston; a young American diplomat, John James Appleton, who had befriended them in Stockholm, agreed to escort her as far as England. Her departure would be a financial blow to Longfellow, who had counted on her family's contribution as part of his European budget.

Amid this shock and disruption of plans, Longfellow made as much as he could of his two weeks in Denmark, where he had been welcomed at once into a circle of scholars and bibliophiles of the sort he had failed to find in Sweden. His original plan had been to spend the winter in Berlin, whose university was rapidly becoming the most highly regarded in Europe. He decided instead to travel by water up the Rhine, perhaps seeking winter quarters in one of the smaller university towns, such as Bonn or Heidelberg. Living expenses would be less there, he learned, than in Berlin, and his pregnant wife would be spared the travail of a long overland journey in a jostling coach. On September 25, the three remaining travelers boarded the *Frederik den Siette* for Kiel and Hamburg, whence they would sail for Holland and the Rhine, in the hopes of being settled for the winter by the first of October.

One further story of Longfellow's Danish visit merits telling, however, as testimony to his own ability to laugh at himself. He had encountered a wonderful specimen of Jacksonian America in the person of Colonel Johnathan Woodside, the U.S. chargé d'affaires at the Danish court. "He has never seen a European Court before, and seems like a cat in a strange garret," Longfellow noted. The colonel had achieved some renown back home in Ohio in 1830 as the result of a political quarrel with the editor of a politically hostile newspaper. The editor had come after him with a knife, cutting Woodside's right hand so badly he had to learn to write with his left. The editor got three years at hard labor; the colonel, eventually, a diplomatic posting abroad. Woodside showed Longfellow some of his fifteen scars. Glancing over the small ambassadorial library, Longfellow spotted a copy of the first volume of *Outre-Mer* and fished for a compliment.

"Ah, you have a copy of that book, I see."

"Yes. I brought it from London. It is very highly spoken of there, but for my part I do not see much merit in it."

Recovering his composure, Longfellow admitted he was the author. Woodside looked at him blankly. Smiling desperately, Longfellow continued: "I am glad to hear your opinion of the book, before you knew me to be the author of it." Woodside admitted he had spoken more candidly than he would have, had he known who his visitor was, then calmly proceeded to explain to the author what the book's faults were. Too much triviality, for example: "A man of your talents"— (sweetly put in, that)—"might employ his time to more advantage, than writing about such foolish stories as Robert the Devil." Longfellow declined to yield. "These old stories—though trivial in themselves—are not so as scraps of literary history. I put this paper in my book as you put a Chinese ornament on your mantle-piece, not for its intrinsic value, but because it illustrates manners, customs and feelings of another age or country." Woodside appeared unconvinced.

By October 1, the travelers had got only as far as Amsterdam, where they lodged at the Wapen van Amsterdam. Despite some signs of exhaustion on Mary's part (serious enough to seek a doctor's advice), they began their usual routines, Longfellow haunting the bookshops and studying Dutch, and the two young women buying rolls of linen which they hoped to smuggle through American customs. It was Clara's task to hide this "contraband" among the folds of clothing in their trunks. The condition of Mary's health in these days has to be guessed at from some very sketchy references in the otherwise detailed journals kept by Crowninshield and Longfellow. Candid discussion of pregnancy was not a fit subject even for a personal journal, which might at some point be read by family and friends. If Mary kept her own record, it was destroyed. Nothing that has survived suggests any sense of danger. The first indication that something was seriously wrong appears, in novelistic detail, in Crowninshield's diary entry for October 5. She was awakened by a tap at her door. It was Longfellow in search of a candle. His had burned down. "Is there anything wrong?" she asked.

> "Yes," said he, "Mary is sick—worse than ever."
> "Shall I come in?"
> "No," said he, "you can't do any good."

Clara found him a fresh candle and put on her clothes in case she should be needed. She lay on her bed, shivering and dozing until morning.

> I heard Mr. Longfellow's bell ring and much passing up and down the entry, but I lay quietly till Mr. Longfellow came to my door. I went out and he stood a moment at the window. I asked him if Mary had an ague fit. "Something worse than that," said he. "You can't go in just now," said he—so I waited a moment. When I went in I found Mary in the other bed looking very pale. I asked her how she did. She said she felt better but that she had not slept any through the night. After a while Mr. Longfellow took his pipe and walked out and Mary called me to her bed and related the occurrences of the night and there they were in utter darkness.

Longfellow's own entry was more laconic:

> Was up before daylight—Mary being very ill. The very deuce to pay, and all in the dark; for it was a long time before I could muster flint, steel and matches and strike a light. Sent for the Dr. in a hurry; but before he arrived it was all over....

In the dark hotel room she had once again miscarried, probably in her sixth month of pregnancy, attended only by a young husband stumbling about for a candle and trying to staunch the blood. It took Mary two weeks to recover her strength, and by October 22, after sightseeing at The Hague and elsewhere, they reached the Hotel des Pays Bas in Rotterdam, near the mouth of the Rhine. Mary was not well.

They would miss the sights and scents of the vendange; Clara consoled herself with a volume of engravings of romantic Rhine scenery.

Longfellow, knowing that they could not leave Rotterdam until Mary had recovered, set out to make the best use of his time—studying Dutch, buying books for the Harvard library, translating the Danish ballad "King Christian." He told his father that Dutch was the most disagreeable-sounding language he had heard, except for Russian, "but a very important language to me, being of all the modern Gothic tongues, the one which bears the strongest resemblance to the mother-tongue, from which they all come." He was aided in his studies by an English clergyman, the Reverend Dr. Joseph Bosworth, an early authority on Anglo-Saxon who invited Longfellow to contribute to his forthcoming dictionary. Rotterdam they found as pretty as Amsterdam, and Henry had managed to locate a first-class hotel. Their apartments were carpeted (a luxury they had not enjoyed since leaving England) and decorated in the rococo style, with French furniture, chinoiserie panels, and paintings of Apollo and Flora over the fireplace. The rooms were large, quiet, and comfortable, but north-facing, without a ray of sun.

While doing everything possible, with the aid of the local physicians, to hasten Mary's recovery, Henry and Clara went about their daily routines amid no sign that there was any emergency; it was Henry in fact who was suffering, with a very bad cold. On October 27, however, Mary took a turn for the worse. Her doctor found her a nurse, who spoke no English but seemed to know her business, and by the end of the month Mary felt stronger. On October 30, Henry took Clara for a walk—the first time she had been able to leave the hotel for a week—and they looked at the boats on the river and speculated on which might be the most reliable for the long voyage up the Rhine. Mary still had sleepless nights and frequent headaches, but through the first week of November gave no one cause for alarm. Clara busied herself sewing, studying German, reading to Mary, and sketching; Longfellow criticized her drawing for its unsteady "feminine style." Even the life of a hotel *de luxe* was beginning to wear: Clara yearned for plain bread and butter instead of the delicacies regularly set before them: "four kinds of meat, cauliflower, brockily and salad, *appelmoes*, tarts, and then the dessert, consisting of 8 dishes, among them grapes, delicious ones, nice pears, nuts, cakes, and bonbons." They awoke on November 9 to find the rooftops covered with snow. Would they be winter-bound? The gloom was settling in. Clara started making flannel drawers for the patient, who by the 11th seemed to her husband "as pale as a snowflake."

By the week of November 22, it was clear that Mary was not recovering. After several days of rheumatism (which Clara treated with pieces of flannel soaked in brandy), nausea (the sweetness of the blancmange Clara had cooked for her over a brazier made her vomit), and feverishness, she was in great pain. On the 24th, Longfellow thought she was "sinking," but she rallied the next day. The doctor was not fooled. As Clara recorded:

> The doctor called at the usual time, said she had a good deal of fever, and knit his brow when he turned from the bed saying "M'est faible, toujours faible." His expression alarmed Mr. Longfellow and he followed the doctor into the entry. I was afraid Mary might hear him and be alarmed, so I went to her bed and talked as calmly as I could that she need not hear her husband's voice. But she missed him from the room and asked where he was. I told her very quietly that he had only stepped into the entry. He came back soon and spoke cheerfully to Mary, but I saw that there was a cloud upon his brow.

By the 28th, she was steadily weakening, and Longfellow tried to cushion the blow as best he could in a letter to his father. "It is the effect of a miscarriage, which happened some weeks ago, in spite of all our precautions. I hope she may yet revive; but my anxiety is very great; and I write this to prepare your minds for what may happen." He added that Clara had been a "great consolation"—"She takes the place of a sister. . . ."

In Mary's final hours, her pain seemed to lift somewhat and, according to Clara, she was bright and attentive. Letters from her family seemed to have cheered her. She was unquenchably thirsty and gasped for breath; but—and there is no reason to doubt Clara's firsthand account—she left her life with the grace and presence of mind of a young woman who had nothing to fear from what was to come.

When she first began to feel her breathing more difficult, she was conscious she was near her end and with the most perfect composure said to Henry, "Tell all my friends I thought of them in my last moments. How my poor father will mourn for me. He has always been so kind to me and so have all my friends." "Because you have always been such a good, gentle girl," said Henry. "Will God take me to him?" "Yes," said Henry. "I shall see my dear mother, shan't I?" Then she clasped Henry's neck with her almost lifeless arm and said, "Henry, it is hard to die and leave you. I remember all your kindness to me." "You are going to your best friend," said Henry. She was perfectly tranquil and this was the only expression like regret that she uttered at the prospect of dying. She said once, "I ought to bless God that he makes one suffer so little."

Henry was sufficiently in control of his feelings to read to Mary from the prayer book; they prayed together when Dr. Bosworth arrived sometime before 2:00 a.m. Henry closed one of Mary's eyes and let Clara close the other. Later, when the nurse had laid out the body, Henry kissed Mary's lips and drew the rings from her hand and placed them on his own. Clara adds: "I gave him some wine and prevailed upon him to lie down upon my bed. I wrapped a cloak round me and reposed as well I could on two chairs. Now that there was no longer cause for restraint he gave vent to his grief and wept bitterly till sleep came to his relief."

The next day Clara set to work separating and packing Mary's things; the odor of spices filled the rooms, for Longfellow had the doctors embalm his wife's body and seal it in a leaden coffin, then in an oaken one. He found a ship bound for Boston and asked that the body be kept at the Mount Auburn Cemetery in Cambridge until he returned and could purchase a plot. He wrote a pain-filled letter to Mary's father on December 1, and the next day he and Clara left in the steamer for Cologne and the darkness of the long German winter.

An Alpine Interlude

IN JULY OF 1836, TWO YOUNG NEW ENGLANDERS
found themselves in the Bernese Alps, each seeking a kind of healing.

The younger, Frances Appleton, was with her father, her younger
sister Mary, her older brother, and a sickly young cousin, halfway
through a two-year European tour. It had turned into a voyage of
convalescence for their cousin William Appleton, a frail, tubercular
twenty-one-year-old whom they had long treated as a member of their
immediate family. At nineteen, Fanny, as she was called by her intimates, was perhaps more handsome than beautiful—brown-haired,
serious, self-possessed, and the sort of young woman whose arrival
in the spa towns and European capitals was an event of note, for she
and her sister were expected to be heiresses on a scale that could have
repaired many an aristocrat's fortunes. Their father was Nathan
Appleton of Boston, a leading member of the dominant Whig Party in
New England and a pioneer in the development of that region's lucrative textile industry. Joining them for much of their journey was another young cousin, Isaac Appleton Jewett, part of a clan of Appletons
that was making its influence felt in every aspect of Boston life. Their
tour was being conducted on a princely scale—Fanny would be presented to Louis Philippe in Paris and would attend a soiree at the
Court of St. James (catching a glimpse of the young Princess Victoria,
Fanny pronounced her "a short, thick, commonplace, stupid-looking
girl")—but it had been undertaken in a rehabilitative spirit by the entire party. Fanny's mother, Theresa Gold Appleton, had died of consumption in 1833. The European tour had originally been conceived
as a coming of age gift for Fanny's brother Charles, who had died of the

same disease in 1834, weakening her father's hopes that he had an heir capable of taking over his vast network of business and civic interests.

The other young New Englander had also sought a change of scenery—more literally, a change of atmosphere after the damp German spring—by ascending, as soon as the snows had melted in the Alpine passes, into Switzerland. The British had discovered its scenery some fifty years earlier and made it a place one had to visit. It was a country that still had an enticing air of remoteness, for the railroads had not yet arrived, ushering in the modern age of European tourism. Travel was by horseback, or in slow coaches, or in little lake steamers. Still, it was a land that had lost some its ability to awe travelers by the frightfulness of its mountains; it was being reconceived as picturesque. Longfellow had spent the winter at Heidelberg, on the Necker, a small university town of great charm, rendered romantic by the brooding ruins of its castle. He had gone through the motions of attending classes, buying books, making calls in genteel society, and serving as companion and chaperone to Clara Crowninshield, who was at the start of what would be her own lifelong love of Germany. Longfellow's fascination with the more sentimental side of German romanticism had deepened, as he sought refuge from his own sorrow in the poetry of Novalis and Uhland and Jean Paul. He was tormented by guilt, blaming himself for exposing his late wife to the dangers of foreign travel. His life seemed pointless. "Good God, what a solitary, lonely being I am," he wrote in his journal when he reached the lakeside medieval Swiss town of Thun. "Why do I travel? Every hour my heart aches with sadness." As the glacial meadows blossomed, he sought an end to his *Winterreise* of the spirit through the sheer physical exertion of tramping through the green Alpine foothills.

On July 20 at Thun, Fanny Appleton noted in her journal: "Prof. Longfellow sends up his card to Father. Hope the venerable gentleman won't pop in on us, though I did like his Outre-Mer." Finding the Appletons out of the hotel, Longfellow continued by water to Interlaken, where he met them on the 31st. "A young man after all," she noted, "or else the son of the poet." For almost three weeks, amid the

Balthusian landscape of the Thunersee, they were in and out of each other's company, walking, reading and translating German romantic poetry, discussing art, sketching, and boating. Longfellow's spirits lifted. He had met intelligent and attractive Americans who shared his interests. They liked him enough to invite him to travel for the time being with them. Perhaps because of his experience in nursing Mary in her final weeks, he felt a special affinity for William Appleton, whose lungs were beyond any healing the dry mountain air might have accomplished. And he was charmed by the witty (and sexually ambiguous) Thomas Gold Appleton, the most artistic and poetical of the family; indeed a Jamesian American *avant la lettre*, who would become one of Longfellow's closest friends and a much sought-out social figure on both sides of the Atlantic.

This Alpine idyll abruptly ended at Schaffhausen on July 17. Clara Crowninshield, eager to arrange for her return home to America, had summoned him back to Heidelberg. Longfellow could find at least some consolation in knowing that he would see the Appletons again, although perhaps not for another year, in Boston—except for William. Longfellow, who had spent many hours reading to him, paid a final call. Fanny wrote that "she was quite sorry to have him go; he has been so kind to William and helped keep up our spirits." On August 19, she wrote: "Miss Mr. L considerably." On the 24th, William died at Schaffhausen and was buried there. The Appleton party set off for Paris. On the 30th, while sitting at the window of their inn at Strasbourg, Fanny saw Henry walking down the street, with Clara and the wife and daughter of William Cullen Bryant (the Bryants were spending a year in Europe and had befriended Longfellow in Heidelberg). But they would not meet again until the fall of 1837, when the poet-professor would discover an old truth about the nature of holiday romances.

But what kind of romance had it been? The traditional accounts of Longfellow's life tend to assume that he had fallen passionately in love with Miss Appleton more or less as soon as he saw her at Interlaken. He wooed her—a bit awkwardly, it is implied in these accounts—by reading German poetry aloud and translating it for her on the spot. Yet Paolo and Francesca they were not. Longfellow seems to have spent as much time with Mary Appleton, not to mention Tom, as with Fanny. The increasing certainty of William's death must have rendered somber most of those days. More important, would a man as self-controlled as Longfellow have allowed himself to pursue an eligible young woman only six months after his own young wife had died in horrific circumstances?

We do not know the significance of the confidences exchanged, the words deliciously lingered over, in those afternoons between Interlachen and Zurich. Here is one way of viewing the encounter. Longfellow, a deeply wounded man, had met a young woman who had borne her own share of sorrows, and they discovered that they could console each other, not least through reading poetry together. After her mother's death, Fanny had taken on much of the responsibility of running her father's large and complicated household and had no intention of falling quickly in love with anyone. She had found a role that fulfilled her. In Longfellow, she had met a new social type for her—the idealistic, poetry-besotted young professor—and had allowed herself to be charmed by him and diverted by him, even educated by him, in the midst of another unfolding tragedy for her family. Longfellow cannot have been unaware that he had stumbled upon a very important band of Bostonians whose friendship he would do well to cultivate. He perhaps underestimated the social gap between even a Harvard professor of good family and the Appletons of 39 Beacon Street (although in truth the Appletons' fortune had been made with dazzling rapidity). Might he have been infatuated by the Appleton glamour, as much as by Miss Appleton herself? He had plenty of time to think about it, on his own slow voyage back to America in 1836. His tentative, self-defeating attempt later that fall to rekindle what he imagined a flame suggests that the "crystallization" (in Stendhal's sense) of this hopeless affair may have taken place in the emptiness of his rented rooms at the Craigie House. A glimpse of Fanny in some

Beacon Hill drawing room, her figure in the distance on the promenade on the Common, an overheard reference to one of her many suitors in Boston—anything might have served to quicken his pulse. He knew, at any rate, that he was living in a house worthy to receive such a bride.

Six

CASTLE CRAIGIE

U PON RETURNING TO AMERICA, the first thing was to find a place to live. Longfellow had spent the previous two years in hotels and rented lodgings or on shipboard, and he was eager to establish himself in quarters that were both comfortable and suitable to the dignity of the Smith Professorship. His Cambridge friend and colleague Cornelius Felton, who had played a large role in bringing him to Harvard, told him of a vacancy on the third floor of Professor Stearns's house, where he lodged, on Kirkland Street. Longfellow took it, for the 1836–37 academic year, but soon tired of boarding-house life and began looking in earnest for more spacious and private quarters. The terms of his professorship required him to live in Cambridge—his predecessor Ticknor had annoyed his colleagues by insisting on staying in his Park Street, Boston, mansion—yet did not require him to be within sight of campus. Since New England college professors who lived near their colleges frequently got pulled into nocturnal student disturbances as disciplinarians, if not targets, some distancing made sense. He strolled out along Brattle Street one day in the spring of 1837 and asked the Widow Craigie for rooms. Evidently he had not quite assumed the full dignity of Smith Professor, for she thought he was a student and turned him down. When he insisted that he was indeed one of the faculty, and author of the book *Outre-Mer*, the first volume of which sat on her side table, she relented, and perhaps the most famous link between an American writer and an American house began.

The dignified Georgian house at what is now 105 Brattle Street had been built in 1759 as a country retreat by a rich merchant, John Vassall, on a raised terrace overlooking the water meadows of the Charles River, about half a mile from the center of Cambridge village. In the two decades before the Revolution, this bucolic neighborhood along the Watertown Road had proven so popular among Boston's wealthier citizens, it became known as "Tory Row." The Vassall House, with its broad, symmetrical, pedimented facade and commanding site, was the most imposing Brattle Street dwelling of all. Like other great merchants with family and commercial connections in Britain, Vassall remained loyal to the Crown when the Revolution erupted, and he had to flee for his personal safety in 1774. His property was confiscated, and his Cambridge estate was occupied by the Marblehead Regiment of rebel troops. In July of 1775, General Washington made the house his headquarters during the Siege of Boston. He stayed for nine months, taking command on Cambridge Common of the new and unproven Continental Army, and in December welcoming his wife Martha and her son and daughter-in-law. The house seemed safe, but Martha reported to a friend in Virginia that on "some days we have a number of cannon and shells from Boston and Bunkers Hill...." According to a letter written in 1843 by the aged John Trumball, who had served on Washington's staff, the general lived in the two eastern second-floor rooms and, on the first floor, made the southeast room his study and dining room, the rear eastern room his staff office, and the southwest room his wife's parlor.

Amid the rigors of war, the Washingtons managed, according to family tradition, to live there in some style. John and Abigail Adams, Henry Knox, Nathaniel Greene, Benedict Arnold, and a host of other Revolutionary War luminaries crossed its threshold. Here, Washington struggled to turn his undisciplined, ill-supplied New England troops into a real army, amid his own doubts about whether the revolution would succeed. Here, the general learned of the providential arrival, thanks to the twenty-four-year-old General Knox (a former Boston bookseller), of the cannon from Fort Ticonderoga, laboriously dragged across the mountains on the hard-packed snow. Mounted overnight on the heights of Dorchester, facing Boston from the south, the guns forced the surprised British to evacuate the city or face the destruction of their fleet.

The general, his aides, and his family left in April of 1776. After a series of owners, in 1791 an ambitious land speculator, Andrew Craigie, bought the house. Craigie had done well in the war, as first Apothecary General of the United States, and went to some trouble and too much expense to return the estate to its pre-Revolutionary splendor. His lavish habits nearly ruined him, and his widow in 1819 found herself encumbered with debt. She managed to keep the house, however, and began taking in lodgers to pay off her late husband's creditors. Her tenants included two future Harvard presidents, Edward Everett and Jared Sparks, and enough students to persuade her by Longfellow's day to rent only to adults. Meanwhile, Elizabeth Craigie herself had become a local eccentric. She slept late and read well into the night; she wore a turban and loved Voltaire. She had a passion for flowers, cats, and most living things. As the Longfellows wrote in a private history of their house in the 1840s, "When the canker-worms came spinning down from the elm-trees, she would sit by the open window and let them crawl over her white turban. She refused to have the trees protected against them & said, Why, sir, they have as good a right to live as we—they are our fellow worms." She and her new tenant became friends. At the ring of his bell, her servant, "Miriam the giantess," brought the young professor his breakfast (Felton called her "Miriam the Profit-ess" because of her high charges) and, at 5:00 p.m., his dinner; later he shared meals with another tenant, Sarah Lowell, James Russell Lowell's maiden aunt. He was very pleased with his new quarters. He slept in General Washington's chamber and worked in his sitting room. He wrote to George Washington Greene in August of 1838:

> I live in a great house which looks like an Italian villa: have two large rooms opening into each other. They were once Gen. Washington's chambers. I breakfast at seven on tea and toast: and dine ... generally in Boston. In the evening I walk on the Common with Hillard or alone; then go back to Cambridge on foot, drinking at every pump on the

way—six in number. If not very late, I sit for an hour or two with Felton or Sparks. If late, go to bed.... Most of the time am alone—smoke a good deal. Wear a broad-brimmed black hat—black frock-coat—boots—trousers with straps—black cane. Molest no one. Dine out frequently.

Although he had no reason to believe that he could stay at "Castle Craigie" indefinitely, the house was clearly more than just a dwelling to him. The Washington connection was a powerful one; a large part of Longfellow's self-fashioning drew on his family's experience in the Revolution. Despite Washington's Virginia origins, he was nowhere more revered than in New England—not only as a tribute to his historical accomplishments, but as an iconic reminder of how far the nation had fallen politically as a result of Jacksonian democracy. Federalism had withered as a political force, but not as a part of the consciousness of genteel New Englanders. Longfellow's own family was a case in point in its sacralization of the Father of the Country. An engraving of "The Apotheosis of Washington" hung in a place of honor over the parlor mantel in Portland. When Longfellow's grandfather Wadsworth had been in Congress, Zilpah's sister Eliza had begged for a lock of the late General Washington's hair. Martha Washington obliged, and the hair became a Longfellow family heirloom, passed down upon Eliza's early death to Zilpah, then to Henry (who had it encased in a gold locket), and then to his daughter Alice, who gave it to the Maine Historical Society, thereby returning it to the family home. In a similar spirit, Stephen Longfellow, when in Congress in 1825, sent to his sons at Bowdoin a fragment of cedar from the site of Washington's tomb at Mount Vernon.

That same letter in which Longfellow described the house to Greene went on to express a vague sense of malaise, even in such august surroundings. "Do not like this sedentary life," he wrote. "Want action—want to travel—am too excited—too tumultous inwardly—and my health suffers from all this." To some extent, he had not recovered from the events of 1835, the memory of which lingered as a kind of chronic ache. His daily experience as a Harvard professor soon con-

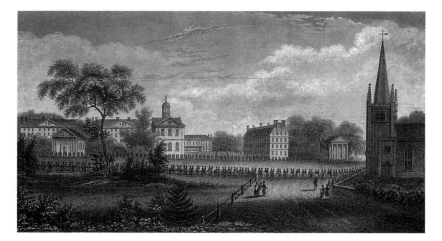

FIGURE 4: The procession of the alumni in Cambridge, honoring
Harvard University's two-hundredth birthday, September 8, 1836,
from Josiah Quincy's *History of Harvard University*, Vol. II (1840).

tributed to his unhappiness. He had certainly expected to flourish
there on a larger scale than at Bowdoin, and he had not been disappointed. His social circle was far wider, far more worldly and learned,
than what he had known in Brunswick or Portland. Yet his expectations of the teaching profession, and his insistence that it could be pursued in tandem with a literary career, found less sympathy among the
Harvard faculty, not to mention the Boston worthies who served on
the Harvard Corporation. Literature was respected, he found, without being particularly esteemed.

Harvard College's reputation in the antebellum years has never
quite recovered from Henry Adams's account of his student days in the
1850s:

> For generation after generation, Adamses and Brookses and
> Boylstons and Gorhams had gone to Harvard College, and although
> none of them, as far as known, had ever done any good there, or
> thought himself the better for it, custom, social ties, convenience, and,
> above all, economy, kept each generation in the track. Any other edu-
> cation would have required a serious effort, but no one took Harvard
> College seriously. All went there because their friends went there, and

the College was their ideal of social self-respect. . . . Four years of Harvard College, if successful, resulted in an autobiographical blank, a mind on which only a water-mark had been stamped.

Adams's sardonic remarks are meant by way of contrast to the post–Civil War Harvard of President Eliot—and briefly Professor Adams—when German learning had finally reached these shores, and the graduate seminar and well-stocked laboratory had become the defining feature of higher education. But Adams was right, right about all the early New England colleges, and their desire to socialize the local elite and send them back into the world "with all they needed to make respectable citizens, and something of what they wanted to make useful ones." Far more deflating of antebellum Harvard's self-esteem is Nietzsche's alleged remark: What a philosopher Emerson would have made, if only he had had an education.

As a teacher of modern European languages and their literatures, Longfellow might seem to confirm both writers' disparaging view of the college. He could not press his young gentlemen too hard, except in grammatical drills, and if he had—what could he have offered them? For all his love of the arcana of languages, he was not a trained philologist in the German-university mold. If he could not really teach his students in any rigorous way, he knew that he could charm them, within limits entertain them, perhaps even inspire in them the love of foreign literature that had so enriched his own inner life. In 1837, this was far more difficult than it might sound. His chief obstacle was Harvard College itself. Ticknor had exhausted himself in a long battle with the institution over the teaching of modern languages. Each small victory had been followed by a new defeat. Coming into this quarrel with his idealism still intact, Longfellow found that most of his energies were quickly dissipated simply in running his department, which depended for basic instruction on the poorly paid labors of four European emigres, one each for Spanish, French, Italian, and German. As Smith Professor, Longfellow was supposed to oversee this labor, but, as the result of the vagaries of hiring and firing, he ended up doing much of the basic language drill himself, in some years. If this was not wearisome enough, he had to engage in what almost always proved losing battles with the tight-fisted Corporation for small sums to purchase books for the College Library, and in only slightly less demoralizing arguments with his own colleagues over the curriculum.

During Longfellow's eighteen years as a Harvard professor, the consensus of the Corporation remained virtually unassailable: classical languages were the essence of a liberal arts education; modern languages, merely a social accomplishment or a diversion. There was a rationale for this: at a time when virtually every educator believed in "faculty psychology"—the notion that the brain comprises various "faculties," for each human attribute or skill—studying Latin and Greek was considered difficult; hence, it "exercised" the various faculties of memory and understanding, in a way that French or Spanish did not. It did not matter that in all the "classical seminaries" in America, there was scarcely a classicist of any real accomplishment teaching. It was the drill, the mental exertion, the gymnastics of the mind that mattered. But this generally unexamined belief hid a greater anxiety. If colleges began experimenting with their curricula, allowing greater choice of electives or replacing the traditional recitations with real teaching, who knew where it might lead? Whether run by Unitarians or Congregationalists or Presbyterians, colleges remained bastions of orthodoxy in their thinking.

Longfellow managed, nonetheless, to make a few small improvements. He is said to have been the first Harvard professor to address his students as "Mr. __." This gesture of respect seems to have been appreciated; again, as at Bowdoin, his relative youth made him seem more approachable than some of his colleagues. His greatest innovation, however, was to introduce a new kind of course (though Ticknor had touched on it, at least in regards to Spanish literature), one in which foreign languages were not an end in themselves but a way of understanding a culture. In the 1830s this was a radical pedagogical notion. Drawing on his own experience of several European cultures, Longfellow offered advanced language courses as well as more general lectures in which, for the most part, he read significant passages from a European author, translating as he went along, and offering his own opinions on their literary merits as well as enough historical context to help his students comprehend what they were hearing. These were a prototype of the "survey of Western culture" courses which, until a generation ago, formed the backbone of liberal education in most American colleges, but they were also ventures in comparative literature, a very new field on either side of the Atlantic.

Longfellow's notes for many of his lectures survive; the most interesting and complete are those for a series on Goethe in 1837–38. Here, as elsewhere, the degree of preparation he invested in his teaching was unusual for an antebellum college. The lectures are written out, although with many pauses for him to refer to the text of, say, *Faust* (his well-annotated copy of which also survives at the Houghton Library). Knowing that Goethe is only a name, if that, to many of his students, he takes a slow biographical approach, stopping to sketch each important work and assuring his New England audience that reports of Goethe's immorality are exaggerated. *Faust* Part I he champions as a work of world-class importance; *Faust* Part II he admits he really does not understand. Goethe's many-sidedness makes him difficult to pin down, he admits, but this should not frighten off readers.

> It seems to me very strange that anyone should deny to Gothe the attribute of great genius. Yet this has been done. Persons have not been wanting, who would fain have dethroned the monarch of Letters. Friend and foes have waged fierce war together: and so great is the dust of battle, that we cannot see clearly how the victory goes. And here, it seems to me, lies the difficulty of estimating justly the character of this extraordinary man. There is such a din in our ears and such a smoke before our eyes, that we are blinded and confused. From the midst of the battle we hear the shouts and war-cries of the combattants—on one side;
>
> "The dear, dear Man"—
> "The Life-enjoying Man"—
> "The All-Sided One"—

"The Representative of Poetry on earth"—
"The Many-Sided Master-mind of Germany".
And on the other side the fierce epithets of
"Old Humbug" and
"Old Heathen"
"Magnificent Impostor"
which hit like pistol-bullets.

Thus are opinions divided. Some think him a charlatan—others
"the greatest man that ever lived."

This is as close as we can get to the actual voice of Professor Longfellow in the lecture hall. He presents his evidence, over the course of
several lectures, and allows his auditors to make up their own minds.
What emerges, amid the literary and touristic detail, is his portrayal of
Goethe as a citizen of the world who nonetheless encapsulates every
aspect of his own nation's culture. It was a model he always held before
him (literally: a statuette of Goethe stood on his writing desk). Many
of Longfellow's comments in these lectures on Goethe, as well as the
ones on Dante and Cervantes and Molière, read today like a crib; he
certainly never displayed the intuitive grasp of post-Kantian idealism
that Emerson and Margaret Fuller enjoyed, and he had no taste for academic philosophy. But, once again, he made a pioneering effort to
popularize writers and ideas that had been hitherto appreciated by
only a handful of Americans. In the context of the old-fashioned college, this was an extraordinary achievement; characteristically, the
Corporation discouraged his efforts to open up the lectures to the
general public, as was the practice in some European universities.

It is hard to judge the effect of this teaching on the eighteen classes
of Harvard men Longfellow taught between 1836 and 1854. Surely
some became better readers. Perhaps a detail here or there stuck. He
mentioned, in passing, for example, that Goethe liked to write with
a pencil. Attending those lectures in 1837 was a young man from
Concord, the son of a pencil manufacturer. His name was Thoreau.

Goethe became one of the great intellectual influences in his life as a result of Longfellow's lectures.

There are some contemporary witnesses to his teaching style. For example, Edward Everett Hale—the most celebrated orator of post–Civil War Boston—was a close friend of Longfellow's brother Samuel when both were undergraduates in the class of 1839, and he commented on the lectures in his journal for September 18, 1837:

> At 11 A.M. went to Prof. Longfellow's first lecture on Goethe's Faust. The lectures are to be extemporaneous translations of the German with explanations; as he called it recitations in which he recites and we hear. He made a long introduction to the matter at hand, very flowery and bombastical indeed, which appeared to me very much out of taste. I believe however that it was entirely extemporaneous and that he was carried away by the current of his thoughts. In fact he appears to say just what comes uppermost. The regular translation and explanation part of the lecture was very good.

A more sympathetic account can be found in Thomas Wentworth Higginson's reminiscence in *Old Cambridge* (1899):

> I had the good fortune to study French under him, not in the general recitation room, but in what was called the Corporation Room, where we sat round a long table as if guests at his board. His lectures, which were to us most interesting, were sometimes criticised as too flowery by our elders, who had perhaps been accustomed to gather only dried fruit; and I remember how he fixed in our memories the vivid moral of any French books that happened to be provided with that appendage, as for instance "Le Peau de Chagrin" of Balzac.

Higginson also remembered the day in 1839 when a printer's boy came in and laid between Longfellow and himself the proof of the title-page of *Voices of the Night*. "It was as if I had seen a new planet in process of making."

This notion of the young professor's "floweriness," his perhaps too European mode and manner for what was still a New England village, comes through in comments on the elegance of his clothing. Even the unconventional Mrs. Craigie thought so, declaring that he had "somewhat too gay a look." As the Baron cautions Paul Flemming in *Hyperion*, "they say that your gloves are a shade too light for a strictly virtuous man." Longfellow made a joke of this criticism of his dandyism, writing to Sumner in England, "If you have any tendency to 'curl your hair and wear gloves,' like Edgar in 'Lear,' do it before your return."

There was in nearby Cambridgeport one living link with Europe that he did pursue seriously. Washington Allston—once regarded by many as the closest thing to a genius the new republic had produced—had settled in a modest studio there while trying to complete work on his gigantic canvas of *Belshazzar's Feast,* a project supported by subscriptions from some of Boston's leading men. Longfellow visited him frequently. Allston was by this time a somewhat pathetic figure, but in his youth he had been the most celebrated American painter of the new century (as well as a poet). In his years in Italy, he had befriended Irving, and in 1805 had become even closer to Coleridge. The visits were an occasion for reminiscence by both travelers, but for Longfellow they represented something more. Allston had a lesson to teach: he had shown in his heyday that an American could have a transatlantic career, even a Euro-American style. In creating a body of work that assumed a high degree of cultural literacy on the part of the viewer, that idealized rather than realistically depicted, and that grew out of a strong feeling for history and mythology, the painter was showing the way to the poet. He also represented a more cautionary lesson: do not take on a project beyond your talents. He never completed *Belshazzar's Feast,* despite years of promises to his patrons. When they entered his studio after his death in 1843, only a fragment remained, partly effaced by its own creator. "A melancholy ruin," Longfellow's friend Sumner called it.

⚜

Despite the frustrations of teaching and his sense of loneliness, which at times seemed almost unbearable, Longfellow found considerable comfort in the society of a small group of other young men who gathered in his rooms at the Craigie House or dined with him in the chop houses and oyster bars of Boston. They were so frequently in each other's company, they were dubbed the "Five of Clubs," in a sort of Pickwickian way. The organizing spirit seems to have been Cornelius Conway Felton, whom Longfellow had met on Boston visits while teaching at Bowdoin and who had recently become Eliot Professor of Greek. Chubby and effervescent, Felton combined good humor and a keen sense of academic politics (he later became president of Harvard). Another regular was Henry Cleveland, whose health was poor but who had married well and lived on an estate at Brookline. Less prosperous yet already a central figure in the Boston literary world, and later a great supporter of Hawthorne, was a young lawyer named George Hillard. His partner in Court Street was the fifth member of the club, another Harvard-educated lawyer with strong literary inclinations and not many clients, Charles Sumner, who was to play a role in Longfellow's life over the next thirty years that went far beyond these convivial early soirees and oyster-feasts. His immense talents as an orator and political organizer not yet formed, Sumner was an awkward, gangly, highly intelligent young man. He had grown up on the edge of elite Boston (his father was sheriff of Suffolk County, a respectable though not well paid position), yet had so strong and independent a mind that he soon found himself at odds with much of Beacon Hill society, especially on the troubling question of slavery. Abrupt to the point of rudeness, Sumner was ill fitted for a conventional legal career—until a visit to Europe in 1841 made him into a minor local celebrity. Deferential to his British hosts without betraying his New England reformer's idealism, Sumner enjoyed a stunning social success with a long series of aristocrat hosts and hostesses. News of this back home boosted his reputation overnight; however much Bostonians complained about Britain, the good opinion of its ruling social and intellectual elite was of immeasurable importance to them. (Throughout the nineteenth century, a palpable tremor of excitement ran through Boston each week when the packet ship with British let-

ters and journals arrived.) Sumner was well on his way to the political
career that would make him a founder of the Republican Party and one
of the most powerful figures in the Civil War–era U.S. Senate.

From the start, Longfellow exercised a moderating influence on his
easily angered, hypersensitive friend. Sumner in turn kept Longfellow
well informed of both national politics and the great reform movements of the day, and also shared his interests in poetry and the visual
arts. Astonishingly self-absorbed, almost totally devoid of a sense of
humor, Sumner nevertheless was a loyal and generous friend. Longfellow answered his deep emotional neediness. What developed between
them was a romantic male friendship of a type not at all uncommon in
nineteenth-century America. (Lincoln, Webster, Emerson all experienced such friendships with other males.) We lack the vocabulary to
define such attachments, which probably were rarely sexual but which,
in the years before one of the two friends married, satisfied emotional
needs with an intensity that went far beyond mere comradeship. Sumner probably was gay, if you will excuse the anachronism: or, rather,
the biographical record seems to show that he formed his most mean-
ingful relationships with other males, and certainly his attempt late in
life to marry proved a disaster. It is highly unlikely that he acted on
these feelings overtly (a man with so many political enemies after 1850
had every aspect of his public and private life scrutinized for faults),
and both his intense absorption in reform politics and his compulsive
art collecting suggest a sublimation of the erotic side of his pysche.
Longfellow, on the other hand, was an uxorious man with a well-
documented eye for female beauty, yet in this period of his life he
found himself once again experiencing the frustrations and disappoint-
ments of bachelorhood, and he was clearly emotionally vulnerable.

The friendship of Sumner and the three other young men did more
than lift Longfellow's spirits. They provided him as a writer with
his first real audience outside of his family—real in the sense of
immediate, supportive, intelligent, and quick to criticize, the sort of
sounding board he had never found in the distant editors to whom he
mailed his poems and stories. Their feasting and drinking involved

not only literary gossip but impromptu poetry, irrepressible punning, sexual innuendo, and a mild degree of skepticism toward those in authority, especially those at Harvard. It was a reprise of Longfellow's evenings with Preble at Göttingen, possibly of student days for all of them.

Is it a coincidence that his first major poetry appears in these early years at the Craigie House? The traditional biographical explanation is that the shock of Mary's death forced him into purging his grief through poetry. There may be some truth to that, but the existence of an audience of his peers may explain why some of these poems are so good. *Voices of the Night* (1839) included the best first line yet written by an American poet. It opens the poem "Hymn to the Night":

> *I heard the trailing garments of the Night*
> *Sweep through her marble halls!*

Longfellow said later that he had composed the poem one summer night "while sitting at my chamber window, on one of the balmiest nights of the year. I have endeavored to reproduce the impression of the hour and the scene." Among the more insistent of these voices, however, was a poem he had written in a deep depression, had kept in his desk for some time, then read to his class at the end of a Goethe lecture, before publishing it in the *Knickerbocker Magazine*. "A Psalm of Life" has achieved a level of fame that lifts it beyond poetry into the realm of cultural artifact; it quickly became one of the most ridiculed and the most frequently memorized poems in the language, and it popularized more common phrases than any other short American poem imaginable ("footprints on the sands of time" being the most notorious). The resounding exhortation at its end has been taken to be Victorian cheeriness at its worst, but in the context of Longfellow's own life it has a certain poignance:

> *Let us, then, be up and doing,*
> *With a heart for any fate;*
> *Still achieving, still pursuing,*
> *Learn to labor and to wait.*

FIGURE 5: Illustration for "The Wreck of the Hesperus" from Carey & Hart's 1846 edition of *The Poems of Henry W. Longfellow.*

That slim volume—nine new poems, eight reprints of poems he had written in college, and a brief envoi—persuaded much of the literary establishment that the country had finally produced a major poet. America in 1839 knew that one was overdue. The *Boston Quarterly Review* spoke of its "genuine poetic feeling"; the *New-Yorker* declared Longfellow "one of the very few in our time who has successfully aimed in putting poetry to its best and sweetest uses." Willis's *Corsair* gave it "an elevated place in the library of American classics." The *Southern Literary Messenger* placed Longfellow "among the first of our American poets."

Three years later, Longfellow proved that his first volume was not an anomaly. *Ballads and Other Poems* included two instant classics— "The Wreck of the Hesperus" and "The Village Blacksmith"—as well as perhaps the worst poem he ever published, "The Rainy Day." It also introduced what was to be his highly successful antiquarian vein, represented by the fast-paced Viking ballad "The Skeleton in Armor."

The quickness with which the public not only bought this book but memorized the poems (several of which had been originally printed, and widely reprinted, in newspapers and magazines) was without parallel in U.S. publishing history. (Readers of a certain age may recall, by way of parallel, the speed with which some Beatles tunes—say, from *The White Album* in 1969—were being sung everywhere in the country.) "The Wreck of the Hesperus" has suffered too many tub-thumping recitals, but even its author could not resist its gale-force rhythms. As he later explained, he was sitting by his fire, smoking past midnight, "when suddenly it came into my mind to write [it], which I accordingly did. Then I went to bed, but could not sleep. New thoughts were running in my mind, and I got up to add them to the ballad. It was three by the clock. I then went to bed and fell asleep. I feel pleased with the ballad. It hardly cost me an effort. It did not come into my mind by lines, but by stanzas." Longfellow had it printed originally as a broadside, to guarantee a popular audience. The poem was the *Perfect Storm* of its day—almost literally so, for it takes place at the mouth of Gloucester harbor, on the reef of Norman's Woe. Longfellow was having fun with the traditional ballad form revitalized by Burns, and he produced a poem that tapped that deep-seated human urge to hear about disasters at sea. Some years ahead of Little Nell, it also exploits the pathos of a young girl's death. To a modern, to whom the whole thing may at first seem to define kitsch, the poem offers another reading: it is the first hint in his work that Longfellow was going to challenge, in his own quiet way, the gender standards of his time. Living in a patriarchal age, he nonetheless sketches a sea-captain father who is a dolt, the original male-who-never-asks-for-directions. As a result of the father's arrogance, he, his daughter, his crew, and his ship are destroyed on the reef, in a ballad whose insistent "folk" rhythms are linked with a strong sense of fatality.

"The Village Blacksmith" of 1839 is another performance piece that brings back the days, now widely regretted, when young people were expected to memorize poetry. Most readers associate it with the Brattle Street smithy whose spreading chestnut tree was a landmark of mid-nineteenth-century Cambridge, but Longfellow told his father it was a tribute to their seventeenth-century ancestor, the first Stephen Longfellow, who had a blacksmith's shop at Newbury. (The famous tree, incidentally, was removed in 1876, over the protests of Longfellow and others; the Cambridge town fathers had decided it was an impediment to traffic.) "The Village Blacksmith" is a genre scene, a nostalgic evocation of the age of the citizen-artisan, proud, independent, pious, productive—a New England myth-in-the-making as the small towns began to become industrialized and much of the yeomanry moved west in search of better rewards for their labor. It is also an allegory of the poet's craft, as Longfellow saw it, if he did not always experience it quite that way in practice. The suggestion that writing might be as valid a form of work as any other still needed making, and he made it with his characteristic quiet note of resignation:

> *Toiling,—rejoicing,—sorrowing,*
> *Onward through life he goes;*
> *Each morning sees some task begin,*
> *Each evening sees it close;*
> *Something attempted, something done,*
> *Has earned a night's repose.*

And then there is "Excelsior," a poem that was so loved by Longfellow's contemporaries, so loathed by following generations, that it is in a category all its own. He scribbled it on the back of a letter from Sumner at half past three in the morning on September 28, 1841. "Now to bed," he noted. He got the idea from a scrap of a New York newspaper that bore the state seal, a rising sun with the motto "Excelsior," a word of dubious Latinity as used in his poem, translated as "higher."

FIGURE 6: Illustration for "Excelsior" from the 1846 edition of the collected poems.

The shades of night were falling fast,
As through an Alpine village passed
A youth, who bore, 'mid snow and ice,
A banner with a strange device,
Excelsior!

The setting recalls his Alpine summer with the Appletons; the
youth's sad fate—he ends up in even more ice than crusted the maid of
the Hesperus—may be a faint projection of his own foolhardiness as a
suitor. Whether the poem was in the least autobiographical, its ballad
quality caught the imagination of the mid-nineteenth-century public
and, in the next century, the eye of James Thurber, who produced a famously whimsical cartoon on the subject. "Excelsior" was also the first
Longfellow poem to be widely parodied, a compliment in the sense
that it indicated virtually everyone knew the original.

For all his new fame as a poet (which was quickly spreading across
the Atlantic as well) and his sustaining circle of intimates in Cambridge, Longfellow's journal entries for these years present a self-
portrait of a man who frequently is miserable and almost always a little
depressed. He hid this from all but his closest friends, and it is difficult
to know how literally to take the journal, which is rarely confessional
in any deep sense and may have had its own mild therapeutic effect just
as a record of his moods. His grieving for Mary had long since been
diffused, but there is reason to believe—given his chronic complaints
about bad health in this period—that he had internalized an overwhelming sense of guilt over exposing her to such danger and over his
subsequent failure, as a husband, to protect her. If he wished to punish
himself by his pursuit of Fanny Appleton, he had found a perfect vehicle for doing so. This is not to say that his passion for Fanny Appleton
was not sincere. But he pursued it so doggedly and in the face of so
much rejection and even humiliation (for his plight was well known
in Boston and Cambridge) that it goes beyond a mere unreciprocated
romance.

The details are sketchy—some presumably relevant entries in the
journals have been inked over or even cut out—but he had fallen ob-

sessively in love with Miss Appleton. His feeling of isolation as a young widower surely contributed to his emotional vulnerability at that time. Upon the family's return to their town house at 39 Beacon Street, Longfellow called, as he habitually did on a number of Beacon Hill families. He invented occasions to see Fanny (he was under the misapprehension that she very much wanted to learn German), and at some point in 1837 declared his intentions to her, only to be firmly turned down. Retreating briefly to lick his wounds, he soon returned to the pursuit, always taking care not to be so obvious that the Appletons would decline to see him, but obvious enough to expose himself to some good-natured ridicule in Boston society. He became something of a fixture among the extended Appleton family and remained on very good terms with Fanny's sister Mary and her brother Tom as well as various uncles and aunts. Fanny herself treated him with mildly satirical contempt—he was "the Prof" to her and her intimates—but never totally ignored him. His puppyish devotion took the form, for example, of long walks on the Common (which the Appleton house faced) in hopes of catching a glimpse of his "dark ladye" (a bit of poeticizing on his part, for her hair was actually brown).

Then he went too far. Toward the close of *Hyperion*, his quasi-philosophical travel novel of 1839, his hero, Paul Flemming, falls in love, in Germany, with a young Englishwoman, Mary Ashburton, who to his great distress rejects him, despite his obvious merits as an American who understands German culture. *Hyperion* was widely read—Americans in 1839 were eager for someone to explain Germany to them—and on Beacon Hill it was only too obvious who "Paul" and "Mary" were. Fanny was understandably mortified and displayed a new degree of frostiness toward her hapless suitor.

Today, *Hyperion* is one of Longfellow's most obscure works, succumbing to slow acidification on the shelves of secondhand-book shops, and not chosen to be reprinted with the generous selection of Longfellow's prose in the Library of America's 2000 edition of his work. In truth, a modern reader would probably find its vaporous narration and its potted accounts of various German writers and thinkers heavy going. It has about it an air not so much of undergraduate earnestness as of undergraduate self-absorption, despite its touristic ramble through three German-speaking lands and innumerable German books. But whatever its obvious literary shortcomings, it did, after all, stay in print for more than half a century. As late as 1865, the great British photographer Francis Frith produced twenty-four images to illustrate a new edition; only the glimpse of a railroad track in one of them hints that anything had changed since Longfellow's own Rhine-journey.

We need to resist any urge to read *Hyperion* as autobiography, however much Mary Ashburton was Fanny in Longfellow's mind. (By that point, "Fanny" may have been as much a figment of the author's mind as the "dark ladye" of the story.) *Hyperion* is rather a book that represents a particular moment, a particular mood in its author's life—the fall of 1838 and spring of 1839—and it draws, in his familiar Spanish tailor's fashion, from his drawer of memories of the summer of 1836 and from his vast and eclectic reading. In writing it, Longfellow's project turns out to have been twofold: he needed to exorcise the ghosts of that horror-filled night in Amsterdam, and he needed to get Miss Appleton out of his system. He succeeded more with the former than the latter.

Hyperion is a difficult book to synopsize because, in its weird, almost-postmodern way, it stands the usual habits of narrative on their head. Someone is telling the story—someone in Cambridge, Massachusetts, as we discover about halfway through—a trick of detached narration Longfellow probably learned from Carlyle's popular *Sartor Resartus* of 1833–34, along with Carlyle's mix of memoir, dark humor, and mordant philosophizing. The prose lacks Carlyle's zest, to say the least; on the other hand, the smooth tone of the writing made it more marketable to Longfellow's contemporaries. The story has an end—the central figure rides off into a solidly American future—but it is harder to locate a beginning. This elusive hero, a bookish young American named Paul Flemming, has a history: "The friend of his youth was dead," he has "passed many months in lonely wandering," and now he has reached the Rhine, which he knows well from brighter days in his recent past. He suddenly plunges into a swiftly flowing river of folk tales; anecdotes; lecture-room asides on Goethe, Jean Paul, and E. T. A. Hoffmann; and long conversations with a worldly-wise baron and a bibulous Englishman. In the third chapter of the third of *Hyperion*'s four books, he encounters at Interlachen a soft-spoken young lady in black. He asks the Englishman about her:

"What is her name?"
"Ashburton."
"Is she beautiful?"
"Not beautiful, but very intellectual. A woman of genius, I should say."

One can imagine how that was received at 39 Beacon Street. The author does try to cover his tracks by depicting his "dark ladye" as an Englishwoman traveling with her widowed mother, but no one in the know was fooled. He is captivated and pursues her, through an Alpine landscape, and finally declares his love by way of telling her a medieval romance he invents on the spot, in which he and she turn out to be characters. Her proud heart prevails, and Flemming sulks off, like a chastened puppy. His wanderings take him into the Austrian Alps, where he hears more folk tales and legends and grows delirious with fever, then starts his long journey home. But in the inn at Stuttgart, he hears through the thin walls a familiar voice—yes, Mary Ashburton!—and his heart's "wounds began to bleed afresh." He is too proud himself to go say hello, but she appears in a dream that night, embraces him, and vanishes. The postilion and the horses are waiting, the servant brings him his coffee. He throws himself into the carriage, casts one last look at her window, and knows he will see her no more:

No more! Oh, how majestically mournful are those words! They sound like the roar of the wind through a forest of pines!

The Mary Ashburton episodes take up only a small number of *Hyperion*'s pages, however voyeuristic their appeal even at this remove in time. Part of Longfellow's offense was not just in creating this ghostly version of the robust Miss Appleton, but presumably in re-creating with some accuracy the conversations that had passed between them at Interlachen and Thun, only three years earlier (*Hyperion* was published in August of 1839). Some of it is unintentionally hilarious.

> "How beautiful the Jungfrau looks this morning!" exclaimed he, looking at Mary Ashburton.
> She thought he meant the mountain, and assented. But he meant her likewise.

Some of it is merely tedious, as when he lectures her on the poetry of Uhland.

> "He and Tieck are generally considered the best living poets of Germany. They dispute the palm of superiority. Let me give you a lesson in German, this afternoon, Miss Ashburton; so that no one may accuse you of 'omitting the sweet benefit of time, to clothe your age with angel-like perfection.' I have opened at random upon the ballad of the Black Knight. Do you repeat the German after me, and I will translate to you: Pfingsten war, das Fest der Freude!"
> "I should never persuade my unwilling lips to pronounce such sounds."

Miss Ashburton might be forgiven for running for the hills at this point, but she allows Flemming to show off with an impromptu translation. It is easy to make fun of these passages and regret that Longfellow could not temper them with the touches of satire on tourism that enliven other chapters of his romance, but they allowed the author to work through his feelings for Fanny, while giving us a glimpse of the repressed aggression against her that must have mingled with his love.

Hyperion has other attractions, not least some passages of decent travel writing. Taking the night coach to Innsbruck, for example, the half-asleep Flemming remembers afterwards:

> . . . the climbing of hills and plunging into dark ravines; the momentary rattling of the wheels over paved streets of towns, and the succeeding hollow rolling and tramping on the wet earth; the blackness of the night; the thunder and lightning and rain; the roar of waters leap-

ing through deep chasms by the roadside; and the wind through the mountain-passes sounding loud and long, like the indistinguishable laughter of the gods.

Hyperion is filled with the memory of Mary Potter Longfellow as well, from start almost to finish. On the Rhine-journey that we find Flemming making in the second chapter of the first book, he travels through the early morning mists to the riverside village of Andernach. He is puzzled by a little chapel attached to its church, "only a small thatched roof, like a bird's nest, under which stood a rude wooden image of the Saviour on the cross. . . . The face was haggard and ghastly beyond expression, and wore a look of unutterable bodily anguish . . . coarse, harsh, and revolting to a sensitive mind." The face haunts him, however, and an old woman at the hotel, surprised he has never heard of the Christ of Andernach, tells him the story, which she assures him is true.

There was a poor but pious old woman whose roof tiles were broken and let in the rain. One dark, windy night she heard heavy steps on her roof and loud pounding. Terrified, she prayed and prayed then ran to the window to scream for help. Suddenly all was quiet, and she saw a light streaming through the rain and the shadow of a man with a lantern coming down a ladder from her roof. The next morning, the old broken tiles lay in the street, and her roof never leaked again. Others in town also reported nocturnal benefactions: the cooper found new hoops on his wine barrels, a windmill had been repaired, a church gate made new, a leaky and hazardous boat recaulked. Everyone had seen the man with a lantern, but he always disappeared before anyone could identify him.

Now one stormy night a poor, sinful creature was wandering about in the streets with her babe in her arms, and she was hungry, and cold, and no soul in Andernach would take her in. And when she came to the church . . . she sat down on a stone at the foot of the cross and began to pray, and prayed until she fell asleep, with the poor little baby on her bosom. But she did not sleep long; for a bright light shown full in her face; and when she opened her eyes, she saw a pale man, with a lantern, standing right before her. He was almost naked, and there was blood upon his hands and body, and great tears in his beautiful eyes, and his face was like the face of the Saviour on the cross. Not a single word did he say to the poor woman, but looked at her compassionately, and gave her a loaf of bread, and took the little babe in his arms, and kissed it. Then the mother looked up to the great crucifix, but there was no image there; and she shrieked and fell down as if she were dead. And there she was found with her child; and a few days after they both died, and were buried together in one grave.

A woman in the village heard the scream, went to her window, saw the figure hang his lantern, climb up the ladder, and nail himself to the cross, where he remains. The story, we are told, made "a painful impression on [Flemming's] sick and morbid soul."

An image not unlike a fetus appears in the next chapter, although this time it is the ruined castle at Stolzenfels that mysteriously tells the tale. An archbishop who had dwelt there delved into magic and hermetic philosophy, spending a fortune on a failed attempt to create a homunculus in a glass bottle, and died poor and childless for all his efforts.

And toward the end of the fourth book of *Hyperion*, in "The Tale of Brother Bernardus," a widow's child dies suddenly in the night.

Flemming saw a light in her chamber, and shadows moving to and fro, as he stood by the window gazing into the starry, silent sky. But he little thought of the awful domestic tragedy which was even then enacted behind those thin curtains!

The child's funeral follows in *Hyperion*'s penultimate chapter; Flemming attends and is strangely buoyed by the experience. He undergoes an epiphany of sorts. He goes forth strengthened, determined "that he would no longer veer with every shifting wind ... no longer to waste his years in vain regrets ... but to live in the Present wisely, alike forgetful of the Past and careless of what the mysterious Future might bring."

In titling his "romance," Longfellow was not alluding to the Hyperions of Keats or Hölderlin, but to its more Miltonic usage as "the child of the morning." Flemming—despite a name taken from medieval German literature—himself becomes such a renewed being, and it is implied that his real life will take place far removed from the misty, legend-haunted Rhine or the picturesque Alpine valleys. He is the first in a line of American literary heroes who repatriate themselves, after their Wanderjahre abroad. He will return, bright as the morning sun, to a scene not unlike the one Longfellow sketches in one of *Hyperion*'s most abrupt narrative lurches. It is the view from the author's upstairs study window at the Craigie House:

> The elms reach their long, pendulous branches almost to the ground. White clouds sail aloft, and vapors fret the blue sky with silver threads. The white village gleams afar against the dark hills. Through the meadow winds the river,—careless, indolent. It seems to love the country, and is in no haste to reach the sea.

Seven

THE WATER CURE

CRITICS WERE NOT QUITE SURE what to make of *Hyperion*, but reaction to *Voices of the Night* continued overwhelmingly positive, with a few exceptions (notably Edgar Allan Poe, who was beginning his campaign against what he saw as Longfellow's inflated reputation), and *Ballads and Other Poems* brought even louder praise from most of the country's newspapers and journals. Despite this obvious success, Longfellow continued to struggle with his demons, which included the array of chronic ailments that plagued him all his adult life—eyestrain, neuralgia, headaches, influenza—as well as what would now be diagnosed as chronic depression. It did not help that after thirteen years he was very tired of "teaching boys" when he would rather be "talking with men," as he put it. The usual aggravations of departmental work and intramural quarreling took their toll as well. Add to this what was presumably a large element of sexual frustration, and a feeling of deflation after finally admitting to himself that his quest for Fanny's hand had been a quixotic waste of effort, and you had a man almost in a state of nervous collapse.

"I am reluctantly compelled by the state of my health to ask leave of absence from the College for six months from the first of May next," he wrote to the Corporation on January 24, 1842. "In this time I propose to visit Germany, to try the effect of certain baths, by means of which, as well as by the relaxation and the sea-voyage, I hope to reestablish my health." Realizing the seriousness of his friend's plight, Felton had generously agreed to take over his supervisory duties at no extra expense to the college. The request was granted.

Meanwhile, Longfellow's spirits were lifted by the arrival, amid great public excitement, of the thirty-year-old Charles Dickens and his wife on the first stage of an American lecture tour. "He is a glorious fellow," Longfellow told his father.

> He has not a moment's rest;—calls innumerable—invitations innumerable;—and is engaged three deep for the remainder of his stay, in the way of dinners and parties. He is a gay, free and easy character;—a fine bright face; blue eyes, long dark hair, and withal a slight dash of the Dick Swiveller about him.

It is a tribute to Longfellow's charm and growing reputation that Dickens took so readily to him, when so many others were vying for the novelist's attention. Longfellow and Sumner took Dickens to the North End to hear the famous Edward Taylor—the inspiration for Melville's Father Marble in *Moby-Dick*—preach to the sailors. Their tour then took them past the Old North Church to Copps Hill, where the British had placed their guns in 1775, and on through Charlestown, which those guns had destroyed, to Bunker Hill, where New Englanders some twenty years earlier had erected a granite obelisk to commemorate the battle. A few days later, Dickens breakfasted with Longfellow, Felton, and the theologian Andrews Norton before embarking on his lecture tour.

Despite his unhappy memories of the Rhine, Longfellow determined to try the new style of "water cure" offered at Kloster Marienberg, a former convent overlooking the vineyard town of Boppard. His friends were reluctant to lose him but relieved that he had been awarded the leave. Sumner was particularly hard hit. He wrote to Longfellow in New York:

> Dear Henry,
>
> Will this parting note reach you? I write, not knowing; but the chance of again uttering a word to yr soul, before you descend upon the sea, is enough.—We are all sad at your going ; but I am more sad than the rest; for I lose more than they do. I am desolate. It was to me a source

of pleasure & strength untold, to see you, &, when I did not see you, to feel that you were near, with your swift sympathy & kindly words. I must try to go alone; hard necessity in this rude world of ours! For our souls always in this life need support, & gentle beckonings, as the little child when first trying to move away from its mother's knees. God bless you! my dearest friend, from my heart of hearts! You know not the depth of my gratitude to you. My eyes overflow as I now trace these lines. May you clutch the treasure of health; but, above all, may you be happy! . . .

Your ever loving friend,
Charles Sumner

Longfellow did receive the letter: ". . . it made my heart swell into my throat." He assured Sumner, "I treasure your kind, parting words in my inmost soul; and will read your letter over again far out at sea, and hear in it friendly voices from the shore."

Arriving at Le Havre, he revisited Paris then took the train sight-seeing by way of Antwerp, Ghent, Bruges, Brussels, Aix-la-Chapelle, and Cologne, where he embarked for the short boat ride to Boppard, a walled medieval town with Roman ruins at a great bend in the river. By June 6 he was ready for his first "plunge" at Marienberg, an eighteenth-century convent whose nuns had been evicted during the Napoleonic occupation.

The best thing to be said for the water cure is that it probably did no one who submitted to it any harm, unless they got caught in a draft. The rationale was perfectly logical, in a medieval sort of way: disease often "broke" when the body experienced a very high fever. If the conditions of this fever could be replicated—for example, by turning the skin bright red and causing shivers—a healing effect would necessarily follow. This method was recommended by its practitioners for any ailment from gout to impotence to paralysis. It may actually have worked with certain psychological conditions in which the patient felt cleansed or purged or made new by the constant application of water over the body.

The routine, as Longfellow explained to several correspondents, was this: You are awakened at 4:00 a.m. by a servant who wraps you in blankets and quilts. You lie for an hour or more until you perspire freely. You are wheeled in an armchair to the bathing room, where you plunge into a large bath of running water and splash about. You dress, walk in the garden, drink the local spring water, breakfast on bread, butter, and milk, possibly strawberries. Another walk, an 11:00 a.m. shower under a spout, then another hour's walk, then a flowing *Sitzbad* for half an hour, another walk, followed by a frugal dinner at 1:00 p.m. (no wine or spices). Walk, sit, or play billiards until 5:00, when there's another Sitzbad, then a long walk uphill to the neighboring village for a bread-and-butter supper. At 10:00, to bed.

"I think I am growing a little web-footed; which is not wonderful, as I take four cold baths a day; beside an occasional swim in the Rhine," Longfellow wrote to his Cambridge friend Catherine Eliot Norton.

If there was anything physically wrong with Longfellow, he had long since gotten over it. On his twentieth day of treatment, he wrote to Sumner:

> The water begins to work upon my nerves. I had a dream last night, in which I saw you. You mentioned a certain person's name, whereupon, like the Patriarchs in the Old Testament, I fell on your neck and wept, exclaiming "I am very unhappy." The most amusing part of the dream was that we were in bed together, and you were buried up to your neck in tar [?], which absorbed my tears.

There were some sixty patients at the Kurort Marienberg, a few of them seriously ill, a good number of them recovering from an excess of food and drink, and some there simply to be fussed over. As the weeks passed, Longfellow regarded them with growing amusement. They were a cross section of the European minor aristocracy and upper gentry, some from as far away as Russia. He also made friends in the neighborhood and only occasionally lapsed in his faithfulness to the regimen; he could not resist his favorite Rhine wines, especially the nearby Johannisberger.

One major sonnet emerged from his summer at Boppard, although he considered it too personal to publish in his lifetime. "Mezzo Cammin" was written on August 25, 1842, shortly before he began his return home. It is one of the most masterful examples of the form in nineteenth-century American poetry.

> *Half of my life is gone, and I have let*
> *The years slip from me and have not fulfilled*
> *The aspiration of my youth to build*
> *Some tower of song with lofty parapet.*
> *Not indolence, nor pleasure, nor the fret*
> *Of restless passions that would not be stilled,*
> *But sorrow, and a care that almost killed,*
> *Kept me from what I may accomplish yet;*
> *Though, half-way up the hill, I see the Past*
> *Lying beneath me with its sounds and sights, —*
> *A city in the twilight dim and vast,*
> *With smoking roofs, soft bells, and gleaming lights, —*
> *And hear above me on the autumnal blast*
> *The cataract of Death far thundering from the heights.*

Its Dantesque title, its employment of Puritan self-scrutiny, its cautious acceptance of middle age, its oblique reference to both Mary and Fanny, its belated recognition that poetry is in fact his gift, however little he has yet done with it—all these things give "Mezzo Cammin" a weight that surpasses anything in his work to that point. The poem even reflects, with some pardonable license, the topography of Marienberg. The Kloster still stands there, on a hillside overlooking Boppard's smoking roofs and bell towers; behind it, a stream rushes down from the heights.

He wanted to extend his stay, pleading only a partial "cure," but the Harvard Corporation declined to continue his salary beyond the agreed upon term of six months, and he turned homeward in the fall of 1842, by way of London. Two great and unanticipated boons had come from this third European sojourn. At Boppard, he had befriended the radical German poet and translator Ferdinand Freiligrath, who was an important link in introducing Germans to English and American literature; they were to remain lifelong friends. And in London he renewed his friendship with Dickens, who introduced him to his friend (and future biographer) John Forster, who became one of Longfellow's regular correspondents. Dickens escorted him one night on a tour of the bleakest and most dangerous of the East End slums. Both writers made a deep impression on him: Freiligrath for his personal courage in opposing the Prussian authorities (he would soon be exiled), and Dickens for the kind of social conscience that struck a sympathetic chord in a New England Unitarian.

In London he read the just-published *American Notes* of Dickens, based on his travels earlier that year. Dickens was kind to Boston and his hosts there, but scathing about much of the rest of what he saw of the United States, especially its toleration of slavery. Longfellow had the opportunity to hear at first hand the abolitionist views of Dickens and his circle—a position still considered dangerously radical in much of proper Boston—and he determined on the voyage home to express his own feelings on the subject at last. Sumner for some time had urged him to take up the topic. In a letter to Marienberg, he had asked:

> What red-hot staves has your mind thrown up? What ideas have been started by the voyage? A poem on the sea? Oh! I long for those verses on slavery. Write some stirring words that shall move the whole land. Send them home and we'll publish them. Let us know how you occupy yourself with that heavenly gift of invention.

As Longfellow later wrote to Freiligrath from America, it had been a boisterous passage. "I was not out of my berth more than twelve hours for the first twelve days. I was in the forward part of the vessel, where all the great waves struck and broke with voices of thunder." Confined to his cabin, he wrote seven poems on slavery. "I meditated upon them in the stormy, sleepless nights, and wrote them down with a pencil in the morning." They are the most overtly political of his writings, on the part of a poet who has been seen by many of his critics—and admirers—as staying "above" politics. *Poems on Slavery* quickly appeared in December of 1842, in a volume whose slight thirty-one pages betrayed its radical message. It included the shipboard poems and an eighth, previously written one, "The Warning." He had not realized that the Reverend William Ellery Channing—the most famous of New England's Unitarian preachers—had died, but decided to leave in the ode addressed to him as a memorial to a "great and good man." He wrote to his father:

> How do you like the Slavery Poems? I think they make an impression; I have received many letters about them, which I will send to you by the first good opportunity. Some persons regret that I should have written them, but for my own part I am glad of what I have done. My feelings prompted me, and my judgment approved. . . .

He knew he was taking some risk to his reputation, personal as well as literary, since so many of the Beacon Hill families he frequented—including the Appletons—depended for their fortunes on the textile industry, which needed a guaranteed supply of Southern cotton.

Longfellow had had no personal exposure to Southern plantation life, and he relied, especially in the poem "The Quadroon Girl," on some of the abolitionists' favorite tropes of rape and interracial slave families. "The Slave's Dream" presents the pathos of an African king sold into bondage, thinking of his homeland as he lies dying. "The Slave in the Dismal Swamp" tells of a runaway on the Virginia-Carolina border:

> *In the dark fens of the Dismal Swamp*
> *The hunted Negro lay;*
> *He saw the fire of the midnight camp,*
> *And heard at times a horse's tramp*
> *And a bloodhound's distant bay.*

"The Slave Singing at Midnight" compellingly links the psalmist David, the Hebrews of the Exodus, and Paul and Silas in prison with the hopeless slave who sings of Zion. "The Witnesses" offers a chilling image of the bones of the slaves who drowned in the Middle Passage.

Longfellow ended his volume with the strongest of these poems, "The Warning," which closes with prophetic lines, written some two decades before the Civil War:

> *There is a poor, blind Sampson in this land,*
> *Shorn of his strength and bound in bonds of steel,*
> *Who may, in some grim revel, raise his hand,*
> *And shake the pillars of this Commonweal,*
> *Til the vast Temple of our liberties*
> *A shapeless mass of wreck and rubbish lies.*

Poems on Slavery immensely pleased the abolitionists, still regarded as a radical fringe by most upright Bostonians; John Greenleaf Whittier even invited Longfellow to run for Congress on the new antislavery Liberty Party ticket. He politely declined, perhaps remembering his father's unhappy congressional experience and content enough for the moment with the mainstream Whig Party. Moreover, he was temperamentally unsuited for electoral politics, which in antebellum America could prove almost a contact sport. He shunned confrontation and public controversy in every circumstance. But his growing fame—and possibly his public stance against the slaveholders—soon made him the target of a master of invective.

In 1845, in the pages of a new (and short-lived) New York monthly, *The Aristidean*, Edgar Allan Poe launched the most bitter in a series of attacks he had been directing over the past six years against Longfellow and what he considered the New Englander's exaggerated reputation. Reviewing *Poems on Slavery*, Poe dismissed the work as "intended for the especial use of those negrophilic old ladies of the north, who form so large a part of Mr. LONGFELLOW's friends." While admitting there were fine passages in the poems, Poe commented:

> No doubt, it is a very commendable and very comfortable thing, in the Professor, to sit at ease in his library chair, and write verses instructing the southerners how to give up their all with good grace, and

abusing them if they will not; but we have a singular curiosity to know how much of his own, under a change of circumstances, the Professor himself would be willing to surrender.

"The Slave in the Dismal Swamp" was "a shameless medley of the grossest misrepresentation"—Poe denied bloodhounds had ever been used to chase runaways in the South—and "The Quadroon Girl" a tired piece of abolitionist propaganda. Longfellow had written "incendiary doggrel" [sic], and Poe dismissed the volume "with no more profound feeling than that of contempt."

That Poe—irritated by the relentless moralizing of the New England "clique"—was offended by Longfellow's critique of his slave-owning fellow citizens is not surprising. But the depth of his "contempt" was profound indeed, possibly pathological, and it clearly stung Longfellow. He kept above the fray, but several of his friends—including Hillard and Sumner—fired back at Poe in what came to be known as "the Longfellow War."

It had begun in October 1839 with a short review of *Hyperion* in *Burton's Gentleman's Magazine*, a respectable monthly to which Poe regularly contributed. Longfellow's unshapely romance was a "farrago," evincing a lack of "the great labor requisite for the stern demands of high art." In the same columns, in February 1840, Poe took on *Voices of the Night*. He admitted he had admired "Hymn to the Night" upon first reading it in a newspaper and had even concluded that "a poet of high genius had at length risen amongst us." Yet he had had second thoughts upon reading the new collection. "[H]e appears to us singularly deficient in all those important faculties which give artistical power.... He has no combining or binding force. He has absolutely nothing of unity." Some of Poe's criticism hit the mark: he found Longfellow's archaizing inversions of normal word order ("Spake full well ...") "preposterous" for a nineteenth-century poet. But he went on to make a much more serious charge. Longfellow's "Midnight Mass for the Dying Year" had been plagiarized from Tennyson's "The Death of the Old Year." The similarity of metaphor and rhythmical structure in the two poems was no mere coincidence, but an example of "the most barbarous class of literary robbery."

In truth the two poems have little in common other than the familiar poetic conceit of personifying the outgoing year as an old man. But it became clear over the next five years that the vehemence of Poe's attacks on Longfellow's reputation were often in reverse proportion to evidentiary truth. Amid the transatlantic adulation that Longfellow had received by the early 1840s, Poe had managed to find a weak spot: Longfellow was a chronic borrower—of European themes, of traditional European meters, of a poetic diction in which echoes of a hundred other poets sounded. But this was not plagiarism. The previous century would have praised this practice as imitation, in the long-established Renaissance sense of the term. Yet Poe was living at a time when literature was becoming commodified, when the market economy was transforming writers from gentlemen-amateurs into producers who had a right to the products of their own labors. In Poe's day, the issue of international copyright was being debated, and Romanticism too condemned the absence of originality.

Reviews in 1842 of *Ballads and Other Poems* and in 1845 of Longfellow's anthology *The Waif* and of public lectures in New York on American poetry gave Poe the occasion for further critique, much of it delivered with a harshness of phrase that was exceptional even in the rough-and-tumble literary life of New York. Poe not only attacked Longfellow's style and choice of subjects but declared that his very conception of what it is to be a poet was wrongheaded. Poetry, said Poe, was the rhythmical creation of beauty. "Beyond the limits of Beauty its province does not extend," he wrote in *Graham's Magazine* (which he was then editing). Longfellow's insistent didacticism violated this principle. Of course, added Poe, Longfellow would find his defenders "so long as the world is full to overflowing with cant and conventicles"—a trenchant attempt to capture New England intellectual life in a phrase.

In 1844 Poe had joined the staff of the *New York Weekly Mirror*, owned by Longfellow's old acquaintance Willis. A long letter appeared

there on March 1, 1845, defending Longfellow against charges of plagiarism, and signed "Outis," classical Greek for "nobody." Poets often
draw on the same images, even use the same phrases, Outis wrote, and
gave as examples fifteen places where Poe's own "The Raven"—which
had been an instant popular sensation that year—could be said to imi-
tate an earlier poem. Between March 8 and April 5, Poe—who had
moved on to another paper, the *Broadway Journal*—published five extensive replies to Outis, further detailing Longfellow's alleged plagia-
risms. The charges grew more outrageous (at one point Poe accused
Longfellow of stealing parts of *The Spanish Student* from his own
unfinished play *Politian*), but the unrelenting attack on a popular literary figure and his Boston "clique" boosted sales of the newspaper.

That was the purpose, some have argued—a publicity stunt to put
the *Broadway Journal* (of which Poe had become editor) on the literary
map. While earlier students of Poe took the letters at face value, Poe's
recent biographer Kenneth Silverman concluded that, probably with
Willis's aid, "Poe himself concocted the entire exchange," even to the
point of accusing himself anonymously of plagiarism. But there is reason to believe that the "Longfellow War" (Poe's phrase, not Longfellow's) went beyond being a literary hoax. Poe was growing increasingly
irrational in this period, and within the year would have a complete
nervous collapse. Aware of his own genius yet buffeted by circumstance
and a pattern of self-destructive behavior, he had reason to envy the
placid life of the well-to-do Cambridge professor, surrounded by a
crowd of uncritical admirers and able to give the public the moralizing
verse that Poe himself scorned. Growing sectional antagonism added
to the mix. That the prestigious *North American Review* would publish
only New England writers, as Poe and others charged, was cited as evidence of that breach. That Longfellow did not respond to the attacks
surely added to the insult. Moreover, as Silverman notes, Poe himself
had a long history of plagiarism and of reprinting his own earlier work
as new. The Outis letters were in that sense a projection of Poe's own
creative anxieties onto a well-established literary figure.

Poe was not the only critic to attempt to deflate Longfellow's reputation as the leading American poet of the mid-1840s. The South Carolinian William Gilmore Simms, for example, repeated Poe's charges of plagiarism, adding of Longfellow:

It is the grace and sweetness of his verse, and that extreme simplicity of thought which taxes no intellect to scan—which we read as we run—that constitutes his claim upon the reader.

But it was a fellow New Englander, a writer from Longfellow's own social and intellectual milieu, who took up this theme of the poet's shallowness with a chill and deadly touch. Longfellow complained of Margaret Fuller's "bilious attack," which wounded him in a way that the distant and unstable Poe could not. Reviewing his collection *Poems* in 1845, and acquitting him of any charge of copying, she wrote:

We must confess a coolness toward Mr. Longfellow, in consequence of the exaggerated praises that have been bestowed upon him. When we see a person of moderate powers receive honors which should be reserved for the highest, we feel somewhat like assailing him and taking from him the crown which should be reserved for grander brows. . . .

The reason of his being overrated here, is because through his works breathes the air of other lands with whose products the public at large is but little acquainted. . . . Twenty years hence when he stands upon his own merits, he will rank as a writer of elegant, if not always accurate taste, of great imitative power, and occasional felicity in an original way, where his feelings are stirred.

In fairness to Longfellow, we should remember that both Poe and Fuller were judging him on the basis of a few dozen poems, albeit some of them his most popular short lyrics. Had Poe lived beyond 1849, he would have been unlikely to join the ranks of Longfellow's admirers, for their concepts of poetry's true nature were too contradictory. Book-length works such as *Hiawatha* or *Tales of a Wayside Inn* might well have confirmed Poe's detestation of the long poem. But it was a loss to Longfellow—to America—that Fuller (by then the Marchesa Ossoli) died at sea in 1850, depriving him of a supremely intelligent critical voice he would have had to take seriously.

Poe's "Longfellow War" had one touching sequel. After learning of Poe's death from a brain fever, Longfellow wrote in the *Southern Literary Messenger*: "The harshness of his criticisms I have never attributed to anything but the irritation of a sensitive nature chafed by some indefinite sense of wrong." Perhaps on the basis of this generous testimonial, Poe's aunt and mother-in-law, Maria Clemm, living in reduced circumstances in Lowell, Massachusetts, wrote to him in 1850 requesting a copy of *The Seaside and the Fireside*. Over the following sixteen years, they corresponded, Longfellow sending her money and books and doing her other small favors. In her dotage Mrs. Clemm claimed she had stayed in Longfellow's house, but there is no evidence this happened; still, he was genuinely solicitous of her welfare. In 1859 she entreated him: "Please speak kindly of my darling Eddie."

A Wedding in Beacon Street

AND THEN IT SUDDENLY HAPPENED. AT A PARTY at the Nortons' shortly before Tom Appleton sailed for Europe in the spring of 1843, Fanny hinted to Henry that she would soon need company. He took the hint, called at 39 Beacon, was received more warmly than he once thought possible, and wrote her a candid appraisal of his feelings. She replied on April 17, declaring that "a better dawn has exorcised the phantoms" that had separated them in the past. Whether her reference to "those once-haunted walls" meant the memory of Mary Potter or some more recent misunderstanding, her letter certainly marked a great turning point in their relations. "I could not well disguise how some of your words troubled me," she wrote. "I should never have ventured to speak so frankly to you had I not believed that the dead Past had buried its dead, and that we might safely walk over their graves, thanking God that at last we could live to give each other only happy thoughts." It is a curious love letter, expressing at first more of Fanny's gravity of character than any obvious passion. But the stately tone, the graveyard language melt. "I rejoiced to see how calmly you met me, until Saturday when I trembled a little, as we are apt to do for a long cherished hope, but I will put aside all anxiety and fear, trusting upon your promise...."

On May 10, Longfellow received her note accepting him. It had been almost seven years since they had met in Switzerland, perhaps five since he had first given up any real hope of marrying her. He did not hop on a horse or even order a carriage. He walked—from the Craigie House, past the College, through Cambridgeport, and across the West Boston Bridge (its successor is named in his honor). The quickest route from there would have been down Charles Street—in those days still lapped by the river—and then up the hill on Beacon Street, to the bow-fronted house overlooking the Frog Pond. A person of about Longfellow's height can make the trip briskly by foot on modern sidewalks in good weather in about ninety minutes. He explained afterwards that he was too restless for a carriage, too fearful of meeting an acquaintance who might break the mood. In truth, he wanted to stop time. After so much anguish, so much humiliation, he wanted to savor the exquisite hour between the arrival of the news of her acceptance and his heart-pounding appearance at her door.

He of course expressed it differently in his journal. Remembering Dante's first glimpse of Beatrice, he said he walked that day "amid the blossoms and sunshine and songs of birds, with my heart full of gladness and my eyes full of tears! . . . Oh, Day forever blessed; that ushered in this Vita Nuova of happiness."

Why had it taken so long? There are several practical reasons why Fanny might have changed her mind. Her closest friend, her older sister Mary, had married a Scotsman three years earlier—Robert Mackintosh, the son of a well-known diplomat and essayist, Sir James Mackintosh—and had moved abroad. Her next best friend, Tom, had made it clear that he would spend a peripatetic life, dropping in on Boston but much preferring, at least as a young man, to live abroad, in a world of grand hotels and fashionable spas. And her widowed father had recently been remarried, to Harriet Coffin Sumner, a woman about Fanny's age who had taken over her role in running the household and being Nathan's companion. She was facing an unprecedented degree of loneliness, despite the brilliant social world in which she seemed to flourish. For all her disparagement of "the Prof" within her family, Longfellow was nonetheless a familiar and reassuring figure in her small Boston world, and during his sojourn abroad in 1842 she may have realized that she missed him more than she would have admitted. She had also become very religious. She was an unusually "churchly" Unitarian. Had she lived longer, she might have been attracted, like so many Bostonians of her class after the Civil War, by the liturgical richness of High Episcopalianism. It was her seriousness that had made it so easy for her to dismiss the usual suitors, but it may have been this same element in her nature that persuaded her she would not fulfill her life as a Christian woman without a husband. She never explained her decision in any depth—as she wrote to her aunt Martha Gold, "what is there to tell but the old tale that true love is very apt to win its re-ward"—but the notion among earlier biographers that she simply did not "know" her own mind is an insult to her intelligence.

There is no record of exactly what was said when Henry arrived at 39 Beacon, perhaps a trifle red in the face after his hike, on that May morning. It was an occasion he was to celebrate and then commemo-rate each ensuing year of his life. His letter the next day to his mother survives, announcing his engagement "to a very lovely woman—Fanny Appleton—for whom I have for many years cherished a feeling of affection. I cannot say another word—save that she is very beauti-ful—very intellectual—and very pious—three most excellent verys." To his sister Anne, ten days later, he confessed: "Life was too lonely—and sad;—with little to soothe and calm me. Now the future opens its long closed gates into pleasant fields and lands of quiet. The strife and struggle are over, for a season, at least, and the troubled spirit findeth its perfect rest."

On her part, Fanny wrote an affectionate and daughterly letter to Zilpah—she described herself as an orphan longing for a mother—and a pious one to Anne Pierce, in which she acknowledged "your brother's long-tried affection." All parties were aware of the social gulf separating 39 Beacon Street and "The Old Ordinary," on Congress Street, Portland, but there is much evidence over the years to come that Fanny was gifted with enough tact to bridge it.

The wedding was quietly sumptuous. Perhaps aware of her rela-tively advanced age as a bride, thirty-year-old Fanny dismissed the prospect of a "drilled bodyguard" of bridesmaids. The recent death of a cousin precluded too festive a ceremony. Some fifty family mem-bers and close friends gathered in the drawing room at 39 Beacon. The most complete account of the event comes in a letter Mary Longfellow Greenleaf wrote to brother Sam:

... the groom was handsome as usual, in fine spirits, and very happy (as he ought to be). "What do you say the bride was dressed in?" Not the green glass breast pin indeed, but in a rich and simple and little muslin, trimmed with splendid thread lace—the tunic looped up with natural orange blossoms, a bunch on each side of the skirt—short sleeves, two tiny bracelets on one arm and one on the other—wedding gifts—on her head was a plain very delicate lace veil which reached to her feet and partly enveloped her person in a most becoming and graceful manner—a branch of orange blossoms was on the back of her hair. She stood a queen, admired of all. A supper-table was spread in the back-parlor with fruit, ices, and a big loaf cake beautifully dressed with flowers in the center. . . . The couple went out to the Craigie the same night by the light of a full moon, and there they seem as happy as possible.

Eight

A SEASIDE IDYLL

THAT THE CRAIGIE HOUSE was to be theirs was by no means certain. The property had been leased from the Craigie estate by the lexicographer Joseph E. Worcester, who rented in turn to Longfellow the eastern half of the house. Nathan Appleton did everything possible to replicate for Fanny the comforts of Beacon Street—luxurious fabrics, handsome carpets, a Chickering piano, new furniture, even "a patent Shower bath"—but the new couple was aware that their tenancy might be brief. Large, semidecayed Georgian houses were not particularly fashionable in 1843, and it is easy to imagine the Longfellows building (as her father hoped) a comfortable new house in the Italianate or Gothic revival style becoming popular in that decade. Yet "Castle Craigie" grew on Fanny. In a letter to Tom Appleton, she said that her husband's old friend George Washington Greene had convinced them to stay there: "We have decided to let Father purchase this grand old mansion if he will. Our interest in it had been quickened by our present guest, Mr. Greene of Rome. . . . He has excited an historical apreciation [*sic*], or rather reminded us how noble an inheritance this is where Washington dwelt in every room." That September, they asked Fanny's father to buy for them not only the house but the meadow in front extending down to the Charles, lest their vista be spoilt by a block of new houses. "The house is large enough to introduce every modern comfort we should desire," wrote Fanny, "and there is no position in Cambridge that can compare with it for the views and air. It is, moreover, very interesting to us from its associations." The next month, Appleton bought the house and land for ten thousand dollars. The Worcesters became the Longfellows' tenants, in the western half of the house, until their new house farther out on Brattle Street was completed that spring. Fanny embarked on an even more ambitious decorating scheme. Her textile-manufacturing father scolded her for buying European carpets in New York, rather than New England products, but she had her way in the end, with his generous support, and she promised for both economy and patriotism to patronize "the Lowell manufacture" in the future.

"The Craigie house is decidedly conservative [old-fashioned]; and will remain as much in its old state as comfort permits," Longfellow noted in his journal. Fanny assured Tom that, while they were full of plans and projects, they had "no desire to change a feature of the old countenance which Washington has rendered sacred." This was a somewhat novel idea in the 1840s. Americans reverenced their brief past but had not yet imbued its architecture with any particular historical aura. The rescue of Mount Vernon by a committee of determined women—now considered the birth of historical preservation in this country—was a decade in the future, and as late as 1863 Bostonians were careless enough to allow John Hancock's Georgian mansion next to the State House to be torn down.

As historical preservationists, in other words, the Longfellows were ahead of their time. In the front hall they displayed a copy of Houdon's bust of Washington. Over the years, people gave them odds and ends of Washington souvenirs. But, despite erroneous reports in a Boston paper in 1844 that they were assembling a kind of Washington museum, the Longfellows were more interested in preserving the structure that had seen so many great events than in restoring its interiors to some earlier period. In fact, the house quickly came to be filled with that eclectic mixture of eighteenth- and nineteenth-century paintings, sculptures, books, neoclassical furniture, massive Victorian pieces in a variety of revival styles, heavy draperies, and souvenirs of travel that the visitor to the Craigie House sees today. Nonetheless, as Longfellow's fame as a writer increased, so did public recognition that he was living in surroundings sacred to every patriotic American. For

FIGURE 7: "Headquarters of General Washington, now the residence of Professor Longfellow." Mid-nineteenth-century engraving. Courtesy National Park Service, Longfellow National Historic Site.

example, when John Adams Whipple compiled his *Homes of American Statesmen* in 1854—the first American book to be illustrated with a photograph—he included an engraving entitled "Headquarters, Cambridge 1773." The residence still stands, the book noted, "and in worthy occupancy." In the post–Civil War years, as the Craigie House became in the public's estimation more and more a shrine to Longfellow himself, it seemed only appropriate to the poet's many admirers that he should be at home in the same dwelling where the father of his country had acted out the history being commemorated in the master's poetry.

But other things preoccupied the Longfellows in the 1840s: above all, their new family. Given his memories of Mary's death in Rotterdam in 1835, one can imagine the anxiety that Longfellow must have felt about his new wife's first pregnancy. On June 9, 1844—eleven months after their wedding—Fanny gave birth to Charles Appleton Longfellow, with both mother and child in excellent health. Five more children followed over the next eleven years: Ernest Wadsworth in 1845, Frances in 1847, Alice Mary in 1850, Edith in 1853, and Anne Allegra in 1855. All but Frances survived into adulthood.

⚜

To escape the dust and heat of a Cambridge summer—and, in Longfellow's case, to refresh himself with a change of scenery after the travails of the college year—the family tried out a series of vacation retreats before finally settling upon Nahant as a permanent summer residence from 1850 on. In August of 1845, for example, Longfellow sought relief for his chronic eye troubles at Dr. Robert Wesselhoeft's new "Aquatic Institute," a hydrotherapy spa in Brattleboro, Vermont, somewhat reminiscent of the Marienberg. (Four years later, he would send his brother Stephen there, in an unsuccessful attempt to cure him of his alcoholism.) Most of the following August was spent in far western Massachusetts, in the Berkshire town of Pittsfield, where Nathan Appleton summered at the Gold House, the homestead of Fanny's maternal grandmother. (The house is gone, but Longfellow had made use of it in his very popular "The Old Clock on the Stairs," ticking away its "Forever—never!/Never—forever" in the hall, which he had published in 1845 in *The Belfry of Bruges and Other Poems*.) He continued to pay shorter summer visits to Portland, although the old-fashioned house on Congress Street was proving inconvenient for his growing family; Anne, chronically short of money, had never replaced its original outhouse.

In 1847, Longfellow learned that a local entrepreneur, J. Kingsbury, had built a substantial modern hotel and "new watering place" with a splendid view of Casco Bay two miles north of the city, on a small, wooded peninsula known as Oak Grove (today, Martin's Point). The Verandah Hotel—called after its wide piazzas—offered a view in one direction of rocky coastal scenery and the Casco Bay islands and harbor forts, while in the other direction the more tranquil shores of the mouth of the Presumpscot River were visible. At low tide the whole area was a mud flat, but here, too, the tidal pools and shoals of mussels, and the play of light on the rushing waters had their littoral charm. This type of hostelry marked the beginning of Maine's transition from a remote, somewhat hazardous place to visit into the Vacationland of the late nineteenth and twentieth centuries. Kingsbury had realized that well-to-do urbanites would pay handsomely to enjoy ocean breezes, both salt and fresh water fishing, a variety of genteel outdoor sports, and hearty Down East meals—away from the city, but within easy reach of the railway. Longfellow agreed that the place was enchanting, and his family's six-week stay—his longest sojourn in his native state after leaving it in 1835—had a discernible impact on his poetry.

The Longfellows left Boston at 6:00 a.m. on July 15, with Tom Appleton in the party, and were in Portland that afternoon in time to see a ship launched. Longfellow declared the oak-covered promontory "delicious"—relaxing, too, for when he tried to read in the grove, "the seaside drowsiness and dreaminess stole over me; and I sat gazing at the silvery sea...." He bathed in the cold waters in the mornings before breakfast, then bowled with Tom or watched little Charley begin a lifelong fascination with boats. Like many Americans that summer, he and Fanny were reading a new book called *Omoo*, "a series of sketches of wild adventure in the South Sea Islands" by a young travel writer named Herman Melville. (The following summer, they were to rent the eighteenth-century Melvill Farm at Pittsfield, owned by the author's cousin.) Soon, a stream of relatives and childhood friends made their way over from Portland, including Henry's ailing father.

Longfellow was pleasantly surprised one day to find his old Heidelberg friends, William Cullen Bryant and family, also vacationing at the hotel. The summer had its bittersweet moments, however, for Portland was full of reminders of the past (Longfellow met Pitt Fessenen, his late sister's fiancé, on the street one day). There was one genuine tragedy: on August 4, a ropewalk in Free Street caught fire. Before the blaze could be extinguished, a dozen or more houses burned down, among them his brother Stephen's—one further disaster in a life increasingly marked by ill fortune. "We passed most of the day with Marianne [Stephen's wife] looking for her scattered goods."

The summer also brought its holiday intrigues. "There is a party here right out of Wilhelm Meister," Longfellow noted of the Verandah, alluding to the Goethe novel still regarded in that day as scandalous. "Mrs. Coffin, a beautiful woman; Mr. Coffin, her melancholy husband; young Meyer, her admirer, and a good musician; Mrs. Buel, whose husband is in Boston, and Dr. Codman who is very attentive to Mrs. Buel. I could sketch a chapter here for an American Wilhelm Meister, but forbear, out of sheer laziness." He was not too lazy to walk frequently over the bridge and into town, observing those changes in his boyhood haunts that were, a decade later, to give his elegiac "My Lost Youth" its poignancy. There were human landmarks that also attracted him: the once "wild" John Neal, for example, now eking out a living as an editor, and especially the family's longtime minister at First Parish Church, Dr. Ichabod Nichols. "Ah! he is a man of genius. There is great freshness, force and originality in that man, and his long life in the little provincial town has not tamed him, nor made him in any way common-place."

But mostly he looked at the water. "How lovely the view of the harbour, with its pearly sea, and its almost irresistible attraction drawing me out into the ocean. A whole fleet of vessels in the horizon, looking in the vapory distance like the spires and towers of a great city." At sunset he liked to walk with Fanny over the trestled bridge. On July 19, he noted: "The gurgling of the tide among the wooden piers was the only sound audible. Coming back through the grove we heard the evening gun from the fort, and the islands seized the sound and tossed it further and further off, with multiple reverberations, till it died away in a murmur." Another day, after the rain stopped, he watched the sea mist roll away. "White sea-gulls sitting on the flats, with a long reflexion therein. Sunset like a conflagration. Walk on the bridge; both ends of which are lost in the sea-fog, like human life, mid-way between two eternities; beginning and ending in mist." He also drove to Cape

Elizabeth, to visit its lighthouses. He climbed to the top of "the re-volving one"—the whitewashed Portland Head Light of 1791, a bea-con he would revisit in "The Lighthouse":

> Steadfast, serene, immovable, the same
> Year after year, through all the silent night
> Burns on forevermore that quenchless flame,
> Shines on that inextinguishable light! ...

What we see in his journal that summer is the shaping of a vision of the New England coast as distinctive in its own artistry as the sea-scapes of Fitz Hugh Lane or Winslow Homer. He is closer in poetic temperament to Lane—both are students of low tides and late after-noons—but Longfellow could paint with Homer's realism as well:

> The sea-bird wheeling round it, with the din
> Of wings and winds and solitary cries,
> Blinded and maddened by the light within,
> Dashes himself against the glare, and dies. ...

We can see this coastal vision take shape in an unpublished passage of blank verse from his journal for August 18:

> O faithful, indefatigable tides.
> That evermore upon God's errands go,
> Now sea-ward, bearing tidings of the land,
> Now land-ward, bearing tidings of the sea,
> And filling every frith and estuary,
> Each arm of the great sea, each little creek
> Each thread and filament of water-courses,
> Full with your ministration of delight!
> Under the rafters of this wooden bridge
> I see you come and go; sometimes in haste
> To reach your journey's end; which being done
> With feet unrested ye return again,
> But recommence the never-ending task,
> Patient, with whatever burdens ye may bear,
> And fretted only by impending rocks.

This is only a sketch, quickly put to paper, unpolished, diffuse. Its distillation would emerge more than three decades later in that bleak, chilling little masterpiece, "The Tide Rises, the Tide Falls."

> *The tide rises, the tide falls.*
> *The twilight darkens, the curlew calls;*
> *Along the sea-sands damp and brown*
> *The traveller hastens toward the town,*
> *And the tide rises, the tide falls.*
>
> *Darkness settles on roofs and walls,*
> *But the sea, the sea in the darkness calls;*
> *The little waves, with their soft white hands,*
> *Efface the footprints in the sands,*
> *And the tide rises, the tide falls.*
>
> *The morning breaks, the steeds in their stalls*
> *Stamp and neigh, as the hostler calls;*
> *The day returns, but nevermore*
> *Returns the traveller to the shore,*
> *And the tide rises, the tide falls.*

Meanwhile, the Verandah idyll gave Longfellow further opportunity to exercise his skill as a painter of genre scenes. He was struck, for example, by Peter, the hotel driver, his omnibus, Mazeppa, and—despite its name—his un-Byronic horses.

He is a short little fellow with a red face and one leg shorter than the other. In fair weather he wears a brown linen sack, and straw hat; in foul, a browner woolen sack and a glazed, round sailer's hat. He seems always in great perplexity of mind; for having no regular hour of coming and going, he depends on the will of his passengers, and as some want to go, when others want to stay, he never knows what to do. And in addition to this he seems to have weighing on his mind the advertisement of the host of the Oak Grove; "The Omnibus Mazeppa is always at the depot and steamers to convey passengers to the Verandah."

It proved a working holiday despite the distractions, for Longfellow was correcting proofs—between a forenoon sea bath and a billiards game with Fanny—of *Evangeline* in late July. The popular success of his first two volumes of poems, the financial and emotional security brought by his second marriage, and the growing awareness that many of his fellow citizens looked to him as the most representative American writer had given him the artistic confidence to write more poetry. In 1845, Carey & Hart in Philadelphia had published an illustrated edition of his work to date—or most of his work. In the only deplorable act in a long and otherwise blameless literary career, Longfellow had agreed to drop the antislavery poems from this volume, called *Poems*, after his publisher had warned that including them would discourage sales in the slave-holding South. Many of the other works in the edition were already well known from their publication in *Graham's Magazine* and elsewhere; as further evidence of his marketing skill, Longfellow had much of this new work repackaged in *The Belfrey of Bruges and Other Poems*, a literary landmark of 1845.

The Belfrey of Bruges takes its title from one of his characteristic travelogue poems—a panorama of Flemish history as imagined from the famous bell tower, the kind of potted European "color" that later critics would ridicule, but that homebound Americans of Longfellow's day read with eager devotion. (There is a companion poem about Longfellow's day in Nuremberg and an anecdote in rhyme about the minnesinger Walther von der Vogelweide.) "The Arsenal at Springfield" represents him at his most didactic—and his most antimilitaristic—but it also has some biographical significance (rather rare in Longfellow's work over all). On their wedding journey, accompanied by Sumner, the Longfellows had visited the United States Arsenal at Springfield, Massachusetts, where Fanny had pointed out how the stacks of gleaming gun barrels resembled the pipes of an organ and had urged him "to write a peace poem."

> *Ah! what a sound will rise, how wild and dreary,*
> *When the death-angel touches those swift keys!*

What loud lament and dismal Miserere
Will mingle with their awful symphonies!

There is much of interest in the volume, including a sonnet to Dante, and one short lyric, "The Arrow and the Song," in which Longfellow achieves a kind of offhand mastery. He improvised the poem in October of 1845 while standing with his back to the fire, waiting to go to church. The moral is common enough—we do not know where our thoughts, not to mention our writings, may end up once we have launched them—and the conclusion is trite, but how many poets have achieved something so instantly memorizable in three short stanzas?

I shot an arrow into the air,
It fell to earth, I knew not where;
For, so swiftly it flew, the sight
Could not follow it in its flight.

I breathed a song into the air,
It fell to earth, I knew not where;
For who has sight so keen and strong,
That it can follow the flight of song?

Long, long afterward, in an oak
I found the arrow, still unbroke;
And the song, from beginning to end,
I found again in the heart of a friend.

But the small masterpiece in *The Belfrey of Bruges* is the fifteen-stanza topographical poem "The Bridge." It gathers all the strengths of Longfellow's middle period: simplicity of diction, a subtle music in the meter, common yet memorable imagery. It is distinctly rooted in New England topography, yet deals with a universal theme; it is movingly biographical for those who know his personal history, yet intelligible to any reader.

I stood on the bridge at midnight,
As the clocks were striking the hour,

And the moon rose o'er the city,
Behind the dark church-tower.

The narrator stands on the West Boston Bridge over the Charles, which Longfellow had crossed and recrossed with such desperation in his days of rejected courtship; the church is the Old West, on Cambridge Street. Unlike the massively buttressed Longfellow (or "Pepperpot") Bridge now on that site, the nineteenth-century bridge had "long, black rafters" that allowed the tide and the seaweed to surge into the channel, in the days before damming produced the lakelike Charles Basin.

How often, oh how often,
In the days that had gone by,
I had stood on that bridge at midnight
And gazed on that wave and sky!

How often, oh how often,
I had wished that the ebbing tide
Would bear me away on its bosom
O'er the ocean wild and wide!

For my heart was hot and restless,
And my life was full of care,
And the burden laid upon me
Seemed greater than I could bear.

This burden he carries no longer, but the pain and despair he once felt on that site have made him better aware of the tragic lot of his fellow man. Whenever he crosses the bridge's wooden piers and smells the odor of brine, he sees the eternal procession, in an image that goes back to Dante and his amazement at how many men are in Hell, and forward to T. S. Eliot, who expresses the same amazement at the spectral crowd crossing London Bridge in *The Waste Land*. In Longfellow's words:

. . . I think of how many thousands
Of care-encumbered men,

Each bearing his burden of sorrow,
Have crossed the bridge since then.

I see the long procession
Still passing to and fro,
The young heart hot and restless,
And the old subdued and slow!

Yet the poem does not end on the expected bright, upbeat note that brings so much of Longfellow's work to a crashing halt. Water brings out the best in this poet, not least for its refusal to remain fixed in place.

And forever and forever,
As long as the river flows,
As long as the heart has passions,
As long as life has woes;

The moon and its broken reflection
And its shadows shall appear,
As the symbol of love in heaven,
And its wavering image here.

Nine

EVANGELINE

L ONGFELLOW'S POETIC PRODUCTION in the late 1840s still gave
evidence of a writer who did not want to confine himself to short
lyrics and souvenirs of European travel. Not long before his marriage,
he had even written a play. *The Spanish Student* (1843) is not very stage-
worthy (there is record of one performance, in a German translation,
in 1855), but as a closet drama it has a certain charm. The plot, which
owes something to Cervantes's tale *La Gitanilla*, is creaky, with enough
romantic students, Spanish hidalgos, and gypsy brigands to fill several
light opera libretti. But the mood of the piece reflects Longfellow's
warm memories of his Spanish sojourn in 1827, particularly in his portrayal of the gypsy girl Preciosa. Her dance in front of the archbishop
and cardinal assigned to examine her for alleged indecency literally
ends with their throwing their hats into the air in lubricious excitement, a touch of Protestant satire at the expense of the Church, or at
least a triumph of art over dogma. The following year, Longfellow produced a small anthology of verses mostly by other writers, under the
title *The Waif*, followed in 1845 by the first of his ambitious anthologies
of literature in translation, *The Poets and Poetry of Europe*. Many of the
translations were his own—by this point, there was no other American
who was so good at such things—with Felton contributing scholarly
introductions. In a sense, the book was the outgrowth of his comparative literature classes at Harvard, but it embodied his broader,
Goethean ambition of making Americans, even those who could not
read foreign languages, aware of the possibilities of a *Weltliteratur*.

He was ready for a very long poem. The British Romantics, notably
Southey, had championed such narratives a generation earlier, but no

American poet to date had found a subject that matched his or her talents, given that the subject had to be of epic proportions. (There was a list of honorable failures, going back to Barlow's clunky *Columbiad*.) Longfellow's particular project was to be seven years in the making.

We know that Hawthorne, Hillard, and Felton dined at Longfellow's rooms in the Craigie House on April 5, 1840, and there is reason to believe that Hawthorne had brought as his guest a Salem friend, political ally, and Episcopal priest, the Reverend Horace Conolly. After dinner Conolly told a story he said he had heard from a French-Canadian woman. He had urged Hawthorne on several occasions to turn this tale into a novel; the writer had considered it, but finally declared: "It is not in my vein: there are no strong lights and heavy shadows." The story told the tragedy of a young Acadian couple who had been separated, on their marriage day, by British troops in the course of the expulsion of the French-speaking Acadians from Nova Scotia in 1755. She wandered for years throughout New England searching for him, only to find him on his deathbed—a shock that killed her as well, although they were united at last in a shared grave. Hawthorne once again declined to adapt the tale as a novel. Longfellow, according to Conolly in an account written many years later, "followed my narrative with great attention and apparently very deep interest." At its conclusion, Conolly reports, Longfellow declared it "the best illustration of faithfulness and the constancy of woman that I have ever heard of or read." Longfellow asked Hawthorne, "If you have really made up your mind not to use it for a story, will you give it to me for a poem?" Hawthorne agreed.

Conolly adds that Hawthorne soon had second thoughts and, on the way home, broke into a profane tirade over the loss of such good material. This is surely an exaggeration, for Hawthorne had had ample opportunity to use the story, had it appealed to him; when he did write an essay on the Acadian expulsion a year later, he made no mention of it. It is interesting to speculate what Hawthorne might indeed have written, had he taken up what turned into *Evangeline: A Tale of Acadie*—perhaps a story in which, out of some obscure sense of guilt, the bridegroom deliberately avoids his bride during all those years of her obsessive searching, only to be caught at his next to last moment?

Longfellow took a different approach, capitalizing on the pathos of the Acadian expulsion but giving his heroine a far larger field of action. In the Harvard library he found out what he could about the exiled Acadians. Some of them had slipped back into Nova Scotia, but most of their descendants were still scattered along the Atlantic and Gulf coasts, including a large settlement in southern Louisiana and a tiny one in northern Maine's St. John Valley. He learned the basic facts of *le Grand Dérangement*, as the Acadians call their exile, from T. C. Haliburton's scholarly *History of Nova Scotia*, augmented by the Abbé de Reynal's eighteenth-century depiction of Acadie—or maritime Canada—as a pastoral paradise. A great wrong had been done against an innocent people, Longfellow concluded, and he was stirred both by this injustice and by the ambivalent feelings he had always had toward Britain (although, in fairness, he recognized that New Englanders, particularly Massachusetts governor William Shirley, had played a large role in the expulsion and the subsequent seizure of Acadian farmland).

The Acadians offered a tragic example of innocent people caught in the middle of distant European power politics. By the 1750s there were somewhere between twelve and eighteen thousand of them, living on farms their ancestors had cleared a century earlier, and vastly outnumbering the English-speaking Nova Scotian settlement centered on Halifax. They were devoutly Catholic but had tried to maintain their neutrality in the conflict between France and Britain (not easily done, given the fact that Nova Scotia had already changed hands ten times in the wars for North America). Traditionally on good terms with the indigenous Micmac Indians, the Acadians were suspected by the British, fairly or not, of aiding the Micmacs in their raids. While nominally subjects of the British king, most of the Acadians had declined, with what seemed to the British a kind of peasant obstinacy, to abjure their oath of loyalty to his French rival. In 1754 a new governor, Major Charles Lawrence, decided to crack down, first by confiscating the

Acadians' weapons and then by conducting, between 1755 and 1760, a massive deportation of these unreliable subjects to other parts of the Empire.

The effort proved more difficult than expected, and only an estimated six thousand Acadians were in fact exiled, about a third of that number from the fictional Evangeline's district of Grand Pré alone. Le Grand Dérangement became the defining event in Acadian ethnic identity, a tribal memory preserved among exiles scattered as far as the Falkland Islands and West Africa. But amid the far more dramatic events that followed in British North America in the 1770s, the Acadians were largely forgotten in the English-speaking world. Longfellow's *Evangeline* was to put them back on the map. As with the case of the Greeks, the Poles, and the Hungarians, mid-nineteenth-century Americans felt indignant upon learning the stories of such exiles, perhaps because these tragedies seemed so foreign to the spirit of progress among civilized peoples. (In 1847, only a radical would have drawn any parallel with American expropriation of Indian lands or the wholesale kidnapping of Africans into slavery.) It is one of the great ironies of Longfellow's epic poem that while writing about what already seemed a distant, more primitive past, he was unwittingly anticipating the horrors of the twentieth century's ethnic "cleansings."

Was there a real Evangeline or Gabriel? Not that anyone has discovered. It would be more accurate to say that they were a composite, a representative type, whose story subsumes and renders mythic the stories of hundreds of families separated, often forever, amid the chaos of the poorly organized expulsion. (The ease with which the Evangeline legend has been rewritten for their own purposes by various Acadian authors in the generations since Longfellow attests to its versatility.) The British had attempted to break up the Acadian settlement by scattering its members wherever ships could take them, but no one really wanted them, or had the resources to house and feed them, and probably hundreds of them died of starvation, exposure, and disease in the years immediately after 1755. As was his poetic practice, once Longfellow had briefed himself on the factual background, he used his

FIGURE 8: The expulsion of the Acadians from Grand Pré,
from F. O. C. Darley's 1866 illustrations for *Evangeline* (1847).

material with a very free hand. He was a bard, not a historian; what mattered was the basic human truth of his story, not its particulars. He was not even sure what to call his heroine. "Gabrielle" was his first choice. "Celestine" was also considered. Rather late in the day, he settled on Evangeline, an uncommon name which he made world famous.

The poem evolved slowly. There were other projects to distract him. In 1842 he was busy writing *The Spanish Student*, amid the labors of teaching and running his department. Then he went abroad for his water-cure, then got married, then in 1844–45 labored over the eight hundred pages of his poetry anthology. He undertook another, much briefer, anthology in English, published in 1846 as *The Estray*, which was to include as its proem a short lyric called "Pegasus in Pound." It vividly expressed his frustrations with Harvard. When the winged steed of Poetry arrives one day in a quiet village, the villagers throw him into the cattle pound and put him up for sale. Stared at but unfed, he finally has enough and breaks loose to return to the heavens. (He leaves behind a soothing spring, rather generous in the circumstances.)

It was not until 1845 that Longfellow was able to turn his full attention back to his "tale of Acadie," which he decided to cast in the classic measure of epic poetry, unrhymed hexameter—a difficult enough feat in Greek or Latin, but a formidable challenge to a poet writing in English. The long, stately, lumbering lines that resulted tend to put off modern readers (though generations of schoolboys have cracked up at such lines as "Sweet was her breath as the breath of the kine that feed in the meadows"). Yet when read aloud by a practiced voice to a patient audience, the music of the poem remains hauntingly beautiful.

Longfellow struck the bardic note immediately—"This is the forest primeval. The murmuring pines and the hemlocks, / Bearded with moss, and in garments green, indistinct in the twilight"—one of the most famous openings in all of American poetry. He was not, of course, describing the real coast of Acadian Nova Scotia, which he had never visited; the scene suggests the forests of Sweden or Maine, for this was to be framed as a northern epic. Savvy French farmers, the Acadian settlers had in fact chosen the lowlands around the Basin of Minas, where they had with great ingenuity and much effort built dikes to reclaim the rich salt marshes for farmland and pasture—an example of good husbandry, but not the landscape of epic poetry. Interestingly, for a long poem that is consistently so visual, Longfellow had seen none of the far-flung places he wrote about in *Evangeline* except the city of Philadelphia. For his color, he relied on his visit to John Banvard's heroic diorama of the Mississippi, which he had seen in Boston, and on such works as Audubon's *Birds of America*. Neither Homer nor Vergil, he might have pointed out, had actually seen Troy.

Banvard proved particularly useful (as did the Austrian travel writer Sealfield, who had explored the Louisiana swamps). Banvard was an itinerant painter and adventurer who had spent his youth on the Mississippi. In the spring of 1840, he had descended the river with his sketchbook in a small skiff, stopping to draw each point and bend in the then still-wild landscape. He had determined to create the largest painting in the history of the world, a three-mile length of canvas that, turning upon cylinders, would enable the paying spectator to feel as if he had actually traveled down the Mississippi, from the mouth of the Missouri to New Orleans. Longfellow visited the spectacle during its Boston exhibition in the mid 1840s and borrowed heavily from its visual depiction of vine-covered banks, deep forests, mossy bayous, and the prairie country beyond the Ozarks. He may also have relied on a pamphlet describing the panorama in some detail, published in Boston in 1847.

Despite efforts by nineteenth-century critics to say that Longfellow borrowed heavily from Goethe's *Hermann und Dorothea* or even the Biblical story of the Jews' Babylonian captivity, Evangeline is a strikingly original work in concept, if not in poetical diction. The story follows the history books fairly accurately at first, in its account of the forced meeting of the Acadian males in the church at Grand Pré, the draconian orders of Colonel Winslow (whose manuscript journal Longfellow had consulted at the Massachusetts Historical Society), the terrible scenes on the beach as families were separated, sometimes never to meet again. There is genuine pathos in the moment when the abandoned herds return from pasture, their udders swollen with milk, waiting in vain for the milkmaids who will never return to them. To any educated nineteenth-century reader, the flames of the burning village as seen from the crowded shore would have evoked the night of Aeneas's escape from the pillage of Troy. From that point on, the story takes on a phantasmagoric quality as the young Evangeline, first accompanied by the priest Father Felician, then entirely on her own, retraces her bridegroom Gabriel's footsteps across a great swath of North America.

The scenes in the bayous of southern Louisiana are perhaps best known: the couple's near-meeting on the Atchafalaya was a moment that moved Victorian readers to tears as reliably as anything in Dickens. Moored among the willows, made drowsy by the noontime heat and the thickness of the magnolia-scented air, Evangeline and her party fall asleep in their pirogue.

> *Nearer, and ever nearer, among the numberless islands,*
> *Darted a light, swift boat, that sped away o'er the water,*
> *Urged on its course by the sinewy arms of the hunters and trappers.*
> *Northward its prow was turned, to the land of the bison and the beaver.*
> *At the helm sat a youth, with countenance thoughtful and careworn.*
> *Dark and neglected locks overshadowed his brow, and a sadness*
> *Somewhat beyond his years on his face was legibly written.*
> *Gabriel was it, who, weary with waiting, unhappy and restless,*
> *Sought in the Western wilds oblivion of self and of sorrow.*
> *Swiftly they glided along, close under the lee of the island,*
> *But by the opposite bank, and behind a screen of palmettos,*
> *So that they saw not the boat, where it lay concealed in the willows;*
> *All undisturbed by the dash of their oars, and, unseen, were the sleepers.*
> *Angel of God was there none to awaken the slumbering maiden.*

As melodrama, this is hard to beat, however much of a smile it may bring to a modern reader, who can hear the silent-movie-house piano player banging away in the background. Yet it touched deftly—and as quickly as Gabriel's boat—on that great theme of loss that characterizes so much of American sentimental poetry. And it represents a real-life moment—two loved ones narrowly missing each other because of some accident of travel—that must have been a wrenching everyday experience in an age of less than reliable communications. The touch of genius is, of course, that these are not ships that pass in the night (to borrow a phrase from Longfellow's "Elizabeth" in *Tales of a Wayside Inn*): Evangeline and Gabriel miss each other in the full light of the blazing Louisiana sun.

She does not get near to him again for some twenty years, although there are several close misses. But it is in her western wanderings, through the Ozarks and into the Great Plains, among the Indians and the trappers, that Evangeline proves herself a literally epic hero. Her beauty fades, yet her wanderings rival (and in duration surpass) those of Ulysses.

> *Thus did the long sad years glide on, and in seasons and places*
> *Divers and distant far was seen the wandering maiden;—*
> *Now in the Tents of Grace of the meek Moravian Missions,*
> *Now in the noisy camps and the battle-fields of the army,*
> *Now in secluded hamlets, in towns and populous cities.*
> *Like a phantom she came, and passed away unremembered.*
> *Fair was she and young, when in hope began the journey;*
> *Faded was she and old, when in disappointment it ended.*
> *Each succeeding year stole something away from her beauty,*
> *Leaving behind it, broader and deeper, the gloom and the shadow.*
> *Then there appeared and spread faint streaks of gray o'er her forehead,*
> *Dawn of another life, that broke o'er her earthly horizon,*
> *As in the eastern sky the first faint streaks of the morning.*

The depiction of Evangeline's triumph over a hostile environment was Longfellow's great achievement, in a poem too often dismissed as a stale endorsement of nineteenth-century patriarchy and the importance of female loyalty to a husband. His Evangeline is not so much a person as an idea in motion: not simply the conventional idea of feminine constancy, but the larger idea—which manages to be both personal and political—that it is only a woman who can set things to order again, who can mend that which has been ripped apart, who can heal the wounds men have inflicted. When Evangeline, now a nursing sister, finally meets the dying Gabriel in the Philadelphia charity hospital, their reunion stands for the bringing together again of all the scattered Acadians—indeed, of all exiled peoples—in an imagined world where the Christian charity of women has redeemed the misdeeds of men. Certainly this helps explain why Evangeline, an almost totally invented character, became the foundational myth of Acadian ethnic identity in the late nineteenth and early twentieth centuries (and, to a very large degree, remains so today, in maritime Canada, northern Maine, and 'Cajun Louisiana). She was a plaster saint to some, but her very lack of definition made her all the more able to receive whatever meanings Longfellow's many readers sought to pour into her.

Recent scholarship on gender relations in nineteenth-century American culture has revealed *Evangeline* as a much more fruitful and complex achievement than it had seemed in the heyday of purely formalist criticism. For one thing, in celebrating his heroine's constancy in the face of so much ill fortune, so many undeserved setbacks, Longfellow is celebrating his own patient and long-suffering quest for Fanny's love. And he has turned the received notion of gender on its head: in a world that validates male achievement, male heroism, male ingenuity, his Evangeline is a person of considerable agency, a woman who survives by her wits over a sprawling, untamed American wilderness that had crippled or destroyed many of the men who had ventured there. The great American theme of conquest, of marching to destiny's drumbeat ever westward, is subtly undermined by this persistent little Acadian farm girl, who takes on the vast continent and survives, only to return east to her greater destiny. There, amid the cholera victims, the Sister of Mercy finds the aged Gabriel, who survives long enough to recognize her and lay his dying head on her bosom. How long she survives him, tending the sick, the poet does not say, but the implication is that she is soon buried beside him.

> *Still stands the forest primeval; but far away from its shadow,*
> *Side by side, in their nameless graves, the lovers are sleeping.*

Under the humble walls of the little Catholic churchyard,
In the heart of the city, they lie, unknown and unnoticed.
Daily the tides of life go ebbing and flowing beside them,
Thousands of throbbing hearts, where theirs are at rest and forever,
Thousands of aching brains, where theirs no longer are busy,
Thousands of toiling hands, where theirs have ceased from their labors,
Thousands of weary feet, where theirs have completed their journey!

Evangeline: A Tale of Acadie was finished in February of 1847 and heavily edited by the poet's friends Sumner, Hillard, and Felton (who paid particular attention to correcting the meter). By way of relief, Longfellow immediately began his comic prose tale, *Kavanagh*, which was to owe a good deal of its New England village subject matter to his sojourns at the Verandah and, more important, in Pittsfield, in the Berkshire hills of western Massachusetts.

A daughter, named Frances after her mother, was born on April 7—the first recorded use of ether in childbirth in America. ("The effect was magical," Longfellow wrote to his mother. "All pain instantly ceased. . . ." He was so impressed, he went to Boston the next day and had a broken tooth "extracted under the etherial vapor.") It seems particularly fitting that a poet whose work so often attempts to assuage the reader's pain should have encouraged his wife to undergo so controversial a procedure. The controversy was not over anesthesia's unknown risks (it was soon discovered that ether actually prolonged labor), but over the conventional religious view that the pain of childbirth was something God intended women to have to endure.

Evangeline was published by William D. Ticknor & Co. on November 1, 1847, although Longfellow dated some presentation copies October 30 so that he could say that the baby was christened and the new poem published on the same day. Hawthorne soon wrote: "I have read Evangeline with more pleasure than it would be decorous to express. It cannot fail, I think, to prove the most triumphant of all your successes." This may have been pure friendliness, but it proved prophetic: no other work of Longfellow's was to have so deep and enduring an impact on the world. The poem was a popular sensation, even if some critics disliked the hexameters or found the heroine "insipid." By the summer of 1848, with *Evangeline* in its sixth printing, Longfellow was the most famous writer in America.

Hawthorne repeated his praise in public, declaring in the *Salem Advertiser* that a lesser writer would only have brought out the "gloom and wretchedness" of the story; "it required the true poet's deeper insight to present it to us, as we find it here, its pathos illuminated with beauty,—so that the impression of the poem is nowhere dismal nor dispondent, and glows with the purest sunshine where we might least expect it, on the pauper's death-bed." John Greenleaf Whittier, writing in the Washington abolitionist paper, *The National Era*, exclaimed: "Eureka!—Here, then, we have it at last! An American poem, with the lack of which British reviewers have so long reproached us." A learned but anonymous reviewer in the *American Literary Magazine*, on the other hand, felt uneasy about the hexameters (indeed, picked many of them apart) and warned that "it is still a hazardous experiment to force the English language into that mold." Typical of the briefer reviews that appeared in most American newspapers was the *Examiner's* comment: "It is a tale of simple earnestness, very graceful, and amid its unexaggerated truthfulness animated by a tranquil and lofty spirit of endurance." *Evangeline* soon found British admirers as well. *Fraser's Magazine* reported: "This is an American poem, full of beauties of really indigenous American growth; and we hail its appearance with the greater satisfaction, inasmuch as it is the first genuine Castalian fount which has burst from the soil of America."

Longfellow was inundated with letters from admirers. Among those that touched him most deeply was one from Laura Bridgman, the world-famous young woman who was deaf, dumb, and blind yet had learned to communicate with her fingers. She was the star pupil at the Perkins Institute for the Blind, in South Boston, one of the most successful of Samuel Gridley Howe's many reform efforts. (Dickens had written warmly of the Institute in his *American Sketches*.) Early in 1852, her teacher Emma Goodwin had "read" *Evangeline* to Bridgman, who was delighted by the story and talked about it for days. "I am so much interested in thinking of Evangeline who devoted all her time in doing so very much good to the sick and afflicted people during her life," Bridgman wrote the poet. He replied, "Certainly I have never received any commendation of that poem so valuable as this, or that goes so directly to the heart." Her teacher told a newspaper reporter that one of Bridgman's few bad habits was kicking cats, for which she had an antipathy, "though generally humane and gentle." One day she asked Goodwin if Evangeline had ever kicked a cat. "I told her no, Evangeline would never have been rude towards anyone. She looked the picture of humiliation, and has not been so vindictive against her enemy, the cat, since."

Public acceptance of *Evangeline* despite its unfamiliar meter brought great satisfaction to Longfellow, but he was unable to enjoy his good fortune for very long. On September 9, 1848, the day after Longfellow had finished reading a life of Keats, he became alarmed by little Frances's ill health. The doctor was at first reassuring, only to change his mind the next day. "A day of agony, of doubt and fear!" Longfellow wrote in his journal. "The physicians have no longer any hope. I cannot yet abandon it. Motionless, she lies; only a little moan now and then escaping from her lips." He sat with the doctor watching her through the night. "Lower and lower. Through the silent, desolate room the clocks tick loud; they all seem laboring on with the fatal hour!" At 4:30 p.m. on the 11th, she died, aged one year, five months. "Fanny and [her sister] Mary sat with me by her bed side. Her breathing grew fainter, fainter—fainter, and ceased with a sigh, without a flutter—perfectly quiet, perfectly painless. The sweetest expression was on her face. Death seemed lovelier than life." She was buried at noon on the 12th at Mount Auburn Cemetery. The previous day, her elderly nurse had carried her body down the Craigie House stairs, through Longfellow's study, and into the library, where prayers were said and she was placed in her coffin. "For a long time I sat by her alone in the darkened Library. The twilight fell softly on her placid face and the white flowers she held in her little hands. In the deep silence the bird sang from the hall, a sad strain—a melancholy requiem. It touched and soothed me." He found some relief the next day in the routine of college work. Visiting the damp and chilly cemetery that afternoon with the other children, Longfellow was told by Charley that little Fanny had gone up into the sky. "Who told you that?" "Mama." "What is she doing there?" "She is playing with the rain; and throwing it down on me." Longfellow asked himself a few days later if this death had paralyzed his affections for his other children. "Can this be? No, they are but deadened and benumbed for a moment." He was to deal with his grief in the poem "Resignation," one of his most popular short pieces among his Victorian readers.

> There is no flock, however watched and tended,
> But one dead lamb is there!
> There is no fireside, howsoe'er defended,
> But has no vacant chair. . . .

The poem, published in *The Seaside and the Fireside* in 1849, affirms his belief in a Providence whose workings are mysterious but ultimately benign:

> Let us be patient! These severe afflictions
> Not from the ground arise
> But oftentimes celestial benedictions
> Assume this dark disguise. . . .

Death is but a transition, a portal to "a suburb of the life elysian," where little Fanny lives on, "Safe from temptation, safe from sin's pollution." Her family will meet her again, not as a helpless infant, but "a fair maiden, in her Father's mansion. / Clothed with celestial grace."

This struck a plangent chord among his contemporaries. It was somehow reassuring not only that a family so blessed in all those things that should vouchsafe happiness in this world could be afflicted by such a loss, but that a male poet should share his grief so publicly. This would later be condemned as sentimentality. More recently, however, Longfellow's work has been celebrated for that very quality, for we are beginning to understand how powerful and positive a role sentiment played in the reception of poetry among Longfellow's nineteenth-century readers. Most of them would also have found it reassuring to learn that, despite his religious liberalism, Longfellow still believed in a life after death and a reunion of loved ones in some more perfect form. Even a reader who approached this poem unaware of the circumstances of the poet's personal loss would immediately recognize the truth of the sentiments; it cannot be emphasized enough what a role infant mortality played in the nineteenth-century public's eagerness for a certain type of poetry, and how skillfully Longfellow in particular met that need. What Longfellow called "the heart's deep history" had found its chronicler of love and loss.

· Ten ·

"SAIL ON, O UNION..."

O N THE EVENING OF FEBRUARY 12, 1850, the British actress Fanny Kemble stood before an audience of more than three thousand people at the Boston Music Hall for one of her much heralded "readings"—a one-woman dramatization of a play by Shakespeare, on this occasion *As You Like It*, sponsored by the Mercantile Library Association. But the real event that evening was her recital afterwards of a contemporary poem, Longfellow's "The Building of the Ship," which had been published the previous year in his collection *The Seaside and the Fireside*. Standing alone on stage at her reading desk, her hands trembling, her voice palpitating, tears in her eyes, she gave every word, as the poet noted in his journal, "its true weight and emphasis." She explained to the audience that when she had first seen the poem, she had desired to read it to a Boston audience, and there she was. Mrs. Kemble was herself an international celebrity—the Vanessa Redgrave of her day, in her membership in a famous theatrical family, in her unparalleled ability as an actress, in her controversial public stands (against slavery and in favor of a woman's right to divorce)—and she was particularly close to the Longfellow family. In the previous year, Longfellow had surprised the actress at supper at the Craigie House by presenting her with his sonnet "On Mrs. Kemble's Readings from Shakespeare." Now she repaid the tribute. "The Building of the Ship" is a poem that insists on being read aloud, and on that particular evening at the Music Hall the poem found its true echo in the cheering of the crowd.

There were similar reactions throughout the North and West. The year of 1850 was to prove a watershed in the country's movement toward disunion and war. The Fugitive Slave Act and Daniel Webster's apostasy in supporting it were to radicalize many New Englanders. Yet few wanted to believe that war between North and South was actually possible, much less desirable. A nationalist poem such as "The Building of the Ship" touched a deep emotion. Hearing a young man recite the poem one day, Lincoln, too, was moved to tears. "It is a wonderful gift to be able to stir men like that," he said.

It was not the only poem of note in *The Seaside and the Fireside*— "Seaweed" and "The Fire of Drift-Wood" are two of Longfellow's very best lyrics—but none others attracted so devoted a readership. It was as if the Union suddenly had a national poem, and even Southern readers could respond positively to its appeal for transsectional cooperation and sympathy. Looking to Schiller's "Song of the Bell" for inspiration, Longfellow had perfected a metaphor that expressed everyone's prayer that war would not come. He chose the quintessentially New England trade of ship building for his ostensible subject, although, despite his Portland childhood and European voyages, he did not actually know much about marine construction and had to look the details up in an encyclopedia. Nonetheless, the poem sounds authentically nautical. He weaves together two stories—the actual building of a merchant vessel and the romance between the master's daughter and the builder.

> *"Thus," said he, "will we build this ship!*
> *Lay square the blocks upon the slip,*
> *And follow well this plan of mine.*
> *Choose the timbers with greatest care;*
> *Of all that is unsound beware;*
> *For only what is sound and strong*
> *To this vessel shall belong.*
> *Cedar of Maine and Georgia pine*
> *Here together shall combine.*
> *A goodly frame, and a goodly fame,*
> *And the UNION be her name!*
> *For the day that gives her to the sea*
> *Shall give my daughter unto thee!"*

This conflation of the national romance and the personal one continues as the stately vessel takes form. But the section that reduced grown men and women to tears comes at the end, in a stanza that begins with these much-quoted lines:

> *Thou, too, sail on, O Ship of State!*
> *Sail on, O Union, strong and great!*
> *Humanity with all its fears,*
> *With all the hopes of future years,*
> *Is hanging breathless on thy fate!*

Longfellow's work of the 1850s rarely strikes so obviously political a note; compared to Whittier, say, he would have seemed to have avoided politics altogether. Moreover, he famously avoided public speaking, a necessity in those days for anyone seeking office. Throughout the 1840s and early 1850s, he remained a firm if undemonstrative Whig, adhering to the party of respectability and moderate, pro-tariff Beacon Hill conservatism. While his antislavery sentiments were never in doubt, he avoided direct criticism of the South, somewhat in the spirit of "cedar of Maine and Georgia pine." After all, his sister Mary had married James Greenleaf, a Boston cotton broker, and they lived much of the year in New Orleans. Moreover, the Appleton family fortunes were still very much linked to the textile industry, which depended on an uninterrupted supply of Southern cotton for its New England mills. At a low point in his relations with the Appletons, the outspokenly antislavery Sumner had famously denounced Fanny's father and his mill-owning associates for their alliance of "the lords of the lash and the lords of the loom."

In this context, Longfellow's 1849 venture back into prose—the rural sketch entitled *Kavanagh*—can be read as an allegory of the foolishness of political or any other kind of partisanship. Ostensibly a mild satire on small-town convention and unreflective Calvinism, *Kavanagh* traces the paths of the leading residents of a Berkshire-like village over several years. It is so slight a piece—more a pastel than a sketch—that it almost resists paraphrase, but it has considerable wit and charm (in the style its author associated with the German writer Jean Paul). *Kavanagh* sets the tone for a later generation of New England "local color" writing, notably the work of Sarah Orne Jewett, a good friend of Longfellow's after the Civil War, when she shared a house with Annie Fields, the widow of publisher James T. Fields. *Kavanagh* has one other distinction: it depicts what is probably the first lesbian relationship in American fiction. Alice Archer's passion for Cecilia Vaughan is not just a schoolgirl crush: when the tale's male ingenu replaces her in Cecilia's affections, Alice literally wastes away in grief. Longfellow may have been influenced by his own close friendship with the great American actress Charlotte Cushman, whose longterm relationship with a younger woman was widely known and generally unquestioned by her adoring public.

Kavanagh also gave Longfellow the opportunity to make an important statement vis-à-vis the literary politics of the day: whether American literature ought to be exclusively American—in subject matter, diction, audience. Asked what he thought of "our national literature," Longfellow's fictional alter ego Mr. Churchill replies:

> "Simply, that a national literature is not the growth of a day. Centuries must contribute their dew and sunshine to it. Our own is growing slowly but surely, striking its roots downward, and its branches upward, as is natural; and I do not wish, for the sake of what some people call originality, to invert it, and try to make it grow with its roots in the air. And as for having it so savage and wild as you want it, I have only to say, that all literature, as well as all art, is the result of culture and intellectual refinement.... As the blood of all nations is mingling with our own, so will their thoughts and feelings finally mingle in our literature. We shall draw from the Germans, tenderness; from the Spanish, passion; from the French, vivacity,—to mingle more and more with our English solid sense. And this will give us universality, so much to be desired."

While pursuing this ideal of universality in his own poetry and teaching, and especially in his labors as a translator, Longfellow nonetheless never could turn his back on "the matter of New

England." In 1858, for example, he published one of his most popular and influential works, *The Courtship of Miles Standish*, a romantic, in places even comic, "epic" of life in the early Plymouth Colony. Embellishing a story about the courtship of his own maternal ancestors, Priscilla Mullen and John Alden, Longfellow was able to satirize the blustery and vainglorious ways of the Pilgrims' military leader, Captain Standish, a *miles gloriosus* in the tradition of Renaissance comedy. The mild-mannered Alden finally does "speak for himself" and wins the hand of Priscilla, who proves the strongest character of the three. Seated at her famous spinning wheel, she achieves a long life of her own beyond Longfellow's text, as an icon of colonial femininity (at once demure and spunky) and the inspiration for a Colonial Revival wave of "Pilgrim Century" reproduction furniture. In the early twentieth century, her face would launch a thousand advertising campaigns, from detergents to life insurance.

The 1850s represent the happiest period of Longfellow's own long life. Indeed his existence at the Craigie House amid his growing family and his ever-increasing international fame seemed almost too good to be true. His fellow Saturday Club member Oliver Wendell Holmes once told a friend that he trembled every time he drove past the Craigie House, "for those who lived there had their happiness so perfect that no change, of all the changes which must come to them, could fail to be for the worse." One immediate change, however, was for the better: in 1854, Longfellow finally felt he was financially secure enough to cease teaching at Harvard (which, five years later, gave him an honorary degree).

His popularity made him a celebrity on the scale of Jenny Lind and Charles Dickens. He sold twenty-five thousand copies of *Miles Standish* within the first two months (plus another ten thousand copies on the first day in London). Looking over his literary earnings in 1857, Longfellow calculated that he had sold the following number of books:

Voices of the Night	43,500
Ballads and Other Poems	40,470
The Spanish Student	38,400
The Belfrey of Bruges	38,300
Evangeline	35,850
Seaside and Fireside	30,000
The Golden Legend	17,188
The Song of Hiawatha	50,000
Outre-Mer	7,500
Hyperion	14,550
Kavanagh	10,500

The improvements to the Craigie House (whose interior in this decade more or less assumed the form the visitor sees today), the formal garden and new lilacs and elms set out by Longfellow himself, the property acquired between the house and the river to protect his view, the quiet, cool summers in the cottage at Nahant—all these were outward signs of an inner security and an at-homeness with the world. Life had its ennuis, to be sure: the unceasing stream of visitors (virtually anyone respectable who came to the door and asked decently was admitted), the importunate letters from strangers (for autographs, money, criticism of their poetry), the persistent attacks of "neuralgia" (possibly chronic sinusitis) and severe eyestrain (during which Fanny read to him and wrote out his letters). But none of these nuisances spoiled his sense of equilibrium.

This quiet possession of himself comes through in many of the poems collected in the 1850s under the title *Birds of Passage*. The collection included his Portland poems "My Lost Youth" and "The Ropewalk" as well as such small gems as "In the Churchyard at Cambridge" and "Snow-Flakes." It also included one of the greatest American poems of the century, the elegy "The Jewish Cemetery at Newport."

Visiting Newport in 1852, early in its career as a fashionable summer resort, Longfellow had seen not only the bogus "Viking tower" (in fact the ruin of an eighteenth-century mill), which helped inspire his popular "Skeleton in Armor"), but also the somewhat neglected cemetery laid out in pre-Revolutionary times by the seaport's small (and by Longfellow's time long vanished) Jewish community.

> *The trees are white with dust, that o'er their sleep*
> *Wave their broad curtains in the south-wind's breath,*
> *While underneath these leafy tents they keep*
> *The long, mysterious Exodus of Death. . . .*
>
> *How came they here? What burst of Christian hate,*
> *What persecution, merciless and blind,*
> *Drove o'er the sea — that desert desolate —*
> *These Ishmaels and Hagars of mankind?*

The narrator of the poem transforms the eighteenth-century genre of the graveyard elegy into something more piercing, as he reflects on the pride and humiliation of an accursed and mocked people, never at home until they find the grave—and now (as far as he can tell) a dead nation that never will rise again. Amid the crude boosterism and often vicious nativism of antebellum America, the poem stands out as a small beacon of sympathy for the oppressed and the maligned, a celebration of a vanished "race" for whom few others gave a thought.

The decade that had begun with Mrs. Kemble's soaring recitation of Longfellow's plea for national unity soon experienced a crisis of sectionalism that seemed to deepen each year. As the Whig Party fell to pieces amid this sectional strife, Longfellow found himself more and more drawn toward the new Republican Party—a successful coalition of abolitionists, nativists, antislavery Whigs, and Free Soilers, in which Charles Sumner had rapidly emerged as the Massachusetts leader. To the distress of "proper" Boston, Sumner was elected by the General Court to a seat in the U.S. Senate in 1851, and he proceeded to use this national platform as a rallying point for the antislavery cause. The dispute between North and South was suddenly brought home to the Longfellows in 1856 when their friend was almost killed at his seat in the Senate chamber. A deranged South Carolinian, offended by a remark Sumner had made in debate with the assailant's kinsman, approached the Senator from behind as he was writing letters at his desk. He beat Sumner unconscious with a heavy cane. The North was outraged—the incident confirmed suspicions that Southerners lacked self-control and were quick to turn violent and lawless—while the South congratulated the assailant, Congressman Preston Brooks, for teaching a "scoundrel" a lesson. Admirers sent Brooks new canes.

Like most people throughout the country, Longfellow still thought secession could be avoided. Yet, like many of his Boston friends, he privately applauded John Brown's bold though bloody raid and predicted the South would soon reap the whirlwind of slave revolt, which it had sown. When Lincoln won on the Republican ticket in 1860, Longfellow was elated: "It is the redemption of the country. Freedom is triumphant." He did not realize how long that victory would take, or what a price his own family would pay.

Eleven

HIAWATHA

LONGFELLOW'S GREATEST ACHIEVEMENT in the decade before the Civil War might seem at first an attempt to escape into a world of fantasy. *The Song of Hiawatha* is a very odd poem, but there was something inevitable about Longfellow's writing it. From his early youth he had been fascinated by tales of Native Americans. The many thousands of Wabanakis—"the people of the dawn"—who had once inhabited the coast of Maine had dwindled to a few hundred by his day, enduring a marginal existence, often literally on the edge of the line of white settlement, eking out a living as trappers and woodsmen and guides. Yet a communal memory remained among the whites from more frightening times, when the Native Americans and their French allies had come close to driving the English from Maine. "Indian Massacre Creek" passed near Longfellow's grandfather's Gorham farm; stories of the natives' raids in the seventeenth century gave a grim aura to Deering's Woods. The young poet's first work celebrated the heroism of the ill-fated whites at Lovell's Pond.

As a Bowdoin undergraduate poet, Longfellow occasionally turned to Native American themes. As a Bowdoin professor, in 1832, he took the occasion of a review of Sir Philip Sidney's *The Defence of Poesy* in the *North American Review* to champion this uniquely American poetic source. He cited as an example the last words of Pushmataha, the Choctaw chief who had died in Washington in 1824.

> I shall die, but you will return to your brethren. As you go along the paths, you will see the flowers, and hear the birds; but Pushmataha will see and hear them no more. When you come to your home, they will ask

you, where is Pushmataha? and you will say to them, He is no more. They will hear the tidings *like the sound of the fall of a mighty oak in the stillness of the wood* [his italics].

Longfellow, as we have seen, did not retain that degree of aggressive literary nationalism, but his thoughts on the Choctaw chief reflect a view he and most of his white contemporaries held throughout the nineteenth century: the "child-like" indigenous people may have been noble, may have been savage, may have been something of both, but their day had passed, and it was time they either accepted assimilation into Euro-American culture or moved on to less settled lands. They were literally a dying race.

This racial notion had been expressed in a great variety of literary productions during the first half of the century, notably the many theatrical versions of the life and death of the once-feared King Philip, or Metamora, the Native American warrior who had terrorized the Massachusetts Bay Colony. In Longfellow's own case, the paradigm of rise and decline had been confirmed by his reading of the eighteenth-century Italian philosopher Giambattista Vico, in whose cyclical history of mankind poets played the crucial role of first lawgivers. It was also a truism of the Romantic movement, most powerfully expressed by Herder then taken up by many poets in Germany, Britain, and America, that it was in native languages—Germanic, Scandinavian, even North American Indian—that the uniqueness of cultures is expressed. When Longfellow set out in the mid 1850s to write his "Indian Edda," he had these notions of the cycles of civilization and the poetic power of aboriginal languages firmly in mind. Familiar with paintings such as Thomas Cole's *The Course of Empire* of 1836—with its five large canvases depicting the movement of humankind from the savage state, to the pastoral one, and on through consummation, destruction, and desolation—his potential audience was already primed for a world-historical drama of the rise and fall of nations.

Of all of Longfellow's works, *The Song of Hiawatha* is the only one still capable of exciting controversy. A standard reading of it by modern academics is that it is a derivative poem rendered "unreadable" by its failure to understand the true nature of Native American oral literature and its dismissal of the full extent of that people's tragedy. The notion that it is "racist" has filtered down and makes this once-popular work "unteachable" in the school as well as university classroom. The case for the prosecution is summed up by Helen Carr in her *Inventing the American Primitive* (1996). "These assumptions of Indian childlike deficiency form the perceptual grid by which Longfellow patterned his sources. Longfellow consistently altered his material so that he infantilised, de-historicized, and, through excessive idealisation, de-humanized the Indians." Despite the poet's apparent sympathy for his Indian heroes, Carr goes on to say that his "consoling myth was as essential to the dispossession of the Indians as the raucous racism of the frontiersmen, or the legalistic exclusion of the Indian from natural rights in the government's bureaucratic language."

There have been more sympathetic readers. In *Lives of the Poets* (1998), Michael Schmidt calls *Hiawatha* "a literary poem pretending to belong to the oral tradition and guaranteed, when read aloud to small children, to fill them briefly with wonder and then with sleep." More recently, Alan Trachtenberg describes "Longfellow up to his own civilized magic, as if reading the poem were an encounter with first things, the primordial, the aboriginal." Longfellow's own contemporaries tended either to love the poem or to be confused by its meter and its frequent use of only slightly anglicized Native American names. In November of 1855, four months after his famous letter to Walt Whitman praising the "largeness" of *Leaves of Grass*, Emerson wrote to Longfellow: "I have always one foremost satisfaction in reading your books—that I am safe." He called Hiawatha a "wholesome" poem, "sweet and wholesome as maize; very proper and pertinent for us to read, and showing a kind of manly duty in the poet to write." He added: "The dangers of the Indians are, they are really savage, have poor, small, sterile heads,—no thoughts; and you must deal roundly with them, and find in them brains. And I blamed your tenderness now and then, as I read, in accepting a legend or song, when they have so little to give." Longfellow thought otherwise.

To understand *Hiawatha*, it helps to follow Longfellow's path in writing it. He had long pondered an Indian epic. But it was not until his discovery in early June of 1854 of the "charming" Finnish national epic, the *Kalevala*, that he figured out a way to do it. By June 22, his concept had taken shape:

> I have at length hit upon a plan for a poem on the Indians, which seems to me the right one, and the only. It is to weave together their beautiful traditions into a whole. I have hit upon a measure, too, which I think the right and only one for such a theme. At present it delights me. Let us see how it will prosper.

What the *Kalevala* provided him was not a fund of stories to adapt (the approach he had taken to other European sources), but the suggestion of a meter that sounded "primitive" and the organizing principle of a central hero around whom any number of more or less disparate tales could be linked. Although he had a smattering of Finnish, he had to read the epic in a German translation, removing him one more length from the raciness and occasional grotesqueness of the original.

"Original" is perhaps not quite the right word for the *Kalevala*, which is in fact an early-nineteenth-century assemblage of traditional, pre-Christian ballads, lyrics, and folk tales from the far northern region of what became Finland. The folklorist Elias Lönnrot had traveled as a doctor in the Karelian countryside in the early 1830s, collecting material that he published under the title of *Kalevala, or Poems of the Kaleva District* starting in 1835. Lönnrot's work as a folklorist and lexicographer is a case study par excellence in how literature can create national identity: the sense of a distinct Finnish identity (and eventual Finnish political independence) is a direct outgrowth of his work, as it was taken up by Finnish nationalists later in the century. The *Kalevala* can be said to have "invented" Finland.

But whatever clues Lönnrot's epic may have provided to writing an "Indian Edda"—the endings of the two poems, as pagan spiritualism

FIGURE 9: Hiawatha struggles with the giant pike, in Canto VIII of *The Song of Hiawatha* (1855), as illustrated by George H. Thomas in an 1861 British edition.

gives way to Christianity, do have vague similarities—Longfellow needed local material. This he found from a variety of books in the Harvard library and elsewhere, notably the protoethnographical accounts of the Indians of the Great Lakes region collected and published by Henry Rowe Schoolcraft. An Indian agent and geologist who had married a Chippewa, Schoolcraft was unscientific but earnest in his methods, and at least appreciated the fact that the tribal legends and chants that he was recording were in danger of disappearing. He was unusual among white Americans of his day in believing this material had any value. As he remarked, the study of Indian languages had been left to "the business of a class of men who were generally uneducated, and who, imbued strongly with the feelings and prejudices of their employers, sought no higher excellence in their profession than to express the common ideas connected with transactions of trade." As a result, the white population remained ignorant of Indian cultures, assuming such people were savages living as brutishly and as unselfconsciously as the animals of the forests. Schoolcraft began compiling an Ojibwa vocabulary—the source of all the names in Longfellow's poem except for "Hiawatha" (an Iroquois hero the poet confused with Schoolcraft's Manabozho)—and in 1839 published his *Algic Researches* (the name is derived from Allegheny and Atlantic, a reference to his tribes' reputed place of origin before being driven westward).

Longfellow rummaged through a number of other texts—for example, John G. Heckewelder's *History, Manners, and Customs of the Indian Nations* (1818)—and sought visual inspiration in the works of the painter and student of Native American life, George Catlin, whose writings, paintings, and staged performances by actual Indians, here and in Europe, had sparked some interest in their "unspoiled" culture. As a result, Longfellow's Indians dress and behave more like the Plains Indians among whom Catlin had lived than like actual Ojibwas. But Catlin had portrayed these tribesmen as powerful, noble, physically imposing characters, and this heroic idealization is carried over into the poem. And Longfellow remembered the Indians—mostly Fox and Sioux—he had seen visiting Boston in October of 1837. As he had written then in a letter:

> There are Indians here: savage fellows;—one Black-Hawk and his friends, with naked shoulders and red blankets wrapped around their bodies:—the rest all grease and spanish brown and vermillion. One carries a great war-club, and wears horns on his head; another has his face painted like a grid-iron, all in bars:—another is all red, like a lobster; and another black and blue, in great daubs of paint, laid on not spar-

ingly. Queer fellows! One great champion of the Fox nation had a short pipe in his mouth, smoking with great self-complacency as he marched out of the City Hall; and another was smoking a cigar! Withal, they looked very formidable. Hard customers.

On June 25, he began what he tentatively called "Monabozho": "His adventures will form the theme at all events." The next day, he looked over Schoolcraft's three volumes—"ill-digested, ill-arranged, and without any index" and tried writing a few lines. On the 27th, he wrote Monabozho's first adventure and lamentation for his brother. On the 28th, he changed his hero's name to the mellifluous Hiawatha—which he said ought to be pronounced "Hee-a-wa-tha"—in the mistaken belief that both figures were "the same Manito." Work was interrupted by his annual visit to Portland and the disruption of moving the family to Nahant, where the sea air always made it difficult to concentrate. Yet by July 25 he noted in his journal that the poem "goes on rapidly, and takes shape more and more." Three days later, he added, "If I had a hundred hands, I could keep all busy with 'Hiawatha.' Nothing ever absorbed me more." At month's end he exalted: "It is purely in the realm of Fancy."

Adding to his cantos—there would in the final version be twenty-two of them—as his family swam, rowed, picnicked, and read at Nahant (with a new work called *Walden* among the readings) became such a part of his daily routine, he mentioned *Hiawatha* in his journal only to complain of social interruptions. Upon the Longfellows' return to Cambridge, the news that the Harvard Corporation had accepted his long-delayed resignation brought both sadness and relief ("This separating one's self from one's former life! This breaking away from one's Past!"). In mid September he was "working away with Tanner, Heckewelder and sundry books about Indians" in search of further source material, while trying to disentangle a great mass of legends. The time once filled up with college duties, he found, was too often consumed with "other, little nameless things." By early October, however, he was polishing the first canto. Later that month he recorded: "'Hiawatha' occupies and delights me. Have I no misgivings

PLATE 14. Group portrait of, from left, Thomas Gold Appleton, John Gerard Cosler, Julia Ward Howe, Fanny, Henry, and Horatia Latilla Freeman. Newport, Rhode Island, 1852. Unknown photographer. Courtesy National Park Service, Longfellow National Historic Site.

PLATE 15. Albert Bierstadt, *Departure of Hiawatha*, 1868. Oil on canvas. Courtesy National Park Service, Longfellow National Historic Site.

PLATE 16. Carte-de-visite portrait of Frances Appleton Longfellow, c.1860. Unknown photographer. From the collection of Victor Gulotta, Newton, Massachusetts.

PLATE 17. "The Politics and Poetry of New England." U.S. senator Charles Sumner and Longfellow, Washington, D.C., 1863. Carte-de-visite photograph by Alexander Gardner. From the collection of Victor Gulotta, Newton, Massachusetts.

PLATE 18: Private Charles Appleton Longfellow, First Massachusetts Cavalry at White Oak Church, Virginia, March 30, 1863. Unknown tintypist. Courtesy Houghton Library, Harvard University.

PLATE 19. "A Gentleman of Kioto" (Charles Appleton Longfellow) 1872. Unknown photographer. Courtesy National Park Service, Longfellow National Historic Site.

PLATE 20. Charles Appleton's carp tattoo, 1872. Unknown photographer. Courtesy National Park Service, Longfellow National Historic Site.

PLATE 21. Longfellow in his Craigie House study, mid-1870s. Unknown photographer. Courtesy National Park Service, Longfellow National Historic Site.

PLATE 22. The Longfellow family in Venice, 1869. Standing, left to right: Samuel Longfellow, Alice, Thomas Gold Appleton, Ernest, Harriet Spelman Longfellow. Seated, left to right: Mary Longfellow Greenleaf, Edith, Henry, Anne Allegra, Anne Longfellow Pierce. Sorgato Studio. Courtesy National Park Service, Longfellow National Historic Site.

PLATE 23. Chromolithographic cigar box label commemorating Longfellow, c. 1900. From the collection of Victor Gulotta, Newton, Massachusetts.

PLATE 24. Cardboard stationery box in the shape of the Craigie House, c. 1890. The top came off, revealing a scene from "The Children's Hour." Louis Prang. Courtesy National Park Service, Longfellow National Historic Site.

PLATE 25. Longfellow and his daughter Edith in front of the Craigie House, c. 1875. Unknown photographer. Courtesy National Park Service, Longfellow National Historic Site.

PLATE 26. "Longfellow," Freshwater, Isle of Wight, 1868. By Julia Margaret Cameron. Courtesy National Park Service, Longfellow National Historic Site.

about it?—Yes—sometimes. Then the theme seizes me, and hurries me away, and they vanish." He found that a native idiom came naturally to him: Indian Summer he declared "a charming tradition in the Mythology of the Indians, that this soft hazy weather is made by the passionate sighs of Shawondasse or the South!"

In mid November he read some passages to his friend Scherb. "He likes the plan, and the execution; but fears the poem will want human interest. So does Fanny. So does the author. I must put a living beating heart into it." In December the mood left him, and the poem was set aside for almost two months. On January 11, 1855, he tried to take it up again. "But alas! I am out of the harness. How I regret it! The 'Day without a line' is a sad day to me." On the 18th, after having heard the great soprano Carlotta Grisi in *I Puritani* and *Lucrezia Borgia* in Boston, he took refuge from the snow to work at his poem. "It will get itself sung—to speak in Carlylese—one of these days." On the 22nd: "Morning 'Hiawatha.' Evening 'Norma'." He complained three days later: "We are so dissipated with all this Opera-going, that I can hardly bring myself to a working mood." He turned to Prescott on Peru to clear his head. But he could not resist *Don Giovanni* a few nights later. By late February he had completed eighteen cantos. On March 19 he began the last one.

> March 21. Read Sumner some Cantos of Hiawatha, which he likes; "Hiawatha's Sailing," and "Hiawatha's Wooing."
> After he goes finish the last Canto at twelve o'clock. Write to Fields.

He added another intermediate canto on "Picture-Writing" ("rather curious than poetical," perhaps in response to his friends' comments), and began the slow chore of revision. (In a burst of poetical enthusiasm amid an attack of influenza, he also wrote his Portland ode, "My Lost Youth," which came to him as he lay sleepless in bed. He was pleased to work into it two lines he remembered from an old Finnish song: "A boy's will is the wind's will/And the thoughts of youth are long, long thoughts.")

On May 11 he complained: "This re-writing a Poem, so long as

'Hiawatha,' is very wearisome, but very profitable; as one can better
see it as a whole, and fill up gaps. The work is nearly half over." Early
June brought proof sheets—"I am growing idiotic about the Song; and
no longer know whether it is good or bad"—and more opera (*Rigoletto*,
Masaniello, the last act of *Lucia*). The annual Portland visit was followed
by a family holiday in Newport, where he continued to correct proofs.

Longfellow himself had given the press a preview of his work, which
Fields followed up upon with an advance notice on July 24:

> A PROMISED LITERARY TREAT. Among the list of new works
> in press, we notice Ticknor & Fields announce a new poem by
> Longfellow. It is, we understand, a lengthy production, and the subject
> is an American one. We could not chronicle a pleasanter bit of news.

"'Lengthy!' a vile word!" added Longfellow to the clipping he
pasted in his journal.

Newport meant further social interruptions and unaccustomed
routines. He continued "vigorously" at the poem in their Perry Street
hotel. "But it is hard to write poetry in a closet, on a wash-stand, with
glare at the window and flies inside." In early August he saw some ex-
cerpts from Tennyson's new collection—"Very rich and dreamy"—
and some sheets sent by Fields from *Maud*, which he first found
"delicious" but about which he had second thoughts upon hearing
Curtis read it aloud. For all its beauty he found parts where Tennyson
had exhibited "a spirit of ferocity I do not like." Meanwhile negotia-
tions for British publication of his own poem continued: "Ticknor
says Bogue offers one hundred pounds for advance sheets of 'Hiawatha.' Tell him to accept." The question of "ferocity" arose in a different context.

On September 20 he noted:

> In great doubt about a Canto of Hiawatha, whether to retain it or
> suppress it. It is odd how confused one's mind becomes about such mat-
> ters, from long looking at the same subject.

At issue was how far Longfellow—and presumably Fields—thought
a poet selling to a broad popular audience could go in depicting the vi-

olence of the Indian legends. Caution won out. The owners of Ticknor & Fields were optimistic. On October 2, Ticknor presented Longfellow a check for a thousand dollars for the first edition of *The Song of Hiawatha*, already scheduled for a press run of five thousand. Sumner, at his habitual Sunday dinner at the Craigie House, tried to add to the celebration by reading aloud the last half of the poem. But his head cold made him hoarse, and the poem "very lugubrious."

November 10, 1855, was publication day, by which time more than four of the five thousand copies printed had been sold, and a new edition of three thousand ordered. This was an extraordinary success for a book of American poetry, and reports of British sales soon proved just as heartening. "Some of the newspapers are fierce and furious about 'Hiawatha,' which reminds me of the days when 'Hyperion' first appeared." Longfellow's excitement was dulled by weeks of severe headaches—"I have been a martyr to neuralgia," he wrote on November 30—and throbbing mouth pain that made him "a gloomy guest" at Thanksgiving. He noted that the reviewers were in "the greatest pother" about his epic: "It is violently assailed; and warmly defended," with a gratifying number of British papers coming out in his favor. Fields was gleeful, and by year's end some eleven thousand copies were in print. While the literati debated its trochaic meter and Longfellow's more hostile critics accused him of borrowing too freely from the *Kalevala*, the general public took instantly to the poem. It was eminently memorizable (Longfellow would be subjected to recitations from it for the rest of his life), and a skillful declaimer could subtly vary its otherwise insistent tom-tom beat. Above all—though this may seem a curious virtue—it lent itself immediately to parody. There were hundreds, possibly thousands, of parodies playing on its long native names and distinctive rhythm (the best of them in print being Lewis Carroll's "Hiawatha's Photographing"; Alice's White Rabbit comes from Canto II of *Hiawatha*.) Longfellow was bothered by these distortions of his work but took them as a vote of popular confidence. They did not hurt sales. His "Indian Edda" proved the most commercially successful of all his work.

Modern students of the poem—and their number has not been great—have tended to focus on what seems its most distinctive canto, "XIV. Picture-Writing," in which Hiawatha, realizing how fugitive is his people's culture, teaches a method of preserving it. As Angus Fletcher writes, "Hiawatha can be read as an implicit treatise on the nature of language. . . . the poem is all about language." Longfellow had succeeded in transliterating Native American words into pronounceable "English" to a degree, and over a span of verse, unequaled by his predecessors. (More typical was the early contemporary of his who rhymed Androscoggin with "noggin.") By avoiding rhyme altogether and relying instead on alliteration, repetition, and his four-beat measure, he created an aural environment that is neither "Indian" nor "Anglo." As several commentators have noted, Longfellow himself assumes Hiawatha's mantle as teacher, adding a glossary of Ojibwa vocabulary at the end of the poem for the benefit of his readers, and frequently translating names as they are given in the work—Minnehaha, "laughing water," being the most famous of them.

Shelley once said that the virtue of long narrative poems was that moments of true poetic intensity could be found amid all the connective tissue. This suggests one way of reading *The Song of Hiawatha* today. Take, for example, Canto XIII, "Blessing the Corn-fields." Longfellow seems to have instinctively grasped what later anthropologists would record—the prevalence across cultures of female fertility rites—and he paints his nocturne accordingly. But it has a distinctive sweetness of touch, amid its strangeness, which is not ethnologically truthful so much as Longfellovian:

> *In the night, when all is silence,*
> *In the night, when all is darkness,*
> *When the Spirit of Sleep, Nepháwin,*
> *Shuts the doors of all the wigwams,*
> *So that not an ear can hear you,*
> *So that not an eye can see you,*
> *Rise up from your bed in silence,*
> *Lay aside your garments wholly,*

Walk around the fields you planted,
Round the borders of the corn-fields,
Covered by your tresses only,
Robed with darkness as a garment.
Thus the trees shall be more fruitful,
And the passing of your footsteps
Draw a magic circle around them,
So that neither blight nor mildew,
Neither burrowing worm nor insect,
Shall pass o'er the magic circle. . . .

The poem is filled with these quiet moments amid the quasi-Wagnerian stagecraft of its battling monsters and treacherous neighbors, magic mittens and trickster-heroes.

There are at least two other ways of reading the poem. Several commentators have sought to historicize it. During the long preparation of the manuscript, Longfellow's journal is filled with references to runaway slaves, the iniquity of the Fugitive Slave Law, and Sumner's speeches in favor of abolition. With its opening panorama of the great peace-pipe ceremony uniting all the nations through its depiction of disease, famine, and treachery, *The Song of Hiawatha* in this view expresses both its author's hopes for peace and his anxiety that the nation would break apart.

The other approach is to accept the poem as a successful exercise in the passage-of-empire mode that so many of its critics have deplored. By this reading, *The Song of Hiawatha* becomes an anti-Aeneid, the song of the unmaking of a city. Hiawatha sets out to civilize his people, to tame the wild forces of nature that threaten them, to turn them into a settled and literate agricultural nation preserving its own culture while keeping peace with its neighbors. So often criticized for its episodic nature, the poem in fact has an overarching structure, reaching its height at the Wedding-Feast, and already declining—it is difficult to say by whose fault—long before the first sighting of the white man's footstep. But the reader can take no satisfaction in this fateful turn of events. When the white men do appear, and Hiawatha departs in his canoe "to the portals of the Sunset," it is not New Englanders who stand among the aboriginals. It is the Black-Robes, bringing French Catholic Christianity. The disappearance of this "race" in turn from the heartland of North America furnished the great theme for Longfellow's friend, the historian Francis Parkman. Two great empires had struggled for Hiawatha's land; each had failed. Longfellow can be read as asking us: what makes us think that we shall endure?

A Lock of Hair

SURVIVAL HAD ITS DOMESTIC DIMENSION AS
well. The Longfellows had already lost one infant, who died too young
to be photographed or painted, but of whom there remained in the
house a wisp of a blonde curl, wrapped in paper and labeled "Little
Fanny. Sept. 11. 1848." This precautionary tactic—the saving of locks
of children's hair—was more than a sentimental gesture in an age
when a minor illness could quickly turn fatal. When one of the three
girls of "The Children's Hour" had her hair cut on the hot afternoon
of July 9, 1861, their mother went to some trouble to collect a lock of
it, walk into the library, fold it into a little packet of paper, and seal it
with a stick of molten wax, softened over a candle. This was a rather
old-fashioned procedure, by 1861, but the act of sealing confirmed the
solemnity of the gesture. Precisely what happened next is not known.
A gust of wind may have spread the flame. Or Fanny may have brushed
her loose sleeve too close to it. Or the candle may have been knocked
over. In an instant the front of her gauzy summer housedress caught
fire. Its very lightness over its steel hoops hastened the flames, as the
pockets of air caught between the layers of cotton intensified the com-
bustion. She ran through a small vestibule into the front study where
Longfellow was sitting, possibly even dozing in the warm summer
weather. He tried throwing a rug around her, but it was too small. She
broke away, ran for the door, turned and rushed back toward him. The
flames must have been dying, for he was able to hug her in an attempt
to protect her face. By this point her lower body and torso (though not
her face) were badly burned, her dress destroyed; he suffered lesser
burns to his face and hands. Someone ran for the doctor while Fanny
was carried up to her room.

215

FIGURE 10: Ernest Longfellow's sketch of the meadow between
the Craigie House and the Charles River, 1855. Courtesy National
Park Service, Longfellow National Historic Site.

These details come from a letter Felton wrote the next day to
Sumner in Washington; he had presumably pieced them together
from the reports of the servants, the doctor, perhaps the police. Felton
was not certain which of the children were in the house, or how much
they had heard or seen during this rapid sequence of events, or how
much information Longfellow himself was able to piece together immediately afterward. "She bore the agony like a martyr dying at the
stake," Felton wrote. Finally given ether, probably some hours after
the accident, she sank into quiet but remained conscious through the
night. In the morning of July 10 she asked for coffee, lost consciousness, and died at ten minutes after ten.

For many years, this was the "official" version of Fanny's death, repeated by biographers and tourist guides alike as part of the legend of
the Craigie House. It is a gripping story, even in its incompleteness,

and it is reportedly the one thing about Longfellow ("his wife caught fire") that young schoolchildren are sure to remember.

Around 1908, however, Richard Henry Dana III—the son of the seafaring writer and the husband of Longfellow's daughter Edith—heard a different version of the story from the youngest daughter, Annie, who had become Mrs. Joseph Thorp. He had found a large folded paper in which two long curls of Edith's hair had been preserved since that day. He took them that evening to Mrs. Thorp, who instantly recognized the packet, which she had not seen for more than fifty-seven years. She related her version of the accident to Dana.

Her mother that afternoon had been lying on a small sofa on the east side of the library. Because of the warm weather, she decided to cut Edith's curls. When her daughter came downstairs, Fanny moved to a Spanish chair next to the window seat (where there is now a doorway) overlooking the piazza and garden. Five-year-old Annie sat to the right on the window seat, her feet not touching the ground; Edith was at her mother's left. Annie began to play with a box of "parlor" matches —designed to ignite on any rough surface—putting them in and out of their box. One of these matches fell to the floor under Fanny's white muslin dress. Annie slid down to pick it up, but either she or her mother stepped on it, causing the match to flare and the underside of the dress to catch fire.

The packet of hair had been folded but not yet sealed; the little candle used for such purposes had not even been lit. Fanny did not panic but walked through the passageway into her husband's study. He was asleep in the big armchair to the left of the fireplace. She called out: "Henry!" He awoke, seized the hearth rug, wrapped it around her. He told Annie to run upstairs for the servants, who were on the third, or attic, floor. He took Fanny into the front hall, where she fainted at the foot of the stairs. The decorative oil cloth that covered the floor was marked by the still unextinguished flames. Longfellow ran in with the water-pitcher from the dining room. Servants helped carry Fanny upstairs to her bedroom and began what proved a difficult search for a doctor. That was the last Edith and Anne Allegra saw of their mother. They were sent immediately to the Dana house on Berkeley Street, where they stayed until after the funeral. Alice had been out of the house, visiting the Spelmans' daughters, when these events took place, and the two boys were at Nahant.

Dana added in his typed memorandum on this conversation, which is among his papers (along with the locks of hair) at the Massachusetts Historical Society: "Mr. Longfellow never spoke to his children about their mother's death and the next Christmas they received presents marked as from their mother." He went on to say: "Annie felt that it had been her fault and she used sometimes to say she had killed her mother. Her father had to tell her not to say that, that it was not so, that it was an accident, etc. It affected her, however, very much to think that she was to blame and she became so oppressed with this and so solemn that her father said, 'I used to call you Allegra; I shall now call you Penserosa.'

"It is a strange fact that Edith told me that she thought that she was the one playing with the matches and felt that it was her fault, but Mrs. Thorp's recollection is so clear and vivid and she so frequently said that it was her fault before others, that it seems as if her recollection must be better than Edith's. Annie so distinctly remembers the box being near her, her dropping the match, and her slipping down from the seat to pick it up."

Dana, a distinguished and fair-minded attorney, believed Mrs. Thorp's account. "[H]er accurate description of the curls and just how the paper was folded, which she had not seen for 57 years, borne out absolutely by them when discovered, shows how vivid was her recollection."

❧

"Poor Longfellow: he was dreadfully but not fatally burned," Felton reported to Sumner. "He has been under ether and laudanum ever since: wanders: thinks he is growing idiotic, begs not to be sent to an asylum: could not see Fanny when she was dying." There had been very little the doctor could do to save her. According to a medical writer of the day, burn victims fell into two categories: those whose burns were superficial enough to be treated with salves or dressings, and those whose burns were so deep, there was nothing to do but try to ease their pain until they died.

She was buried at Mt. Auburn on July 13, the eighteenth anniversary of their wedding day. The funeral had been held at noon in the library—"the scene of so many pleasures, and of one awful tragedy," Felton told Sumner—with her coffin on a table in the center, covered with flowers, white roses across her breast and a bridal-like wreath of orange blossoms around her head. Longfellow, still heavily sedated, was in bed and unable to attend. At the cemetery Felton pulled a rose from her coffin and enclosed a leaf of it to Sumner.

> The coffin was at length closed, and I slowly walked away, oppressed by a weight of sorrow that no words can tell: yet filled with a sense of the soothing power of nature, the harmony of the scene with the character of Fanny, and the surpassing sweetness of every memory connected with her beautiful and happy life.

> I have not seen Longfellow. He has seen no one yet out of his immediate family. I dread to think of him bereaved of Fanny: she was so perfect a companion of his daily existence, and sharer of his glory. But his children remain, and they must fill in part, her place. God help them all. The world henceforth will be strangely changed for him.

When Felton did see Longfellow four days later, he found him calm and reasonable and still suffering from his burns, especially on his hands, but he told his old friend that he slept best when the pain was greatest. Among the flood of letters, he read only a few, including those from Sumner and Hillard. A week later, his face was still too swollen for him to shave, but the burns on his nose and left cheek had healed, and by mid-August he was recuperating at Nahant. "How I am alive after what my eyes have seen, I know not," he wrote to Fanny's sister in London, in a long letter in pencil from "this haunted sea-shore.

So strong is the sense of her presence upon me, that I should hardly be surprized to meet her in our favorite walk, or, if I looked up now to see her in the room."

He worried about the children, who had suffered a double loss. After Fanny's funeral, her eighty-year-old father, confined by poor health to 39 Beacon Street, sat for the rest of the day holding a lily brought to him from her coffin, saying, "She has gone but a little while before me." A few days later he was buried beside her. The customary routines of life at the Craigie House eventually resumed, but Longfellow had the additional burden of being the only parent there. That summer, Charley was seventeen, Erny fifteen, Alice ten, Edith seven, and Annie five. In time Alice would grow into the role of mistress of the house and, to some degree, a surrogate mother for her sisters; she would in fact devote her life to this calling, never marrying, and taking on for herself curatorship of both her father's memory and his Cambridge house. (On a more modest scale, his widowed sister Anne Pierce would perform a similar commemorative role in the Portland house.) Meanwhile, there were a governess and servants, to be sure, but the children's hour had turned into a full day of responsibilities, followed by long nights of loneliness and grief.

Twelve

CHARLEY GOES TO WAR

I T IS DIFFICULT TO KNOW to what degree, if any, Longfellow's private sorrows were subsumed in the great national drama unfolding of secession and rebellion. Certainly Sumner kept him well informed of events in Washington. The unionist and pacifist hopes of some of his earlier poems having been crushed, Longfellow had already produced one rollicking nationalist war poem—"Paul Revere's Ride," published in the *Atlantic Monthly* in 1860, a year before the firing on Fort Sumter. He would go on to write some minor wartime lyrics, including the balladlike "Killed at the Ford," with its image of a bullet flying from the battlefield and into the home and heart of the dead soldier's loved one. But once again the events of the day failed to stir his poetic imagination, however deeply moved he may have been as a citizen (and he was moved, as numerous journal entries on the secession crisis and wartime politics attest). Nonetheless Longfellow threw himself into work, notably the extensive narratives of *Tales of a Wayside Inn* (published in three parts, starting in 1863) and his resumption of the massive project of translating *The Divine Comedy*.

Yet Felton was right in saying that he would find his world strangely changed. According to a much-publicized family tradition, Longfellow grew his beard to cover the scars left by his burns. This may be true. It certainly would have been difficult for him to shave in the weeks after the accident. Yet photographs of him from the mid 1860s on show no obvious scars, and the fullness of the beard suggests that it grew without the patchiness one would associate with permanently damaged skin. What is most dramatic in these images is the fact that he seems to have aged twenty years, as it were, overnight. The Longfellow of the 1850s is a dapper, erect, sleek-looking man in well-fed middle age, with a fashionable fringe of dark mutton-chop whiskers halfway down his cheeks. Longfellow from 1862 on is a grandfatherly figure, somewhat stooped, deeply wrinkled, hoary, almost woolly—at times looking utterly exhausted, yet on one occasion (the great portrait of him from 1868 by Julia Margaret Cameron) coming across as defiantly bardic. The beard may have been the most conscious symbol of this transformation, his badge of mourning, his announcement to the world that his accustomed life had ended with the death of Fanny. There was, at any rate, more tragedy to come: Felton, who in many ways was the most dependable, and certainly the most high-spirited, of Longfellow's close friends from the old days, had become president of wartime Harvard. He died of overwork in 1865.

Meanwhile, in the motherless family at the Craigie House, there was a more immediate difficulty: what to do about Charley. The restlessness he had shown as a child had not diminished in late adolescence, and he showed little interest in his Harvard studies or in pursuing an Appleton-like career in State Street. He loved to sail, to shoot, to roam the countryside or the riverbanks. He seemed accident-prone; at age eleven at nearby Fresh Pond, his hunting rifle had misfired, blowing off his left thumb. Longfellow had good reason to fear that he would volunteer for the army, as so many of his Beacon Hill contemporaries were doing. The exposure of his eldest child to mortal danger so soon after the family's tragedy was more than Longfellow could bear. An opportunity presented itself in 1862 to give the boy a glimpse of the excitement of the war, from a safe distance, in the hopes perhaps of getting it out of his system. (This was still a time when well-informed people on both sides assumed the war would soon be over.) In March, Charley sailed on a supply vessel, the *Parliament*, owned by their friend William Fay, for Ship Island, the Gulf Coast staging point for the Union Army's planned attack on New Orleans. As it turned out, Ship Island was a wind-swept, disease-ridden sandbar, but Longfellow did not know this and hoped that Charley might be satisfied at least to hear the noise of presumably distant guns. Charley, a splendid sailor, found the whole trip a wonderful lark. He sent back vivid descriptions of the crew, the duck shooting, the inefficiencies of military life, and the occasional sighting of a "secesher," or Confederate. As he was to prove on other occasions, he was better at reportage than his father the writer. After one venture ashore on Ship Island, he sketched this scene of the commanding general's wife:

> We were then introduced to Mrs. [Benjamin] Butler in her little ten foot house which is furnished with rebel furniture captured on its way to New Orleans, the floor is covered with sand and the room is chock full of flies and there Mrs. B. sits in her glory and black silk dress languidly fanning herself and making rather flat remarks.

Aboard another vessel, he met another Northern female far from home. As he wrote back to the Craigie House, "we were introduced to a real live woman and it was very pleasant to se[sic] one after a month's voyage I feel half in love with her although she is married as she is very pretty and only 19, her history is this, she enlisted as a private in the 15 Maine with her husband she was not discovered untill she had nearly got here when they did find her out they made her put on her own clothes and took her into the cabin where she is now staying."

Back home in late spring, Charley was soon packed off with his friend Willy Fay for a European tour, which his father doubtless hoped would outlast the war. It did not, and by fall he was again in Cambridge, feeling more restless and striving to be more independent than ever. On March 14, 1863, Longfellow received a letter postmarked in Portland. Its contents did not surprise him—the postmark was a ruse—but they distressed him perhaps more severely than anything that had occurred since Fanny's death twenty months earlier.

Dear Papa

You know for how long a time I have been wanting to go to war I have tried hard to resist the temptation of going without your leave but I cannot any longer, I feel it to be my first duty to do what I can for my country and I would willingly lay down my life for it if it would be of any good God bless you all.

Yours affectionately,

Charley

The letter had been sent to a friend, George Rand, to be posted in Maine, to give Charley a few days' head start toward reaching the Union front lines, where he intended to volunteer in the first Massachusetts regiment he could find. His motives went beyond mere adventurism or even the patriotism expressed in his note. Like many other privileged young men in New England, he saw the war as the great proving ground of his manhood and courage, a justification of his right to live in a position of honor, respect, and authority in his community. He would struggle for the rest of his not-very-long life to carve out an identity for himself as something other than Longfellow's son. And it is quite likely that he wanted to get out of that house of tears in Cambridge and deal with his own grief for his mother by way of some bold and heroic gesture.

As things turned out, Charley had a short but "good" war, ending with a commission and an honorable, though dicey, wound that could easily have killed him. If Charley succeeded at nothing else, he managed to get his depressed father out of the house and to give him two unanticipated experiences of Washington in wartime. Considering how sedentary in his mourning Longfellow had become, this was no mean accomplishment.

The immediate task was to find the eighteen-year-old and persuade him to come home. On the same day Charley's note arrived, Longfellow wrote to Rand, hoping he knew his son's plans and would forward the letter:

My dear Charley,

Your letter this morning did not surprise me very much, as I thought it probable you had gone on some such mad-cap expedition. Still you have done very wrong; and I hope you will so see it and come home again at once.

Your motive is a noble one; but you are too precipitate. I have always thought you, and still think you, too young to go into the army. It can be no reproach to you, and no disgrace, to wait a little longer; though I can very well understand your impatience.

As soon as you receive this, let me know where you are, and what you have done, and are doing.

All join in much love to you. . . .

Ever affectionately
H. W. L.

Two days earlier Charley had reached Washington, where a considerate artillery captain not only recognized him but took him into his battery (the infantry had rejected him because of the childhood loss of his thumb). The captain immediately wrote Longfellow, who was gratified by the news that his son was safe but alarmed at the thought he would soon be on the Rappahannock. Yet he finally accepted the fact that Charley was not going to come home. He immediately wrote asking Sumner to intervene in any way he could on the boy's behalf, but Charley was sharp enough to put off the senator's invitation to visit by promising to do so after the war was over or his three years were out. Longfellow sought Governor Andrew's help in obtaining a commission, but Charley's "half-aunt" Harriet Appleton seems to have beaten him to it. Charley was not only the poet's son, he was an Appleton, a member of a rich and powerful New England dynasty. It would be unseemly for such a young man to serve with the troops. This was more than a matter of maintaining social status; it was brutally practical, for Civil War armies reflected the class structure of the societies from which they were raised, and in terms of both creature comforts and medical care, even the most junior officers were treated significantly better than enlisted men. Judging by his enthusiastic letters home, Charley loved being in the artillery battery, where mingling with the ranks seemed to gratify his urge to escape the gentility of Boston and Cambridge, but thanks to his family's pull, he soon found himself a lieutenant in the First Massachusetts Cavalry. His father was astonished at the cost of outfitting him, including horse, tack, and servant, but felt so obliged to the artillery captain who had kept an eye on him, that he asked Sumner to have him sent a basket of Champagne.

Life as a cavalry officer proved even more agreeable to Charley, whose jaunty letters home were welcome in one sense but did little to allay his father's fears that the boy was reckless, even foolhardy. To the family's relief, his unit missed the great Union defeat at Chancellorsville, but by early June disaster of another sort had struck. While on a visit with the girls to their Aunt Anne in Portland, Longfellow learned that Charley had a severe case of "camp fever"—a term that covered a range of infectious diseases, from the curable to the quickly lethal. Fortunately—and again the family's influence seems to have eased Charley's way—he was sent to convalesce not in a crowded hospital but in the Washington home of a member of the Sanitary Commission who was a friend of Longfellow's brother Samuel. Longfellow rushed to his bedside and nursed him through his fever for several weeks with beef tea, blancmange, and ice cream. A stream of distinguished visitors called, eager to meet the famous poet even in the sticky heat of the Washington summer. A month amid the cool breezes of Nahant successfully concluded the treatment. That sojourn, incidentally, led to one of the great comic moments in the early history of New England summer resorts. Like most males of all ages at that time, Charley was accustomed to swimming on secluded beaches in the nude. Nahant was not quite as secluded as perhaps he remembered, for the formidable wife of General John C. Fremont, a recent presidential candidate, had taken a nearby cottage. She had Charley and a fellow swimmer arrested for indecency. At trial, however, Charley's lawyer won the case—when he forced Mrs. Fremont to admit that she had been unable to recognize the young men from her house until she turned her opera glasses on them.

Just as we begin to think we understand the Victorians, they surprise us. Despite his own grief, Longfellow was determined to keep the household's spirits up. He had a distinctive talent as a caricaturist, as the "Peter Quince" drawings he made for his children in the 1850s suggest. They portray the picaresque adventures at home and abroad of a Longfellow-like traveler. Even more remarkable is a small bundle of stories and drawings, thirty-two sheets of paper sewn together, entitled "Little Merrythought. An Autobiography with a Portrait." They are not dated, but Civil War souvenirs pasted in suggest completion in 1863 or 1864, and there is a watercolor of a young Massachusetts cavalry officer on horseback who is clearly Charley. But the story must have been begun as much as a decade earlier, and added to from year to year, incorporating as it does the sagas (largely tragic) of the various family dogs and tales of various childhood scrapes. Originally intended to amuse the two boys, the book survived to help the daughters through the family tragedy.

The story starts with the "Birth and Parentage" of its title character. "I was born on Christmas day; on which occasion my mother was invited to dinner, not as a guest but as meat. She was roasted; and brought to table with her gizzard under her wing. When I was taken from her breast she was quite dead. I was immediately put naked into the hands of a little brown-eyed boy, named Erny." Wrapped up in a napkin, the wishbone is taken home to the Craigie House, where he is given a red waistcoat, like Papa's, black shoes made of sealing wax, and a white feather for his cap. He stands "on the green meadow of the table cloth."

This extraordinary foreshadowing of Fanny's death might strike a modern reader as something not to be shown to the children after the events of 1861. Yet Longfellow did not destroy it but rather wove it into a playful series of episodes, many of them illustrated, drawn from Craigie House life. He clearly had one of the most blessed of human gifts, the ability to take the simplest events of everyday life and make them amusing and worth retelling.

Edie's French Lesson
Little Edie was at the head of her class in French, because she was the only one in it!
"Ma mere," said her Papa.
"My Mother," said little Edie.
"Est aimable," said her Papa.
"Ate a marble," said little Edie. "Why! How could she eat a marble?"

You have to know how a Bostonian pronounces "marble" to appreciate that episode.

There is at least one passage that suggests "Little Merrythought" was intended for Papa as well as the children. Erny would have the occasional rage (though not as often as Charley, who is known in the story as the "Infant Terrible"). But Erny finally asks his father to help him be good.

Ah yes! help him to be good! That is what children must need. Not so much chiding and lecturing; but a little more sympathy, a little help to be good. You can see through their transparent faces, the struggle that is going on within. A soft, gentle word often decides the victory!

By August, the leave was over, and a grimmer stage of Charley's Civil War began. Although in his absence the North had won the Battle of Gettysburg, the war dragged on. Charley had still not seen a major battle, though he had frequently been under enemy fire in the course of patrols and skirmishes in the rolling countryside around Culpeper, Virginia. On November 27, riding out of a thicket at New Hope Church, he was struck in the back by a bullet that nicked his spine before exiting on his other side. The bullet just missed his heart and lungs, but he was bleeding profusely by the time he had been carried into the church and laid on the altar. He survived.

On December 1, the telegram reached the Craigie House, where Longfellow had just sat down to dinner. The report was inaccurate but alarming, and Longfellow and eighteen-year-old Ernest quickly packed and spent an uncomfortable night on the Fall River steamer to New York. After aggravating delays, they reached Willard's Hotel in

Washington the next night, and moved the next day to the Ebbitt House, only three doors from Sumner. What followed was the closest Longfellow came to the wartime experiences of his fellow poet Walt Whitman among the wounded and dying. Communications with the army were erratic and unreliable, so Longfellow and his son went again and again to the train station in expectation of finding Charley among those being unloaded from the foul hospital cars. On December 5, much the worse for wear but in good spirits, Charley emerged. He was whisked off to the hotel, where every high-ranking surgeon in the army seemed to want to examine him. Once again, word of Longfellow's presence in the capital had spread. He went with Sumner to attend the opening of the Thirty-Eighth Congress, stopping to greet the man who, nearly forty years earlier, had almost become his brother-in-law, the now influential Senator William Pitt Fessenden of Maine. He was persuaded by another admirer to pose with Sumner for a portrait by Alexander Gardner, now regarded as perhaps the greatest of the Civil War photographers. Gardner published the image over the title "The Politics and Poetry of New England." There they sit—two weathered monuments.

On December 8, the Longfellow party left on the evening train for New York, and Charley's eventful nine months in the Army of the Potomac came to a safe and comfortable end. He completed his convalescence at home and would always have a room there, but the cord had been broken. Charley had inherited a sizable fortune from his mother and grandfather, and he would spend the rest of his far-flung life spending it at a pace that once more alarmed his father. There were many adventures ahead—at sea, in the Himalayas, in Meiji Japan. While Charley in 1866 helped sail his Uncle Tom Appleton's fifty-foot sloop *Alice* across the Atlantic, his father sat in his Cambridge study immersed in his difficult translation of Dante. Longfellow had lived through his own version of Hell, in the tragic events of 1861, and in the alarms and anxieties of 1863. Yet these experiences seemed not to touch his poetry, at least directly, which is perhaps the thing that most puzzles a modern student of his life and work.

There is one exception, although it was never published in his life-time. In 1879, recalling the photograph he had seen of a famous mountainside in the Rockies, Longfellow wrote "The Cross of Snow." The sonnet evokes Dante's *Purgatorio* in its play of light and shadow, and links this with the still uncharted grandeur of the American con-tinent, in a great arc of meaning that triumphantly completes his half-century as a poet. There is no doubt who his Beatrice had been.

> In the long, sleepless watches of the night,
> A gentle face—the face of one long dead—
> Looks at me from the wall, where round its head
> The night-lamp casts a halo of pale light.
> Here in this room she died; and soul more white
> Never through martyrdom of fire was led
> To its repose; nor can in books be read
> The legend of a life more benedight.
> There is a mountain in the distant West
> That sun-defying, in its deep ravines
> Displays a cross of snow upon its side.
> Such is the cross I wear upon my breast
> These eighteen years, through all the changing scenes
> And seasons, changeless since the day she died.

At his lowest moment, Longfellow produced his sprightliest work. Few readers today know more than its opening charge—the resound-ing verbal hoof-beats of "Paul Revere's Ride." Doubtless, they would be surprised to discover that the most famous of his poems is merely the first of twenty-two linked narratives in a great variety of meter and tone, several of them delightfully comic. Long narrative poems are in fact so much out of fashion, that this aspect of Longfellow's accom-plishment is virtually overlooked; modern readers prefer his short lyrics. When noticed at all, *Tales of a Wayside Inn* (published in three parts between 1863 and 1873) is often dismissed as watered-down Chaucer, though in truth it owes more to Boccaccio. Yet there is no

other work that better demonstrates Longfellow's breadth of poetic
interests, his ability to produce highly finished work amid difficult
personal circumstances, and his absolute mastery of English prosody.
Probably only two of the tales can be said to be original in conception,
although saying so does not give the poet the credit he deserves for the
long and fluent connective passages that link the tales and their various tellers. Longfellow's sources range from medieval sagas to Renaissance romances to colonial American history. It is not the tale, he
would have argued, but how it is told that counts.

"Paul Revere's Ride," originally published in *The Atlantic* in 1860
amid the gathering gloom of the secession movement in the South, is
a Carlylean plea for a great hero to come save the union. Its
Revolutionary War details are fictionalized, the real Paul Revere having been only one of many patriots involved in spreading the word "to
every Middlesex village and farm." (By a curiosity of literary history,
the real Paul Revere was one of the Massachusetts officers who
botched the Penobscot Expedition, the Down East debacle in which
the Royal Navy destroyed the American fleet in 1779. Longfellow's
grandfather, Peleg Wadsworth, was one of the few patriots to emerge
with any credit from the episode; he later testified in Revere's pro
forma court-martial.) Had it not been for the poem, Revere would
probably be remembered today only for his skill as a silversmith, but
Longfellow single-handedly elevated him to the Revolutionary pantheon. As Matthew Gartner has pointed out, this development did not
really take place until well after the Civil War, when Revere's story became a central myth in the Colonial Revivalism of the late 1870s and
afterwards. That the poem is so seductively easy to memorize helped
anchor it in the American school curriculum for more than a century.
Thanks to the talent of its many illustrators, the poem (or versions
of it) survives in the children's book market—the only work by
Longfellow that is still widely read, occasionally even learned by heart.

The Civil War context of the whole of *Tales of a Wayside Inn* comes
through even more interestingly in the structure Longfellow chose: a
long series of loosely linked stories related by a representative sam-

pling of Americans. The most strikingly original thing about this work is whom Longfellow saw as representative: a Yankee innkeeper, a college student, a theologian, a poet, a musician, a Sicilian, and a Spanish Jew. This is not a collection of people you would have found fraternizing in many American inns of the 1860s. The gathering, although presented as fortuitous, serves to convey not only Longfellow's personal sense of toleration but his affirmation of the union of his country's varied peoples. It is not truly representative, to be sure—no woman, no African American, no Native American. But that would have been straining verisimilitude in the 1860s. The strength of the poem arises from its demonstration of the power of storytelling to imagine a nation.

Tales of a Wayside Inn has a solid ground in biographical fact. As Longfellow explained in a letter, the Wayside Inn is based on the actual Red-Horse Inn in Sudbury, a stagecoach stop about twenty miles from Cambridge. (The title *The Sudbury Tales* was among those considered but rejected.) In colonial times, a prominent family, the Howes, had built a large house there and, falling upon hard times, a later generation had begun taking in guests. Longfellow had visited it briefly, but he knew more about it as a result of the frequent sojourns there of his colleague and protégé, Luigi Monti, who taught Italian at Harvard in the 1850s. Monti was among a group of friends who escaped in summer from Boston and Cambridge to the rather sleepy but idyllic village, and there must have been many such evenings of swapping stories after the ladies had retired. Monti—who had had a colorful career at Palermo in the Italian revolution of 1848 before escaping to America as a young political refugee—is the model for the Sicilian. The Student is based on Henry Ware Wales, a Harvard bibliophile who died young; the Theologian, on Daniel Treadwell, a Harvard physicist who combined an interest in munitions with an interest in theology; the Poet, on Thomas W. Parsons, a fellow translator of Dante; the Musician, on Ole Bull, an internationally famous Norwegian violin virtuoso and close friend of Longfellow's; and the Spanish Jew, on Isaac Edrehi, a Dutch émigré who had translated various Hebrew texts. The Landlord is a sketch of Lyman Howe, the actual innkeeper and direct descendant of the family that had built the house; his taproom, redolent of the Colonial Revivalism to come, is the locus that pulls together these three foreigners and three rather bookish Americans. (The inn literally became a Colonial Revival artifact when it was bought by Henry Ford in 1923 and renovated into a hotel and restaurant still in business in Sudbury.)

There is much in *Tales of a Wayside Inn* of interest. The metrical virtuosity of the twenty-two episodes of "The Saga of King Olaf" (the first part of the work to be written, some of it going back to 1856) is unsurpassed in nineteenth-century American poetry, and a bracing tang of cold salt air enlivens the work. "The Falcon of Ser Federigo" is a skillful retelling of a sunnier tale from Boccaccio. "Torquemada" in its sadism reveals a strain of verismo we do not usually associate with the "genteel" Longfellow. "Lady Wentworth" and "The Baron of St. Castine" are ventures in colonial American myth making. There is no poem in the series that does not reveal some aspect of Longfellow's craft, and the only real weakness of *Tales of a Wayside Inn*—assuming we do not reject long narrative verse out of hand—is the shapelessness of the project as a whole. As with *Hiawatha*, Longfellow could have gone on adding tale after tale, given the open-endedness of the work.

To suggest that Longfellow was a multiculturalist before his time stretches the term a bit, however much the framing of *Tales of a Wayside Inn* conveys a lack of xenophobia and an eagerness to embrace other European cultures. To suggest that Longfellow was an environmentalist before his time, however, is confirmed by "The Birds of Killingworth," which closes Part One and is the most readable of the poems other than "Paul Revere's Ride." It is one of Longfellow's most Unitarian works as well; its satire on Connecticut religious orthodoxy still had considerable bite in the 1860s, despite its colonial setting. Spring brings flocks of birds to the farmlands of Killingworth, among them the hungry ravens. A town meeting assembles to discuss how to deal with these pests; it provides the poet with an opportunity to sketch the leading citizens, including the grandest:

> *Then from his house, a temple painted white,*
> *With fluted columns, and a roof of red,*
> *The Squire came forth, august and splendid sight!*
> *Slowly descending, with majestic tread,*
> *Three flights of stairs, nor looking left or right*
> *Down the long street he walked, as one who said,*
> *"A town that boasts inhabitants like me*
> *Can have no lack of good society!"*

He is followed by the clergyman, devoted to Jonathan Edwards and slaughtering deer; the idealistic Preceptor of the Academy, daydreaming of one of his pupils, the fair Almira ("Who was, as in a sonnet he said, / As pure as water, and as good as bread."); the slow and ponderous Deacon; and sundry bird-hating farmers. After very little debate, the townsmen—over the protests of the sensitive schoolmaster—vote to rid themselves of the birds:

> *Men who have no faith in fine-spun sentiment*
> *Who put their trust in bullocks and in beeves.*
> *The birds were doomed; and, as the record shows,*
> *A bounty offered for the heads of crows.*

A dreadful massacre follows—"the very St. Bartholomew of Birds!" But summer brings the caterpillars and cankerworms and other devouring insects; soon the fields and orchards are stripped bare.

> *The farmers grew impatient, but a few*
> *Confessed their error, and would not complain,*
> *For after all, the best thing one can do*
> *When it is raining, is to let it rain.*
> *Then they repealed the law, although they knew*
> *It would not call the dead to life again;*
> *As school-boys, finding their mistake too late,*
> *Draw a wet sponge across the accusing slate.*

A colorless autumn arrives, then finally a spring when each branch seems to have been hung with wicker baskets: the town has had to import every bird it could find, to restore the balance of nature. The tale is a delightful parable on the Law of Unintended Consequences, and a typically Longfellovian comment on the narrower strains of the New England character.

※

While the varied episodes of *Tales of a Wayside Inn* were taking shape, Longfellow was engaged in two even more ambitious projects. As early as 1856, his German friend Scherb had suggested that he write a tragic poem on the Puritans and the Quakers. He began his research, extending it to include the Salem witchcraft scare, and at various stages in the late 1850s wrote scenes for what he came to call his *New England Tragedy*, which was privately issued in a prose version in 1860. In the 1860s he slowly recrafted this prose into blank verse. The two-part tragedy—"John Endicott," dealing with the persecution by the Boston authorities of the peaceable Quakers, and "Giles Corey of the Salem Farms," dramatizing an incident in the witch trials—was published as *The New England Tragedies* in 1868. It was intended to form the third part of a massive (and never completely finished) work known as *Christus: A Mystery* (1872). Its first part was *The Divine Tragedy*, a retelling in dramatic verse of the Jesus story; its second, *The Golden Legend*, a dramatization of a medieval legend about the Emperor Henry II and a pious young woman who is willing to sacrifice her life for his survival. Together these works absorbed an enormous amount of Longfellow's time and creative energy in the 1860s, but it is hard to find anyone who believes the results merited the effort. Like many literary figures in the nineteenth century, Longfellow loved the theater and saw tragic drama as the highest art form. Like Henry James, however, and unlike Victor Hugo, he lacked any sense of stagecraft or dramatic pacing. *The New England Tragedies* are of some interest, nonetheless, because they are so out of character with the figure we usually think of as Longfellow. As bleak as anything Hawthorne ever wrote about seventeenth-century New England, and far more brutal, they seem to represent a moment of questioning of the origins of the New England polity, even of organized Christianity itself. They are unstageable as drama because their individual scenes are so underdeveloped, but they cry out to be set to music.

Longfellow's other great project in these years was far more welcomed by his public. In 1862 he took up again a project he had tried his hand at on several occasions during his Harvard years: the translation of Dante's *Divine Comedy*. It has often been said that his purpose was to overcome his grief following Fanny's death—the daily effort of translation giving him a regular chore to distract him—but this seems rather superficial. Dante had been a central interest of his since his visit to Italy in 1828 and the focus of much of his Harvard teaching. As part of his greater project of introducing Americans to European high culture, he knew the need for a new translation of this central work in the Western tradition. The discovery of Doré's illustrations in 1862—"a prodigality of horrors," he called them—and his efforts to teach his children Italian were other incentives to take on the task. What really propelled him, however, was the existence close at hand in Cambridge of a small group of literati who knew Italian well and took keen interest in his progress.

This was the famous Dante Club, which formally began in 1865 but which had existed on a more ad hoc basis for several years. It met weekly in Longfellow's study. As the youngest member of the group—William Dean Howells—later recalled, the regulars were James Russell Lowell and Charles Eliot Norton. Others were invited from time to time. The practice was for Longfellow to read the canto he had just translated, while the club followed in the original and offered suggestions or alternatives. Longfellow was determined to translate the poem as literally as possible, even though this meant abandoning Dante's terza rima. The sessions were serious, but they were also convivial, and they became even more so when the work was over and the party (often joined by latecomers) adjourned to the dining room for a supper of oysters and some plain New England fare—cold turkey (which Longfellow carved) or a haunch of venison or canvasback duck, accompanied with wine of the first class from the poet's fabled cellar. The club often continued into the early hours of the morning.

The young Howells was too shy to speak out in such august company—his one attempt at a correction was passed over, he said—but he left an entertaining account of the group:

> When Longfellow read verse, it was with a hollow, with a mellow resonant murmur, like the note of some deep-throated horn. His voice was very lulling in quality, and at the Dante Club it used to have early effect with an old scholar [possibly George Washington Greene] who sat in a cavernous arm-chair at the corner of the fire, and who drowsed audibly in the soft tone and gentle heat. The poet had a fat terrier ["Trap"] who wished always to be present ... and he commonly fell asleep at the same moment with that dear old scholar, so that when they began to make themselves heard in concert, one could not tell which it was that most took our thoughts from the text of the Paradiso. When the duet opened, Longfellow would look up with an arch recognition of the fact, and then go gravely on to the end of the canto. At the close he would speak to his friend and lead him out to supper as if he had not seen or heard anything amiss.

The club in Longfellow's study ended with the publication of *The Divine Comedy of Dante Alighieri* in 1867 but continued at Norton's house with his translation of the *Vita Nuova* and eventually formed the basis of the Dante Society of America, still very much in existence. Longfellow's Dante soon became a fixture in every American household with any claim to high culture; while its diction now seems very old fashioned, it has been praised by later and freer translators, and functions as a very useful crib for anyone trying to read Dante in the original. It was not to be Longfellow's last venture into things Italian.

Throughout his life in Cambridge, Longfellow had yearned, from time to time, to return to the Mediterranean, which glowed in his memories of 1827 and 1828. But the mood would pass (often, as soon as the weather improved), and he had long resisted the temptation to make one more European voyage. In truth, he was too accustomed to his usual routines—each July going to Nahant (with a short, often one-day, side trip to Portland), each September returning to Brattle Street—to be able to summon up the physical and psychic energy such a voyage would demand. It is a tribute to his devotion to his children, however, that in 1868 he finally made such a trip for their benefit. The footloose scholar of the 1820s was now part of an entourage of eleven, including not only the five children but his two sisters, Uncle Tom, Ernest's brand-new wife, Hattie (it was to be their wedding trip as well), and their former governess, Miss Davie. (Charley sailed with them but quickly took off on his own.)

It was the conventional Grand Tour, made more laborious by the fact that everywhere he went, Longfellow found himself showered with honors and attention. Degrees from Oxford and Cambridge, a visit with the Queen at Windsor Castle, an evening with Liszt in Rome, two days of talk with Tennyson on the Isle of Wight—it was a flattering but exhausting round. As his brother Sam recorded: "He breakfasted with Mr. Gladstone, Sir Henry Holland, the Duke of Argyll; lunched with Lord John Russell at Richmond; dined with various hosts, received midnight calls from Bulwer and Aubrey de Vere." (One wonders if Bulwer was reminded of the morning in 1835 when Longfellow called on him?)

The trip lasted from June of 1868 until September of 1869. While the children busied themselves with sightseeing, Longfellow merely went through the motions of accompanying them. He was quickly bored with museums and churches, and dwelt instead with the memories that Rome, Venice, the Bernese Alps, the Rhine brought flooding back. The trip did result in several memorable portraits. In Rome, G. P. A. Healy, working from a photograph of Longfellow and Edith, painted them into a topographical view of the Arch of Titus—the learned poet escorting the innocent young American through the ruins of ancient civilization. And Edmonia Lewis, a young African-American sculptor in the circle of Charlotte Cushman and Harriet Hosmer, sculpted a bust (now at Harvard) in which the poet took on the monumentality of a river god.

On his visit to Tennyson at Farringford on June 23, 1868, his friendly British rival walked him over the downs to Dimbola Lodge, the seaside home of the formidable Julia Margaret Cameron. She took the best photograph of him ever made. Recognized today as one of the master photographers of her century, she was regarded as an eccentric, though an interesting one, by many of her vast circle of friends and relatives. In the tradition of Victorian country-house amateur theatricals, she wrapped her photographic subjects in dramatic costumes, in the former hen-house that served as her studio. The image she captured does not look like Longfellow so much as her romantic idea of what Longfellow ought to look like: wild, bardic, craggy, just off the moors. But it is a masterpiece. His clawlike hand holds the dark robe to his shoulder; in profile, he glares defiantly at some distant object, his mass of wind-tossed white hair and jutting beard dominating the dark background of the portrait. It is not Longfellow, but Lear.

Thirteen

MORITURI SALUTAMUS

A<small>LTHOUGH HE CONTINUED</small> to write poetry until almost the last weeks of his life, Longfellow's project in his final decade seems to have been to revisit images and themes he had worked with earlier, to see what could still be drawn from them. He expressed this condition with stunning conciseness in the two stanzas of "Aftermath," published in a small volume with that title in 1873. Building on a metaphor both personal and writerly, he describes the process of going over the mown fields in early winter to gather what the harvesters have left behind.

> *Not the sweet, new grass with flowers*
> *Is this harvesting of ours;*
> *Not the upland clover bloom;*
> *But the rowen mixed with weeds,*
> *Tangled tufts from marsh and meads,*
> *Where the poppy drops its seeds*
> *In the silence and the gloom.*

This was a literal description of the river meadow between the Craigie House and the Charles, which Longfellow rented out to a farmer whom he must have seen making just such a final sweep each November. In a few deft strokes, the poem also invokes the mental landscape of a poet who, during the twenty-one years that he survived Fanny, struggled through the half-light of memory and desperation.

Two years later, he tackled this problem of aging in a far more vigorous, New England–like way. The occasion was the fiftieth reunion of the famous Bowdoin Class of 1825. Longfellow had returned infrequently to Brunswick after 1835, and he had a lifelong aversion to speaking or reciting before crowds, but he finally accepted President Joshua Chamberlain's invitation. (Chamberlain, who became famous in the 1980s as a result of several modern books and films about his Civil War heroics, was leading the struggling college at a particularly low moment in its fortunes; he, too, as a youth had taught modern languages there.) Longfellow took his title from Gerome's painting of the gladiators saluting Caesar in the Colosseum. In the fall of 1875, he read "Morituri Salutamus" aloud (in a voice few people could hear) in Brunswick's First Parish Church, where almost twenty-five years earlier Harriet Beecher Stowe had experienced her vision of Uncle Tom, and where Longfellow was relieved to learn that he could stand at the pulpit. ("Let me cover myself as much as possible; I wish it might be entirely.") The poem is both elegy and gentle jeremiad. Despite copious classical and local allusions—including a handsome tribute to the sole surviving professor from 1825, Alpheus Packard—the diction is in the easy middle style of Longfellow's best narrative poems. The poet pulls off the difficult feat of sounding both learned and enthusiastic.

> *The scholar and the world! The endless strife,*
> *The discord in the harmonies of life!*
> *The love of learning, the sequestered nooks,*
> *And all the sweet serenity of books;*
> *The market-place, the eager love of gain,*
> *Whose aim is vanity, and whose end is pain!*

The scholar, he suggests, can escape, or at least delay, such a wasted end far better than other men.

> *Ah, nothing is too late*
> *Till the tired heart shall cease to palpitate.*
> *Cato learned Greek at eighty; Sophocles*
> *Wrote his grand Oedipus, and Simonides*
> *Bore off the prize of verse from his compeers,*
> *When each had numbered more than fourscore years,*
> *And Theophrastus, at fourscore and ten,*
> *Had but begun his "Characters of Men."*
> *Chaucer, at Woodstock with the nightingales,*

At sixty wrote the Canterbury Tales;
Gothe at Weimar, toiling to the last,
Completed Faust when eighty years were past.
These are indeed exceptions; but they show
How far the gulf-stream of our youth may flow
Into the arctic regions of our lives,
Where little else than life itself survives.

In his own life he had lived up to this charge: he had published a second series of *Tales of a Wayside Inn* (1870) and *Three Books of Song* (1872), and in 1874 he sold "The Hanging of the Crane" to a New York newspaper for four thousand dollars (a deal brokered by Sam Ward, and the highest price ever paid to that date for a single poem). That same year, he began one of the most ambitious publishing projects in the history of poetry: what eventually became the thirty-one volumes of his *Poems of Places*, a wide-ranging anthology in translation of representative, often topographical, lyrics drawn not only from every major European literature but extending into Asia and the Arab world as well. If Longfellow can be said to have "invented" comparative literature for the American university at Harvard in the late 1830s, then *Poems of Places* gives him standing as nineteenth-century America's most ambitious multiculturalist. Five more volumes of his own poetry were to appear, combining dramatic verse, lyrics, incidental verse, and sonnets on a variety of subjects: *The Masque of Pandora* (1875), *Keramos* (1878), *Ultima Thule* (1880), *In the Harbor* (1882), and *Michael Angelo: A Fragment* (1883 and 1886).

The quality of this work varies, but for all his personal troubles and the often aggravating demands of others for his time and attention, Longfellow continued until the end to experiment with poetic form and take on a daunting array of subjects. Many of the minor poems are charming and of biographical interest (notably the tributes to Parker Cleaveland, Hawthorne, and Agassiz); some are even topical, including Longfellow's expression of shock at President Garfield's assassination and his quick response to the massacre at Little Big Horn—"The Revenge of Rain-in-the-Face," a poem that suggests some sympathy

FIGURE II: Eugene L'Africain, Authors Group, 1883. The lithograph includes
images of the famous American writers' houses and was distributed by
the Travelers Insurance Company. Courtesy Maine Historical Society.

for the Indians' point of view. The works that deserve to endure are his
more than thirty major sonnets, all written in the Petrarchan form,
most particularly the six collected as "Divinia Commedia" (originally
written as introductions to his Dante translations). The series begins
just as his work as a translator begins:

Oft have I seen at some cathedral door
A laborer, pausing in the dust and heat,
Lay down his burden, and with reverent feet
Enter, and cross himself, and on the floor
Kneel to repeat his paternoster o'er;
Far off the noises of the world retreat;
The loud vociferations of the street
Become an undistinguishable roar.
So, as I enter here from day to day,
And leave my burden at this minster gate,
Kneeling in prayer, and not ashamed to pray,
The tumult of the time disconsolate
To inarticulate murmurs dies away,
While the eternal ages watch and wait.

It is a poem that confirms Henry James's observation (in *William Wetmore Story and His Friends*, 1903) that Longfellow is "perhaps interesting for nothing so much as for the secret of his harmony (harmony of situation and sense I of course mean) and for the way in which his 'European' culture and his native kept house together."

The other major poetic accomplishment of his later years is his meditation on the life and art of Michelangelo, which links his 1828 sojourn in Rome to his own situation as an artist facing death. The painter-poet asks:

How will men speak of me when I am gone,
When all this colorless, sad life is ended,
And I am as dust? They will remember only
The wrinkled forehead, the marred countenance,
The rudeness of my speech, and my rough manners,
And never dream that underneath them all
There was a woman's heart of tenderness;
They will not know the secret of my life,
Locked up in silence, or but vaguely hinted
In uncouth rhymes, that may perchance survive
Some little space in memories of men!

In growing his beard, Longfellow began the transformation of himself from a distinguished citizen of Cambridge into an American icon, whose face would peer down—often between Lincoln's and Washington's—from the photolithographs high on the schoolroom wall, managing to convey beneath his whiskers something both patriarchal and benign. Despite the enviable productivity as poet and translator sketched above, Longfellow found himself increasingly drawn in his last two decades toward playing a public role that he both welcomed and regretted. The sheer volume of his correspondence—much of it from strangers requesting autographs (which he unfailingly sent, often in multiples) or seeking his comments on their own poems (which he politely declined to do)—consumed much of his workday. With a kind of grim determination he took on these tasks—as well as dealing with publishers and printers—on his own, not seeking secretarial help until his last years. Meanwhile, amid a steady flow of distinguished visitors (ranging from Trollope to Emperor Pedro of Brazil) and a large circle of Boston and Cambridge friends, total strangers came to the door or peeped in the windows of the Craigie House. He often invited them in. It was as if to show himself in the flesh was part of his role as the nation's premier poet. There would have been something almost sacerdotal about it, had he not been so modest a man. He had an especially appreciative eye for handsome younger women—there are vague hints in the late 1860s and 1870s of mild flirtations, perhaps one serious flutter of the heart—and, as always, he kept an open door for children.

When the schoolchildren of Cambridge presented him, on his seventy-second birthday in 1879, with an armchair for his study made from the remnants of the village blacksmith's "spreading chestnut-tree," he had achieved a degree of celebrity that went beyond merely literary fame. His influence was spilling over into other aspects of American life, most notably the decorative arts. For the next fifty years or more, there were people who sought to live in replicas of the Craigie House (in the early twentieth century, Sears Roebuck would sell scaled-down house plans for it). The tall-case clocks that had stood in eighteenth-century parlors were moved to stair landings in "correct"

Colonial Revival interiors, as a result of the popularity of "The Old Clock on the Stairs," inspired by Fanny's mother's family home in Pittsfield. Even more ubiquitous was the spinning wheel, Priscilla Mullins's contribution to the antiques trade. It sat in the Colonial Kitchen, perilously close to the open hearth (which "The Hanging of the Crane" had helped to popularize) and beneath all those bundles of drying herbs and the ancestral musket (shades of Miles Standish!). It is an irony of Longfellow's career that a writer so open to the cultures of other lands would have so profound an effect on what might seem a narrowly local (and exclusionary) historical revivalism.

In other regards as well there is a sense that Longfellow in these years felt his reputation slipping beyond his control. He was universally well regarded, and much feted, but at the same time increasingly seen as a children's poet. His melancholy in these years—aggravated by chronic ill health and the deaths of close friends (Hawthorne in 1864, Dickens in 1870, Sumner in 1874, Fields in 1881)—may owe something to a feeling that the world he thought was taking shape had not survived the Civil War. Darwinism and the rapid industrialization of the North, with its insatiable need for cheap foreign labor, had undermined the mental world so well represented by antebellum Unitarian professors, championing the argument for creation by design and the placid, predictable universe of the Scottish Common Sense philosophy. Longfellow never had a literary "program" that he put directly into words. Yet there emerges from his writings and from his life a certain vision of America that he hoped that he, or at least his children, would live to see realized. It was a very New England vision, indeed a distinctly Boston one, Whiggish yet cautiously progressive. In religion it was conventionally Unitarian, in politics democratic up to a point, or at least willing to judge people by their talents. It was based on a quiet belief in a hierarchical (and deferential) social order, but one imbued at the top with a strong sense of public duty and a willingness to make sacrifices for the public good. It saw the spheres of men and women as reasonably well defined but complementary. The true role of woman was not just as wife and mother but as a civilizing force on man, whose manners were to be softened while his heart was taught tenderness. There were social evils, but men and women of good will would not rest until they were assured these wrongs would be set right. There was more to life than the counting house. The role of poetry was an idealizing one, by turns celebratory and comforting, and it furnished an important tool in the civilizing mission of women. The role of the poet was public, even when his language was private. The role of the citizen was to love his country and honor its past, but to seek out other lands and cultures as well, certain that their art and literature had important things to teach him. To know foreign languages and literatures was one definition of being educated. God was benevolent, if inscrutable, and the world was a safe place, despite the terrible griefs flesh was heir to. These would be assuaged in the world to come. Heaven might very well resemble Annie Fields's literary salon on Charles Street, with Ticknor & Fields's authors and all one's loved ones there.

Longfellow had the misfortune to live long enough to see this vision begin to crumble. His country became xenophobic, fearful of strangers but quite ready to exploit their labor or conquer their lands if the chance presented itself. The government was run by spoilsmen and vulgarians. Even polite society was obsessed by moneygrubbing and the scramble for place. The streets were full of apparently unassimilable immigrants. Men were taught to harden themselves, to see gentleness as weakness, to prepare themselves for the brutal battle of life (beginning on the collegiate sports field). The pieties of both the literature and science of Longfellow's youth were challenged from many fronts. It was a deeply unsettling world.

Like many other Americans, Longfellow sought refuge and solace from these changes in his own extended family, which included his children, their governess, his widowed sisters, Uncle Tom Appleton, and—when he could get away from battling his fellow Republicans in the Grant administration—Sumner. It also included in his last decade George Washington Greene, a friend from Longfellow's first trip to Europe and one of the few people alive who remembered the poet's first wife. After a lifetime in Rome, Greene had returned to America in poor health and a failure as a writer. He became a frequent and long-term houseguest in the Craigie House. Longfellow paid to have his work published, gave him money, and literally nursed him through a series of illnesses. Greene was a living link with his lost youth.

As the children matured, the family circle began to loosen. Charley never settled into a career, but spent summers racing the *Alice* and winters at the Somerset Club. He traveled widely, pig-sticking with British Army officers in India and living from 1871–73 in Japan, where—if his photo album (recently published) is any indication—he went native and lived surrounded by geisha. To his father's alarm, he spent heavily on Japanese art and decorative goods and finally had to come home because he was so rapidly exhausting the money his mother had left him. Ernest proved more conventional, even stuffy, and pursued a not very successful career as a painter. He and his sisters Anne and Edith married well; Alice continued in the role of chatelaine of the Craigie House, never marrying, and becoming in her later years a formidable figure in Cambridge and one of the founders of Radcliffe College. Edith's husband was the boy next door, Richard Henry Dana III, son of the author of *Two Years Before the Mast* and himself a lawyer dedicated to civil service reform and other good causes. In later years, he remembered his frequent visits to the Craigie House, reflecting on how kind and ever interested a host his father-in-law invariably was, yet also struck by the impenetrable reserve of a man who exhibited a certain distance even from his own children.

Longfellow had increasing difficulty eating in his final years, but typically tried to put a good face on things: Dana remembered him coming down to breakfast, pouring a cup of tea and buttering a piece of toast, but not consuming either; it was all a show of normality for the family. Toward the end, he lived on milk and bread. In March of 1882, the weather turned mild enough for him to walk, as had long been his custom, on the piazza, but he took chill and went to bed with severe stomach pain. He endured another six days, in the end heavily opiated for the pain. On the afternoon of Friday, March 24, after broken episodes of consciousness, he died, surrounded by family. The immediate cause of death was listed as peritonitis, but the symptoms suggest cancer of the stomach.

On Sunday his closest surviving friends and immediate family gathered in the library, where he was laid out, not far from the spot where Fanny had suffered her fatal accident. A single line of passion flowers rested on the broadcloth covering his plain coffin. After brief remarks by his brother Samuel, the funeral cortege of seventeen carriages moved down Brattle Street to the Indian Ridge Path at Mount Auburn Cemetery, where he was interred, next to both of his wives. A much larger public memorial service was held that afternoon at Harvard's Appleton Chapel.

Among the mourners at the Craigie House was Emerson, erect but mentally enfeebled and himself soon to die. Looking at the coffin, he said to his daughter, "I cannot recall the name of our friend, but he was a good man."

Fourteen

AFTERMATH

WASHINGTON IRVING ONCE CLAIMED that while other men live on through the unsteady medium of history, literary men have an advantage, for the intercourse between an author and his public is "ever new, active and immediate." He was taking his own readers just then on a stroll through Westminster Abbey—in the pages of his *Sketch Book* of 1819—and had paused in Poets' Corner. He noted that visitors to the Abbey lingered longest there, "as about the tombs of friends and companions; for indeed there is something of companion-ship between the author and the reader." At the time of Longfellow's death, this intimacy between the poet and his admirers remained an unmistakable feature of the Anglo-American literary landscape. But it was to prove as ephemeral as the historical fate that Irving assigned to the ordinary run of mortals, despite the bust of Longfellow placed in Poets' Corner within two years of his death.

It would have overstretched the imagination of the young Bowdoin student daydreaming over Irving's travel essays to consider that he himself would someday join Shakespeare and Milton in that pantheon. It would have surprised most Americans at the height of Longfellow's fame in the 1860s, when relations between upper-class Britain and pro-Unionist Americans had turned sour. But by the 1880s, Longfellow's substantial reputation among the British reading public and a desire—not unrelated to the racial politics of Empire—to seek ways of affirm-ing the transatlantic tie had persuaded the British establishment to honor him by so grand a gesture. In March of 1884, in the presence of two of his daughters and the American Minister, James Russell Lowell, the idealized bronze bust was unveiled, making Longfellow the first

American to be so honored. (And to this date, the only native-born, lifelong American poet: Auden was a naturalized citizen, and Eliot gave up his U.S. citizenship.) The sculptor Thomas Brock had crafted it on the basis of photographs of the elderly poet. The Prince of Wales had served as Honorary Chairman of the four-hundred-member Longfellow Memorial Committee, and Gladstone had written a letter of support. But much of the cost had been raised by contributions from "ordinary" readers. The Honorary Secretary, W. C. Bennett, expressed hope that Lowell might see "in the presence of his friend in our Poets' Corner how dearly we cherish the thought of the unity of the two great communities of our race." Lowell replied that he hoped that "the Abbey might become the Valhalla of the English-speaking race."

Back home, similar commemorations took shape. A replica of the bust was unveiled at the Portland City Hall in 1885 as a hundred members of the Haydn Association sang "Excelsior." Franklin Symonds's handsome neoclassical seated figure of the bearded poet appeared three years later at a busy intersection that Portland renamed Longfellow Square. Meanwhile, various institutions—the Alumni Association of Bowdoin College, the Massachusetts and the Maine Historical Societies, Harvard University—had published generous memorial tributes. In Washington in 1909, in the presence of Chief Justice Melville Fuller and the U.S. Marine Band, the poet's youngest grandchild, Erica Thorp, pulled a silken cord to unveil William Couper's Longfellow statue at the intersection of Connecticut Avenue and M Street N.W., a space also named Longfellow Square. The statue was the gift of the Longfellow Memorial Association, for which Theodore Roosevelt served as Honorary Regent.

More popular demonstrations of that "companionship between author and reader" also took place. In 1883, for example, *tableaux vivants* representing Longfellow's works were staged in several American cities. Sixteen hundred tickets at two dollars each (to benefit the East Side Library) were sold for the New York spectacle at Chickering Hall. Later that year, almost two hundred men, women, and children appeared in costume at the Music Hall in Woonsocket, Rhode Island, in a similar production called *Longfellow's Dream*. "Childe Henry" falls asleep in Deering's Woods and is visited by the Spirit of Poetry. She shares her harp, and the youth slips into a dream. "Various characters glide past an opening in the wood, the creations he is to embody in his future verse. They are introduced by Chorus," as the program explains. From Hiawatha's "Puk-Wudj'ies" to the Slave Singing at Midnight, from Giles Corey of the Salem Farms to Vittoria Colonna of the Michelangelo poem, from Sallie Manchester in *Kavanagh* to the poet's three daughters in "The Children's Hour," the tableaux touched upon every aspect of his poetical career, closing with Longfellow's meeting with Queen Victoria. What is impressive is not only the scale of the production, but the close familiarity with the poet's work, including his prose, that the producers could assume among their local audiences. This notion of Longfellow celebration as a communal event also had its British manifestation: in the late 1890s, performances of the Hiawatha settings by the Afro-British composer Samuel Coleridge-Taylor became increasingly popular, culminating in a 1900 production at the Royal Albert Hall, with the Royal Choral Society. Coleridge-Taylor's rousing "Hiawatha's Wedding Feast" became a special favorite, inspiring huge choral performances in the early twentieth century on both sides of the Atlantic. It remains the best vocal setting of any of his works. Meanwhile, an even greater composition reflected the Longfellow legacy. In 1892, Antonin Dvorák composed his Ninth Symphony, *From the New World*—his most popular work— with a copy of Longfellow's poetry on his music stand. The symphony (above all its Largo movement) owed an even greater debt to African American music, particularly slave songs, but the composer gave credit to *Hiawatha* above any other American literary source. He did not quote black or Native American music, he was insistent on pointing out. "I have simply written original themes embodying the peculiarities of the music."

Add to these official and unofficial tributes the extraordinary amount of Longfellow material and memorabilia made available to the public between the poet's death and the Second World War—ranging from his childhood home in Portland, deeded by Anne Longfellow Pierce to the Maine Historical Society in 1902, to cigar wrappers, Staffordshire plates, brass buttons, a 1940 commemorative postage stamp, and many other consumables. It would seem that Longfellow had been enshrined not only in Westminster Abbey but at every level of American culture, to a degree surpassed by no other American writer.

How quickly it all evaporated.

Longfellow had never lacked critics—no one has ever done so thorough a job on him as Margaret Fuller did in the 1840s—but on the whole, and considering the range of his work and his willingness to experiment with meter, he had been respectfully treated in the literary and popular journals here and abroad. This friendly tone lingered well after his death, but with a growing note of reservation, even on the part of sympathetic critics. A good example is George Saintsbury, a man who certainly would have found Longfellow good company (Saintsbury is best remembered now for his famous *Notes on a Cellar-Book*, the first serious attempt in English to write knowledgeably about the experience of enjoying vintage wine.) In a thoughtful 1907 essay, Saintsbury dismisses many of the better-known poems but could still praise Longfellow for his sureness of touch in "adorning and exalting the familiar" rather than "seizing and making familiar the strange." It was an uncommon gift, he added—"this unpretentious and apparently easy gift of communicating something of poetical treatment, something of poetical effect, to everything, or almost everything, that is touched."

Yet the mere mention of "poetical effect" soon was enough to tarnish the brightest reputation. As Carol Christ has suggested, the invention of something called Modernism required the invention of something called Victorianism, which it "defeats, displaces, overcomes." In attacking the weaknesses of the latter—its tired rhetoric, its blatant appeal to sentimentality, its lack of irony, its deflation of lyric intensity, its sheer literal-mindedness, not to mention its preachiness and religiosity—the early Modernists were confirming their own aesthetic of the spare, the fragmented, the ambiguous, the ironic.

Yet from the vantage point of our own time, the Modernists' agenda seems not only dated, and on occasion self-deluding, but more closely linked to High Victorianism than anyone in 1910 would have thought possible. Whose twentieth-century poetic practice more closely resembles Longfellow's than Ezra Pound's? The didacticism, the ransacking of European and other cultures, the penchant for quotations in the original languages—allowing for the substantial difference of idiom and tone, the practice is similar. By a nice irony, Pound was teased in England in the 1920s for being "Longfellow's great-nephew." He was in fact a distant relation; his mother back in Idaho was a Wadsworth from New England and quite proud of it. (Her parents thought she had married beneath her.) Likewise, whose attempt in the twentieth century to assume the mantle of Goethe, as the exemplar of an entire culture, surpassed that of T. S. Eliot?—an act of cultural bravado virtually unchallenged for a generation, and one that linked him with Carlyle, Arnold, Tennyson, Browning, and even Longfellow. Moreover, can the Harvard-educated Eliot's lifelong fascination with Dante be divorced totally from Longfellow's championing of the poet and the Medieval Revivalism from which this fascination emerged? (Charles Eliot Norton forms the link between the two poets.) And was not Wallace Stevens's ability to balance a successful business career and a high literary one a recapitulation, in some sense, of Longfellow's eagerness to prove that a poet could be a respectable citizen? Alan Tate's self-conscious mythologizing, Hart Crane's search for an epic vision, James Merrill's virtuosity with meter, Billy Collins's ability to illumine the everyday—to take a selection of very different poets—do these not reflect something of Longfellow's poetic practice? And it is difficult to imagine Robert Frost's career—not as a poet so much as an icon of New England—without Longfellow's example.

At the time, however, rebellion against the genteel tradition allowed no quarter. Longfellow, if anything, was too weak a target for the big guns to be wasted upon, and the mopping-up operation was left to the foot soldiers of Modernism. One of the most vociferous of these was Ludwig Lewisohn. "Who, except wretched schoolchildren, now reads Longfellow?" he asked in 1932. His attack is worth examining in detail because it spells out so plainly the opinion of a literary generation:

> The thing to establish in America is not that Longfellow was a very small poet, but that he did not partake of the poetic character at all.... Twice he came near poetic speech, once in the pathetic sonnet on his dead wife, once in "The Warning"—"There is a poor blind Sampson in this land"—when the antislavery struggle aroused even him. The ballads and the moralizing lyrics are all written from without, are all lacking the organic connection with one shaken soul and are therefore outside of the soul of the world. He can fall as low as Ella Wheeler Wilcox in "The Rainy Day"; he can rise as high as Webster in the final lines of "The Building of the Ship." He never touches poetry. He borrows forms and accepts content from without. The longer works are all strictly patterned upon the works of others. The plays are weary imitation of the Elizabethans; "The Building of the Ship" and "Keramós" lean almost slavishly on Schiller's "Lied von der Glocke," itself hardly a poetic masterpiece, nor has it been sufficiently observed how almost to the point of the popular and of course absurd notion of plagiarism "The Golden Legend" copies "Faust."... He was really not unlike those minstrel artificers of the middle ages who borrowed freely from each other methods of dressing up a common substance and had not yet risen to the notion of expression as an individual act and therefore of literature as individual property. Doubtless this large body of narrative verse as well as certain lyrics of pleasant sentiment and easy rhythm still give pleasure to a subliterary public. But men are not contemporaries though the same decades embrace their lives. To minds concerned with the imaginative interpretation of man, of nature and of human life, Longfellow has nothing left to say.

It would perhaps be unkind to ask who now reads the once prolific Ludwig Lewisohn. Yet his diatribe, however unfair at many points, suggests how wide was the gulf that separated Longfellow and serious poetry for much of the twentieth century—whatever the preferences of the "subliterary public." There were occasional rumors of a revival. None proved true. The one development that did preserve some degree of literary respectability for the poet was Newton Arvin's re-

assessment, *Longfellow: His Life and Work*, in 1963. For a major Amer-
icanist to write on the subject was remarkable enough, and throughout
the book Arvin can be seen struggling with his own devotion to New
Criticism and his respect for the richness and variety of Longfellow's
oeuvre. Moreover, his motivation for taking on such a project may have
been more personal than strictly literary: he was trying to pull his life
back together after the homophobic witch hunt that had cost him his
professorship at Smith College. Attention to Longfellow was perhaps
a bid to link his own name with someone irreproachably "normal."
Whatever Arvin's motive, his book remains the most significant critical treatment of the poet's work to date.

Other cautious admirers from time to time appeared. For example,
the poet Howard Nemerov, introducing a collection in the Laurel
Poetry Series in 1959, saw Longfellow as "stretching a relatively small
gift over a very large frame." But he spoke warmly of "The Fire of
Driftwood" and "Aftermath," helping to initiate the late-twentieth-
century view that even if Longfellow was hopelessly old fashioned,
several of his short lyrics were still worth reading. (An allied line of
thought praised his skill as a writer of sonnets, perhaps the greatest
of any nineteenth-century American poet.) "Aftermath" in particular drew the close attention of Lawrence Buell in *The Environmental
Imagination* (1995)—a glimpse of Longfellow as "greener" than we
had thought—just as *The New England Tragedies* had been treated with
an unprecedented degree of analytical seriousness in Buell's *New
England Literary Culture* (1986). The exuberant and influential essay
"Longfellow in the Aftermath of Modernism" by the poet Dana Gioia
in *The Columbia History of American Poetry* (1993) offered a rallying cry
for a revisionist campaign. But it is significant that the Library of
America's ample selection in 2000 of Longfellow's poetry and prose,
edited by the poet J. D. McClatchy, got more intelligent critical attention in Britain than in the United States, perhaps evidence of the different reverberations the word "Victorian" produces on opposite sides
of the Atlantic.

When Victor Gulotta, the leading contemporary collector of

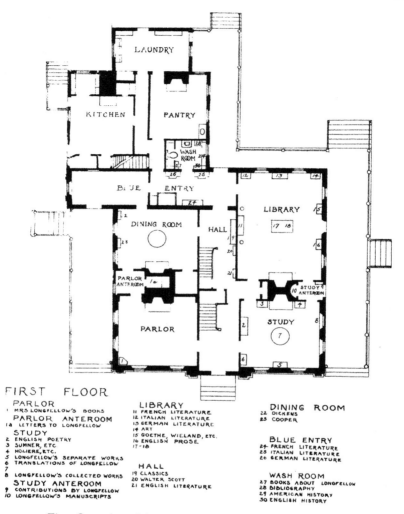

FIGURE 12: First-floor plan of the Craigie House, showing the location
of portions of Longfellow's library, 1948. Courtesy National Park
Service, Longfellow National Historic Site.

Longfelloviana, sold his collection to Harvard's Houghton Library in
2001, he admitted that he had been able to acquire the materials over
the past fifteen years because lack of interest in the poet had kept prices
down. Yet, as Gulotta explained to Nicholas A. Basbanes in *Among the
Gently Mad* (a guide to modern book-collecting), what particularly

interested Harvard was his treasure-trove of realia—photographs, souvenirs, lithographs, portrait busts, advertising ephemera—amid the first editions and autograph letters. Similarly, when the Maine Historical Society in 2002 organized the first museum exhibit ever devoted to telling the whole story of Longfellow's life and career, a large portion of the exhibit space was occupied by extraliterary cultural artifacts, from Colonial Revival chairs made of spinning wheels to the Kennebunk Brewing Company's recent Longfellow Ale.

Today, there is also evidence that Longfellow is being treated with greater academic respect, even if he is not likely to regain a place in anybody's canon, much less be taught in any serious and consistent fashion. At least he is no longer a joke. Historicist trends, the new scholarship on sentimentality, the suspicion that some veins of the American Renaissance have long since been exhausted—all these may contribute to more attention being paid in the years ahead to a cultural producer as fecund as Longfellow. Moreover, in an academic culture that privileges the work of Benedict Anderson, there is something to be said for anyone so skilled at imagining communities and producing so abundantly the literary artifacts that help construct nations. And in a country beginning to discover that "English-speaker" and "American" are not necessarily synonymous, it is significant that Harvard chose to give the evocative name of Longfellow to its new institute devoted to literatures written in this country in languages other than English. Meanwhile, a new generation of scholars—Christoph Irmscher, Matthew Gartner, Mary Louise Kete, Kirsten Silva Gruesz, Eric Haralson—are keeping Longfellow's name in the academic discourse of the twenty-first century. And in the field of popular culture, the young Danteist and novelist Matthew Pearl drew considerable attention in 2003 to Longfellow's Craigie House circle of the late 1860s with his ingenious literary detective story, *The Dante Club*.

⁂

It is among Lewisohn's "subliterary"—extraliterary is a more polite way of putting it—audiences that Longfellow seems to endure.

Granted, the last generation of wretched school children to have been required to memorize "The Wreck of the Hesperus" or "The Village Blacksmith" has now reached retirement age. But Longfellow keeps popping up in popular culture, from "A Psalm of Life" on the Celestial Seasonings tea packages to the recent version of *Hiawatha* filmed by Native Americans (and starring activist Russell Means) who figured out they could do better by appropriating the poem as their own than by following the usual academic path of trashing it. As Gioia notes, "Longfellow remains the one poet the average, nonbookish American still knows by heart—not whole poems but memorable snatches." Everyday language is rich with his legacy—from "ships that pass in the night" (from *Tales of a Wayside Inn*) to "footprints on the sands of time" ("A Psalm of Life").

It is with two manifestations of this *survivance*—as Evangeline's people call it—that Longfellow's story for now can end.

Auden famously said that poetry makes nothing happen. With *Evangeline*, Longfellow proved—unwittingly—that it can. The uprooting of the Nova Scotian Acadians by the British and the New Englanders in 1755 could have been a minor incident in the complex story of the struggle between Britain and France for North America. The Acadians themselves might have retained some tribal memory of their origins and their dispersal, but the ones who returned to Canada could easily have been swallowed up, culturally speaking, by the far more numerous Québecois French or the English speakers of New Brunswick. Those who settled elsewhere might have survived in the anthropological sense that the Amish have survived. But it was Longfellow's world-famous, much translated, hugely selling poem that put the Acadians, and the plight of the Acadians, on the map. In the second half of the nineteenth century, as Acadians in Canada and northern Maine began to assert a distinct ethnic identity, the by-then mythical figure of Evangeline became the focus of popular attention. Many younger Acadians today have mixed feelings about a foundational myth created by a Protestant, English-speaking poet and based so inexorably on a sense of loss, but in the early stages of the construction of Acadian identity, Evangeline herself proved a powerful and effective symbol. The site of her Grand Pré, on the Basin of Minas in Nova Scotia, is commemorated today as a shrine to her memory, visited on pilgrimage by Acadians from all parts of the Atlantic world.

A parallel phenomenon took place on the bayous and prairies of southern and southwestern Louisiana, a region that attracted hundreds of Acadian exiles in the eighteenth century. In the course of contact with their Creole and Anglo neighbors, "Acadian" eventually became "Cajun." When this community's desire to solidify its ethnic identity took shape around 1900, its intellectual elite also took up the name of Evangeline (a name Longfellow had invented) as a rallying cry. Theirs was a slightly different Evangeline—she returns to Louisiana in one version and drops dead when she discovers that Gabriel has married another woman; in another version, they marry and live happily ever afterward—but her usefulness in presenting Acadian culture to the world proved itself again and again. There were even exchanges of visits between Nova Scotia and the bayou country. Today, the Lafayette, Louisiana, yellow pages list some two dozen entities named for Evangeline, from a Boy Scout troop to a laundromat. Today, Cajun culture—not too long ago held in friendly contempt by its English-speaking, Protestant neighbors—has been highly successfully commodified and exported internationally. Every time you *laissez les bons temps rouler*, you have—somewhere in the cultural studies penumbra—Longfellow to thank for it.

❦

Longfellow's power to endure is very much rooted in place—not only the imagined New England and Acadia of his poetry, but an actual landscape, stretching loosely from Casco Bay in Maine and the sandy plains of Brunswick to Plymouth and Newport and Cape Cod. The success of the two Longfellow historic sites—in Portland and in Cambridge—as tourist attractions (as well centers for scholarly research) attests to the way we link the poet and the world most familiar to him.

And in Boston, we can literally follow in the footsteps he laid out for us.

"The Freedom Trail"—one of the most popular tourist experiences in New England—is not exactly chronological, for it incorporates later buildings (Bulfinch's gold-domed State House, for one) and presents no logical sequence of historical events. But as a physical experience it is powerfully informative. It starts on a great public space on the slope of a hill—the Common, where British troops once encamped—and takes you into a lowland (at the moment much chewed up by the pharaonic "Big Dig" highway and tunnel project) and up another hill before thrusting you across the river, by way of the Charlestown Bridge, to that stark but triumphant symbol of the Early Republic, the Bunker Hill Monument. On the way, you pass through Longfellow Country—the ghosts of the Tremont House and the Albion Hotel, the successor of the Saturday Club's Parker House; that seedbed of Boston Unitarianism, King's Chapel; the Old South Church, which the poet helped save; the Old Corner Book Store, from which his fame once radiated throughout the world; Court Street, where his friends Sumner and Hillard practiced law. The Old State House and Faneuil Hall, Quincy Market and Father Taylor's Seaman's Bethel—all evoke the human-scaled, waterfront Boston of brick and granite now overshadowed by the office towers. At the top of Salem Street you reach the handsome Georgian facade of Christ Church, the Old North Church of Paul Revere fame.

In crossing the river you reenact the events of the night of April 18, 1775. According to Longfellow's crafting of the legend, Revere himself rowed across with muffled oar, beneath the nose of a Royal Navy frigate, to await the signal from the church tower that would give birth to a new nation. His adventure is at the heart of the Freedom Trail lesson and, despite every well-intentioned effort to correct it historically, Revere's story is for all practical purposes the one Longfellow created for him.

As they come down Hull Street from the church to the Copps Hill Burying Ground (where the British placed their artillery), the crowds rush, stumble, straggle, trip over each other taking photos, speak in a dozen languages, ask how much farther "it" is (whatever it may be: lunch, a bathroom, the car), stand in awe, breathe deeply, sweat, shiver, laugh, occasionally cry—a pure democracy of motion. It was no accident that Longfellow and Sumner brought Dickens there to Copps Hill, too, when the North End still looked like an eighteenth-century port (though one beginning to fill with Irish immigrants, who would be followed before the end of the century by East European Jews and southern Italians). Beneath the noise of the modern traffic "a hurry of hoofs in a village street" still makes itself heard.

It would be an exaggeration to say that Longfellow invented America. But that he imagined and perfected and made memorable so many aspects of how America is conceived remains his most enduring achievement.

❧ NOTES ❧

Abbreviations

BC: Special Collections, Bowdoin College.

Hilen: Andrew Hilen, *The Letters of Henry Wadsworth Longfellow*. 6 vols., 1966–1982. [References are to letters by sequential number, not by page.]

LNHS: Longfellow Family Papers, Longfellow National Historic Site, Cambridge, Mass.

LP: Longfellow Papers, Houghton Library, Harvard University.

MHS: Wadsworth-Longfellow Papers, Maine Historical Society, Portland, Maine.

ZLP: Zilpah Longfellow Papers, Longfellow National Historic Site, Cambridge, Mass.

Craigie House

the subject of Salome Longfellow had depicted Salome dancing for the head of John the Baptist in "Herod's Banquet Hall," *Christus: A Mystery. Part I: The Divine Tragedy* (Boston, 1872).

Queen Victoria at Windsor Quoted in Ellmann, *Oscar Wilde*, 181. For details of the tour, see Lloyd Lewis, *Oscar Wilde Discovers America, 1882*. Manchester, N.H.: Ayer Co. Publishers, 1967.

himself a beautiful poem Holland, *The Complete Letters of Oscar Wilde*, 137, note 4.

The City by the Sea

Longfellow had not been born in this house On the later fate of the now demolished birthplace in the hands of an early-twentieth-century Portland eccentric, see Barry, "Arthur Charles Jackson," *Down East* (April 1990), 52–55, 61–63.

the Falmouth Gazette Butler, "The Wadsworths," 4–5.

his letters from Washington Wadsworth Papers, MHS, Box 1, Folder 3.

trotting on the knee ZLP, LNHS, Sept. 27, 1807.

the only American officer Leamon, *Revolution Downeast*, 122–23.

a party of Loyalist raiders His daughter Zilpah said her mother had told her the general had been "greatly distressed" by having to order the execution. Zilpah, like her son Henry, opposed capital punishment, saying "there exists no power on earth to empower one man to take the life of another." She was writing her son-in-law, who had sent her the autograph of Gen. Wadsworth's proclamation of martial law in 1780. ZLP, LNHS, Feb. 5, 1834.

To add to the sufferings Dwight, *Travels*, Vol. II. Reprinted in MHS Collections, VII, 232.

Preferring death to slavery Samuel Longfellow, *Life*, I, 3–4.

My dress was simple ZL to Nancy Doane, April 25, 1799. ZLP. For the cultural significance of Zilpah's presentation, see Ulrich, "From the Fair to the Brave," in Sprague, *Agreeable Situations*, 215–25.

It is now evening. ZLP, LNHS, Nov. 29/Dec. 19, 1797.

the room in which we used to read ZLP, LNHS, Dec. 31, 1801.

I presume you know of which room I speak ZLP, LNHS, Sept. 1, 1801.

growing old ZLP, LNHS, Aug. 9, 1801.

the family name had provoked mirth Willis, *History of the Law*, 360.

His interleaved almanacs Clifford Shipton, *New England Life in the Eighteenth Century: Representative Biographies from Sibley's Harvard Graduates* (1742), Cambridge, Mass.: Belknap Press of Harvard University Press, 1996, 157.

in his addresses to the jury Willis, *History of the Law*, 360.

there was money to be made On the legal culture of the District of Maine in the early republic, among many other topics, an essential source is Jordan, *Index to Portland Newspapers*, passim. On the debate over Maine's statehood, see Banks, *Maine Becomes a State*, passim. On the cultural differences between coast and backcountry, see Taylor, *Liberty Men and Great Proprietors*, 9–10.

no political event in American life Theodore Dwight, *History*, 1. The standard modern account argues that the Federalists at Hartford were for the most part moderates, seeking to amend the Constitution but not to leave the Union. Banner, *To the Hartford Convention*, 294–350. Zilpah showed better political instincts than her husband or father: Gen. Wadsworth thought it prudent for the delegates "to deliberate with closed doors." But Zilpah asked Stephen: "... would not a secret consultation give more plausibility to the cry of treason? ... We are assured here that we shall have peace before spring." ZLP, LNHS, Dec. 17, 1814. She correctly predicted the public reaction.

Do you not want to kiss Henry? ZLP, LNHS, Oct. 4, 1809.

Henry is ready to march Lucia Wadsworth to Stephen Longfellow, May 6, 1812. Copy in Materials on Childhood, LP, Box 166, MHS.

Writing amid his legislative duties LP, MHS, Box 166.

the American brig Enterprise The battle is described in the *Eastern Argus* (Portland), Sept. 8, 1813.

Henry's closest brush ZLP, LNHS, July 30/Aug. 6/Aug. 17, 1815.

another painful accident ZLP, LNHS, Sept. 25, 1817.

This certifies Portland Academy certificate, Materials on Childhood, LP, Box 166, MHS.

some friendly gesture Note dated 1821, Materials on Childhood, LP, Box 166, MHS.

He was a very handsome boy Elijah Kellogg, *Bowdoin Orient*, February 1885, BC.

Henry took delight in Don Quixote Samuel Longfellow, *Life*, I, 11.

Deering's Woods For a description and history, see Theo Holtwijk, ed., *Bold Vision: The Development of the Parks of Portland, Maine* (Greater Portland Landmarks, 1999), passim.

Every reader has his first book HWL, "Remarks...upon the death of Irving." 1859. Reprinted in Samuel Longfellow, *Life*, I, 12.

Henry was visiting that evening Samuel Longfellow, *Life*, I, 23. Lawrance Thompson confuses the eighteenth-century poetic practice of imitation—the rewriting of an admired work in one's own language—with plagiarism in "Longfellow's Original Sin of Imitation," *The Colophon*, New Series, I (Autumn 1935), 97–106.

Neither poem is good Thomas Cogswell Upham, "Lovellspond," *American Sketches* (New York, 1819); HWL, "The Battle of Lovell's Pond," *Portland Gazette*, Nov. 5, 1820. Reprinted in Samuel Longfellow, *Life*, I, 21–22.

A Small College in Maine

an excursion into the woods ZLP, LNHS, June 16, 1825.

the brightly colored book Wadsworth Papers, Box 1606, MHS.

In Lawrence Buell's words *New England Literary Culture*, 30.

make the desert bloom Calhoun, *A Small College in Maine*, 3–27.

Writing from Hiram ZLP, LNHS, 1809.

This dear son ZLP, LNHS, Sept. 25, 1817.

a Mrs. Brown ZLP, LNHS, May 10, 1824.

the education of your sons ZLP, LNHS, Jan. 10, 1824.

the truth and the whole truth Letters from Zilpah Longfellow, LP, March 9, 1824.

feel great anxiety ZLP, LNHS, Jan. 25, 1824.

My dear husband ZLP, LNHS, March 4, 1824.

a few hours in your society ZLP, LNHS, Nov. 20, 1824.

What can have made the difference ZLP, LNHS, Feb. 20, 1825.

Henry James was to dismiss Bowdoin James, "Hawthorne," 332.

a country college Hawthorne, *Fanshawe*, 3.

his sister Elizabeth Hilen 28 (Oct. 12, 1823).

the Peucinian librarians The only known surviving copy is in BC.

his first public criticism Loring Hart, "The Beginning of Longfellow's Fame," *New England Quarterly* 34:1 (1963), 67.

I most eagerly aspire Hilen 56 (Dec. 5, 1824).

The Passionate Pilgrim

enlivened only by their chattering Hilen 93 (June 15, 1826).

divers fits of laughter Hilen 94 (June 15, 1826).

Paris is a gloomy city Hilen 97 (July 10, 1826).

the takeover of the college Calhoun, 84–90.

little else than run Hilen 96 (July 10, 1826).

a jauntier letter Hilen 100 (July 23, 1826).

you have changed your costume Letters from Zilpah and Stephen Longfellow Sr., LP, Sept. 24, 1826.

your elastic step ZLP, LNHS, May 7, 1826.

great confidence in your uprightness ZLP, LNHS, Dec. 19, 1826.

Your expenses are much more Letters from Stephen Longfellow Sr., LP, Aug. 11, 1826.

You cannot conceive Hilen 100 (July 23, 1826).

the village's dark streets Hilen 102 (Aug. 17, 1826).

by breaking off the head Hilen 108 (Oct. 26, 1826).

He was alone Hilen 152 (June 18, 1829).

Your ulterior objects Letters from Stephen Longfellow Sr., LP, Dec. 3, 1826.

the most beautiful city Hilen 113 (Feb. 26, 1827).

the great literary mart Hilen 114 (March 20, 1827).

who put you at ease Hilen 114.

Nor was I doomed Mackenzie, *A Year in Spain*, 174.

The Spanish woman Mackenzie, 391.

our fairy life at Naples George Washington Greene Letters, LP, April 7, 1865.

all at the hotel Hilen 141 (Dec. 19, 1828).

the misery of the people Hilen 137 (Sept. 1, 1828).

his Aunt Lucia ZLP, LNHS, 1828.

he exploded in a letter Hilen 141 (Dec. 19, 1828).

melancholy and down-hearted Hilen 143 (Dec. 27, 1828).

In one account of the University Letters from Zilpah Longfellow, LP, Oct. 26, 1826.

In the antechamber Journal for 1829, LP, Feb. 23, 1829.

his Bowdoin memorialist Edward Preble File, Alumni Records, BC.

a vehicle of amusement The only known surviving copy of the *Old Dominion Zeitung* (Göttingen, 1829) is in LP.

a noble river Hilen 156 (May 15, 1829).

Bungonuck Days

a true Christian Letters from Zilpah Longfellow, LP, May 7, 1829. Stephen's comments are added to Zilpah's letter.

a timid feeble girl Letters from Zilpah Longfellow, LP, May 7, 1829.

the guardians of the Institution Letters from Zilpah Longfellow, LP, April 24, 1829.

wrote to the president Hilen 155 (Aug. 27, 1829).

he accepted the professorship Hilen 156 (Sept. 2, 1829).

an ideal university Hilen 147 (March 10, 1829).

the public controversy Calhoun, 84–90.

New curricular arrangements Catalogue of Bowdoin College, 1829.
The prospect before me Hilen 161 (Dec. 20, 1829).
small comedies in French Hilen 158 (Oct. 15, 1829).
the life of an instructer Hilen 161 (Dec. 20, 1829).
nostalgia for Italy Hilen 173 (Jan. 27, 1830).
a Little Man in Gosling Green Reprinted in Hatfield, "An Unknown Prose Tale,"
    American Literature 3:2 (May 1931), 136–48.
His Bowdoin classmate Cheever, *American Common-Place Book of Poetry*, 203.
Its chief characteristics *North American Review* LXXIV (April 1831), 316.
To Englishmen *North American Review* LXXIV (October 1831), 325.
the peculiarities of national character *North American Review* LXXV (April 1832), 36.
the language of a nation *North American Review* LXXV (October 1832), 283.
how other nations have thought *North American Review* LXXV, 283.
the spirit of the age *North American Review* LXXV (January 1832), 59.
You can have no idea Letters from Zilpah Longfellow, LP, May 27, 1827.
the reviews were friendly Loring Hart, "The Beginnings of Longfellow's Fame,"
    New England Quarterly 36:1 (1963), 67.
a kind of Sketch-Book Hilen 150 (May 15, 1829).
pure heart and guileless disposition Hilen 179 (Sept. 26, 1830).
much pleased with this engagement ZLP, LNHS, April 19, 1831.
surrounded by shrubbery Zilpah Longfellow Papers, LNHS, July 14, 1833.
a "black girl" ZLP, LNHS, Oct. 10, 1833.
a wild drama Journal for 1834, LP.
he contemplated a tragedy Journal/Commonplace Book for 1829–34, LP.

The Journey North

an exceedingly agreeable man Hilen, *Longfellow and Scandinavia*, 14.
pleasant little thing Crowninshield, *Diary*, xii–xxxi.
Shall I go? Hilen, *Longfellow and Scandinavia*, 15.
how little can be accomplished here Hilen 307 (May 14, 1835).
ländlich, sittlich Journal for 1835–36, LP, May 22, 1835.
a true dandy Journal for 1835–36, LP, May 21, 1835.
went to a soiree Journal for 1835–36, LP, May 23, 1835.
naked almost to the waist Journal for 1835–36, LP, May 23, 1835.
a sweet, simple, lovely woman Journal for 1835–36, LP, May 22, 1835.
tall and awkward Crowninshield, 11.
a face that reminds you of Burns Journal for 1835–36, LP, May 30, 1835.
a work of rare merit Journal for 1835–36, LP, May 31, 1835.
Breakfasted at Mr. Carlyle's Journal for 1835–36, LP, June 3, 1835.
Our conversation glanced Journal for 1835–36, LP, June 3, 1835.
his great goggle eyes Journal for 1835–36, LP, June 2, 1835.

Lamps gleaming Journal for 1835–36, LP, June 9, 1835.

a feeling of gloom and loneliness Journal for 1835–36, LP, June 17, 1835.

a classical smell Journal for 1835–36, LP, June 22, 1835.

There is no night Journal for 1835–36, LP, June 28, 1835.

two persons gone from town Journal for 1835–36, LP, July 1, 1835.

The moment you leave Journal for 1835–36, LP, July 1, 1835.

leaning over the railing Crowninshield, 75.

Everybody takes a dram Hilen 318 (Aug, 10, 1835).

near a stable yard Journal for 1835–36, LP, Aug. 12, 1835.

blazing from its open mouth Hilen, *Longfellow and Scandinavia*, 125–28.

If I were not in such a hurry Journal for 1835–36, LP, Sept. 8, 1835.

How different this city looks Journal for 1835–36, LP, Sept. 10, 1835.

an unpleasant sound Journal for 1835–36, LP, Sept. 10, 1836.

I began to read aloud Crowninshield, 114–15.

like a cat in a strange garret Journal for 1835–36, LP, Sept. 20, 1835.

Mary is sick Crowninshield, 136.

Was up before daylight Journal for 1835–36, LP, Oct. 6, 1835.

the most disagreeable sounding language Hilen 331 (Oct. 25, 1835).

four kinds of meat Crowninshield, 167.

The doctor called Crowninshield, 176.

a miscarriage Hilen 333 (Nov. 28, 1835).

her breathing more difficult Crowninshield, 183–84.

I gave him some wine Crowninshield, 184.

An Alpine Interlude

short, thick, commonplace Wagenknecht, *Mrs. Longfellow*, 44.

Why do I travel? Journal for 1836, LP, July 20, 1836.

sends up his card Wagenknecht, *Mrs. Longfellow*, 32.

so kind to William Wagenknecht, *Mrs. Longfellow*, 35.

Miss Mr. L Wagenknecht, *Mrs. Longfellow*, 36.

Castle Craigie

the dignified Georgian house For the story of the house's previous owners, see Dana, "The Craigie House," in *Henry Wadsworth Longfellow*.

a local eccentric The Craigie House Ms. Notes, LP, 12.

I live in a great house Hilen 437 (Aug. 6, 1838).

For generation after generation Adams, *The Education of Henry Adams* (Boston: Houghton Mifflin Company, 1971), 54.

a long battle with the institution For details, see Johnson, *Professor Longfellow*, 1–15.

the attribute of great genius Lectures on Goethe, Harvard College, 1837–38, LP.

first lecture on Goethe's Faust Hale, *A New England Boyhood*, xx.

good fortune to study French Higginson, *Old Cambridge*, 142.

too gay a look Craigie House Notes, 10.

curl your hair Hilen 421 (April 30, 1838).

genuine poetic feeling Hart, 74.

it came into my mind *Complete Poetical Works* (1894), 13.

their 17th-century ancestor Hilen 555 (Oct. 25, 1840).

on the back of a letter *Complete Poetical Works*, 19.

one of Longfellow's most obscure works *Hyperion* was not included in the Library of America 2000 edition of Longfellow's poetry and prose. A paperback edition was published in 2002 by Wildside Press, Doylestown, Penn.

The Water Cure

I am reluctantly compelled Hilen 659 (Jan. 24, 1842).

a glorious fellow Hilen 660 (Jan. 30, 1842).

Will this parting note reach you? Charles Sumner Papers, Houghton Library, April 23, 1842.

it made my heart swell Hilen 681 (April 26, 1842).

growing a little web-footed Hilen 690 (June 8, 1842).

to work upon my nerves Hilen 694 (June 24, 1842).

not out of my berth Hilen 743 (Jan. 6, 1843).

How do you like the Slavery Poems? Hilen 739 (Jan. 1, 1843).

negrophilic old ladies Poe, *Essays and Reviews*, 762.

A Wedding in Beacon Street

a better dawn Wagenknecht, *Mrs. Longfellow*, 83–84.

amid the blossoms Journal for 1844, LP, May 10, 1844. Longfellow's journal for 1843 does not survive.

true love is very apt to win its reward Wagenknecht, 84.

a very lovely woman Hilen 780 (May 11, 1843).

Life was too lonely Hilen 781 (May 21, 1843).

long-tried affection Wagenknecht, 86.

the groom was handsome as usual Wagenknecht, *Longfellow: A Full-Length Portrait* (New York, 1955), 231.

A Seaside Idyll

this grand old mansion Wagenknecht, *Mrs. Longfellow*, 92. Longfellow's instincts as a preservationist had deep roots: one of his earliest poems is his 1824 protest against the replacement of his family's church by the present building. See "Old Parish Church," Little, *Longfellow's Boyhood Poems*, 43–44.

every modern comfort Wagenknecht, 93.

decidedly conservative   Journal for 1844, LP, April 9, 1844.

which Washington has rendered sacred   For details of their work on the house, including painting it yellow, see *Historic Furnishings Report: The Longfellow House* (U.S. Department of the Interior/National Park Service, 1999), esp. 45–51 and passim for individual rooms. Copy in Longfellow National Historic Site Archives, Cambridge, Mass.

so many great events   Among these was a literary event whose significance was not appreciated until much later: While living at the Craigie House during the Siege of Boston, General Washington wrote his now famous letter to the young African American poet Phillis Wheatley. Whether she accepted his invitation to call is unknown.

Nahant as a permanent summer residence   Linked to Lynn by a narrow causeway, Nahant combined cool summer weather with easy access to Boston by carriage or steamer. The small peninsula attracted so many prominent but plain-living summer residents that Tom Appleton labeled it "cold roast beef Boston."

the seaside drowsiness   Journal for 1847–48, LP, July 16, 1847.

her scattered goods   Journal, LP, Aug. 14, 1847.

right out of Wilhelm Meister   Journal, LP, Aug. 20, 1847.

a man of genius   Journal, LP, Aug. 14, 1847.

How lovely the view   Journal, LP, Aug. 18, 1847.

an unpublished passage   Journal, LP, Aug. 18, 1847.

a short little fellow   Journal, LP, July 28, 1847. For more details of Longfellow's hometown, see Joseph Conforti (ed.), *Creating Portland* (forthcoming, Northeastern University Press).

that later critics would ridicule   Most unkind of all is surely John Betjeman's "Longfellow's Visit to Venice. [To be read in a quiet New England accent]."

He improvised the poem   Note with poem, *Complete Poetical Works* (Cambridge Edition, 1894), 68.

Evangeline

Conolly told a story   Journal for 1840–41, LP, April 5, 1840. Hawthorne and Dana, The Origin and Development of Longfellow's "Evangeline," 10–13. This essay—by grandsons of Longfellow and Hawthorne—is the fullest account of how the poem came to be written.

Hawthorne soon had second thoughts   Hawthorne and Dana, 13. A copy of Conolly's not very reliable journal is at BC.

the Evangeline legend has been rewritten   Most notably by Felix Vorhees, whose *Acadian Reminiscences* (1907) has a happy ending, and by Antonine Maillet, whose *Pelagie-la-Charette* (1979; English trans., 1982) is probably the most famous novel in Acadian French, a work of magic realism telling how a young woman with a cart undoes the Acadian disapora, reuniting her people. It won the Prix Goncourt in 1979.

Banvard's heroic diorama   For the artist's career, see Collins, *Banvard's Folly*, 1–24.

a pamphlet describing the panorama   "Description of Banvard's Panorama of the Mississippi River..." (Boston, 1847). Copy at the Boston Athenaeum.

foundational myth of Acadian ethnic identity   See, for example, Griffiths, "Longfellow's *Evangeline*: The Birth and Acceptance of a Legend," and Brasseux, *In Search of Evangeline: Birth and Evolution of the Evangeline Myth*. For Acadians in the St. John Valley, see National Park Service, *Acadian Culture in Maine*.

Hawthorne repeated his praise   Hawthorne and Dana, 39. Neither the personal nor the literary relationship between the two writers has been much studied. Yet there are intriguing echoes of *Evangeline* in *The Scarlet Letter* (1850), where in "A Forest Walk" Hester experiences "the mystery of the primeval forest" (as David Hochheiser has pointed out to me). In *The Blithedale Romance* (1852), the poet Coverdale lives in circumstances remarkably similar to Longfellow's at the Craigie House in the early 1840s: "My pleasant bachelor-parlor, sunny and shadowy, curtained and carpeted, with the bed-chamber adjoining; my centre-table, strewn with books and periodicals; my writing-desk, with a half-finished poem in a stanza of my own contrivance; my morning lounge at the reading-room or picture-gallery; my noontide walk along the cheery pavement...my dinner at the Albion [the Boston hotel in which, before his remarriage, Longfellow often took his meals]." Library of America edition, 666.

Laura Bridgman   The Bridgman-Longfellow letters and related news clippings are in the Gulotta Collection, Houghton Library. For a perceptive if less than flattering account of the poet's close friend, Samuel Gridley Howe, see Gitter, *The Imprisoned Guest*. Howe married Julia Ward, Sam Ward's sister, now remembered as author of "The Battle Hymn of the Republic" but in her day a formidable belle; many of his friends hoped Longfellow would marry her. Howe was also the object of Charles Sumner's adoration.

A day of agony   Journal for 1847–48, LP, Sept. 10, 1848.

first recorded use of ether in childbirth   Pittinger, "The Anesthetization of Fanny Longfellow...," 368–69.

Evangeline was published   The event cemented Longfellow's long relationship with the firm that by 1855 was internationally known as Ticknor and Fields and his close friendship with the publisher James T. Fields. The firm's authors included Tennyson, Whittier, Child, Holmes, Hawthorne, Thoreau, and Emerson. For details of every aspect of its operation, see Winship, *American Literary Publishing in the Mid-Nineteenth Century: The Business of Ticknor and Fields*.

more pleasure than it would be decorous to express   Hawthorne and Dana, 39. The hexameter bothered some critics; the best account of Longfellow's use of it is in Allen, *American Prosody*, 180–85, along with analysis of Longfellow's other verse forms and meters.

a family so blessed On the exemplary nature of the Longfellow family in the mid-nineteenth-century American imagination, see Gartner, "Longfellow's Place: The Poet and Poetry of Craigie House," especially for his explanation of how the poet lowered the barrier between public and private by "inviting" the public, as it were, *into his home.*

condemned as sentimentality There is now a vast literature on sentimentalism as a literary movement in the sense that romanticism and realism are considered movements, much of it in reaction to Anne Douglas's dismissal of nineteenth-century sentimental writing as evidence of female intellectual enfeeblement. Very little of this new scholarship concerns sentimental male writers, despite the success of Dickens and Longfellow in this vein. Two important contributions are Haralson, "Mars in Petticoats: Longfellow and Sentimental Masculinity" and the essays in Chapman and Hendler, *Sentimental Men: Masculinity and the Politics of Affect in American Culture*, especially Bertolini, "The Erotics of Sentimental Bachelorhood in the 1850s."

"Sail On, O Union"

its true weight and emphasis Journal for 1849–50, LP, Feb. 12, 1850.

Lincoln, too, was moved to tears McClatchy, 39.

conflation of the national romance and the personal For an analysis of the poem, see Kete, *Sentimental Collaborations: Mourning and Middle-Class Identity in Nineteenth-Century America*, where she compares Longfellow and Lydia Sigourney as "sentimental nationalists."

the Appleton family fortunes Starting life as a New Hampshire farm boy, Nathan Appleton had become one of the richest men in New England as a result of his investment in the Lowell, Mass., textile mills (whose famously literate "mill girls" were among Longfellow's most enthusiastic readers). The mills depended on an uninterrupted supply of Southern cotton; among their products were cheap clothing sold to plantation owners for their slaves. For Appleton's career, see Dalzell, *Enterprising Elite: The Boston Associates and the World They Made.*

the outspokenly antislavery Sumner Boston's Whig political elite, including Robert Winthrop and Nathan Appleton, found Sumner an irritant; Sumner, for his part, seemed genuinely surprised when people he had harshly criticized turned against him. In the 1840s he combined antislavery with a belief in the peace movement; he had accompanied the Longfellows on their 1843 wedding trip to Springfield, where they visited the U.S. Arsenal (which still exists as a museum). Fanny suggested an antiwar poem using the image of the gun barrels as organ pipes, playing the death-angel's tune; her husband obliged.

Without the slightest trace of irony, the museum displays a copy of the poem next to an organ-pipe-like construction of rifles.

the first lesbian relationship in American fiction Faderman, "Female Same-Sex Relationships in Novels by Longfellow, Holmes, and James," 315–18.

life in the early Plymouth Colony See John Seelye, "Feminizing the Rock," *Memory's Nation: The Place of Plymouth Rock*, 361–95.

Holmes once told a friend The Saturday Club was organized in 1855 to bring together for monthly dinners men of literary interests in the greater Boston area; it soon became the most famous of such clubs in the country, a symbol of the prestige of the New England literati. Meetings were long and convivial; Longfellow and Hawthorne sat quietly while such champion talkers as Emerson, Holmes, Felton, and Tom Appleton held forth; it was also a place to show off Boston to distinguished visitors, especially Englishmen. For the membership, see Emerson, *The Early Years of the Saturday Club*, passim.

his literary earnings Allibone, *A Critical Dictionary*, II, 1128–29. See also Charvat, "Longfellow's Income from His Writings, 1840–1852."

severe eyestrain Throughout his middle years, Longfellow suffered terribly from his eyes, at some points becoming unable to read or write (Fanny served as his amanuensis). The condition eventually cleared up, suggesting a temporary disorder of the macula, such as central serous chorioretinopathy. I am grateful to Dr. Frederick S. Miller III for this suggestion.

The Jewish Cemetery at Newport For a less admiring account of the poem, see Harap, *The Image of the Jew in American Literature*, 91–93.

John Brown's bold though bloody raid Howe was one of John Brown's financial supporters and had to flee temporarily to Canada in 1859. Longfellow sympathized: When Brown was hanged, he exclaimed, "This will be a great day in History! The date of a New Revolution; quite as much needed as the old one!" Journal for 1858–59, LP, Dec. 2, 1859.

the redemption of the country Journal for 1860–62, LP, Nov. 7, 1860. His journal over the next months is filled with enthusiasm for the North and complaints about South Carolina and other secessionist states.

Hiawatha

inhabited the coast of Maine Maine's Indians had not been eliminated but had retreated, in small numbers, to the live in the margins of white settlement; see Bourque, *Twelve Thousand Years*, for a detailed account. By Longfellow's youth they were regarded as a curiosity; in the first volume of the Maine Historical Society's Collections (1831), William Willis anticipated the race's extinction but urged study of their character, manners, and history (Introductory Remarks, 8). Longfellow himself took a sympathetic stance in his 1823 collegiate "dialogue" between an "emigrant" and a "savage." See his letter to Zilpah, Hilen 31 (Nov. 9, 1823).

As a Bowdoin professor   *North American Review* (January 1832), 75.

cyclical history of mankind   Robert Stafford Ward, "The Influence of Vico upon Longfellow," *ESQ* 58:1 (1970), 57–62.

The case for the prosecution   Carr, *Inventing the American Primitive*, 127, 141. On the other hand, the American Indian Film Institute gave a prize in 1996 to *The Song of Hiawatha*, starring Russell Means, a film "based on the epic poem."

a literary poem pretending to belong to the oral tradition   Schmidt, *Lives of the Poets*, 439.

his own civilized magic   Trachtenberg, "Singing Hiawatha: Longfellow's Hybrid Myth of America," 12. The best introduction to the poem itself is Fiske, "Mercerized Folklore."

Emerson wrote to Longfellow   Quoted in Trachtenberg, 17. Emerson and Longfellow are two people who enjoyed each other's company but neither ever understood the other.

I have at length hit upon a plan   Journal for 1853–55, LP, June 22, 1854.

The folklorist Elias Lonnrot   For his career and modus operandi, see Magoun, *The Kalevala.*

the study of Indian languages   Schoolcraft, "General Considerations," *Algic Researches*, 10.

There are Indians here…   Hilen 394 (Oct. 29, 1837), to his late wife's sister, Margaret Potter. In 1849, in Boston, he met the Ojibwa preacher and poet Kah-ge-ga-gah-bowh (George Copway).

his long-delayed resignation   Longfellow cited his eye troubles and "the wearinesss of doing the same things over and over again for so many, many years." Johnson, *Professor Longfellow of Harvard*, 82.

My Lost Youth   Robert Frost entitled his first collection of poems *A Boy's Will* (1913). Longfellow's evocation of the Portland of his childhood ranges from the topographic ("The shadows of Deering's Woods") to the sociological ("Spanish sailors with bearded lips") to the imaginary (he could not possibly have heard the battle off distant Monhegan Island between the H.M.S. *Boxer* and the U.S.S. *Enterprise* in the War of 1812).

A PROMISED LITERARY TREAT   Journal, LP, July 24, 1854.

hard work to write poetry in a closet   Journal, LP, July 31, 1854.

Very rich and dreamy   Journal, LP, Aug. 1, 2, 5, 1854.

Bogue offers one hundred pounds   Journal, LP, Sept. 14, 1854.

the violence of the Indian legends   The deleted canto is "The Wrestling of Kwasind," Hiawatha MS, Printer's Copy, Vol. 2, 123–49, MsAm 1340 (97), Houghton Library.

Some of the newspapers are fast and furious   Journal, LP, Nov. 18, 1854.

a martyr to neuralgia   Longfellow's Cambridge journals combine ecstatic descriptions of good weather, terse notes on the quality of the preaching he hears, tantalizingly brief descriptions of his social and literary encounters, lists of his voluminous reading, occasional paens to female beauty and political outbursts, and a litany of physical complaints, mostly regarding his teeth and head. It is not a journal intime, in other words, but he kept it more or less faithfully for most of his adult life and felt guilty when he skipped days.

Hiawatha's Photographing   The parody is printed in Gernsheim, *Lewis Carroll, Photographer*, 113–17. The animal first appears in Canto II ("The Four Winds"), 7: "From the Land of the White Rabbit" and reappears in the deleted canto.

an implicit treatise on the nature of language   Fletcher, "Whitman and Longfellow: Two Types of the American Poet," 141.

who rhymed Androscoggin with "noggin"   The difficulty of poeticizing Native American place names had bedeviled American poets until Longfellow—and Whitman. Try finding a word to rhyme with "Massachusetts."

its author's hopes for peace   The years preceding *Hiawatha* had been difficult for Longfellow in several respects: in a public sense in Daniel Webster's support for the Fugitive Slave Law, more personally because of the death of his father in 1849 and his mother in 1851 (both after many years of being invalids). Within his circle there was great shock over the drowning of Margaret Fuller Ossoli, her new husband, and infant in 1850 on their return from Italy, and even greater anguish over the arrest in 1849 and eventual hanging of Harvard medical professor John Webster for the murder of George Parkman.

A Lock of Hair

the three girls of "The Children's Hour"   "Grave Alice, and laughing [Anne] Allegra, / And Edith with golden hair." The three were painted in a widely reproduced group portrait by Thomas Buchanan Reed; the pose gave rise to a popular story that Anne Allegra had only one arm. One of the most striking artifacts among the Longfellow memorabilia at the Maine Historical Society is a locket belonging to an unknown soldier, bearing a photographic copy of the painting, "found on the battlefield at Gettysburg."

She bore the agony like a martyr   Quoted in Stanley C. Patterson, "The Second Act of Life's Drama," unpublished MS, 474. Copy at Longfellow National Historic Site Archives. The image of the burning woman has proved powerful: see, for example, James Schuyler's 1988 poem "Light from Canada." (My thanks to Carl Little for this reference.)

a different version of the story   "Circumstances of Mrs. Longfellow's Death, 1861." Dana Family Papers, Box 44: R.H. Dana III, Massachusetts Historical Society.

How am I alive   Hilen 1889 (Aug. 18, 1869).

Charley Goes to War

The Longfellow of the 1850s   The poet's appearance is noted in a *Record of Family Faculties* (Francis Galton, Macmillan: London, 1884), filled out by his children, which reports that he was five foot eight inches tall, with brown hair and blue eyes; "Erect, alert, graceful & gracious & gentle." Fanny is described as five foot six or seven, hair dark brown, eyes dark; "Tall, dignified, beautiful, very reserved." Her temperment: "Calm & dignified & self controlled. Great magnetism, but romantic & deeply enthusiastic." Private collection. Longfellow's physiognomy also attracted the attention of phrenologists: L. N. Fowler's *Illustrated Phrenological Almanac* for 1859 used him, with two images of his head, as an example of the "literary faculties." BC, Miscellaneous Pamphlets: Psychology.

We were then introduced   Charles Appleton Longfellow Letters, LP, bMS Am 1340.2 (3503), April 4, 1862.

she enlisted as a private   Charles Appleton Longfellow Letters, LP, [April 10, 1862].

a letter postmarked in Portland   Printed in Hilen, "Charley Longfellow Goes to War," No. 1, 59. Hilen's two-part essay is the most thorough account of Charley's military service; this chapter is much indebted to it.

Longfellow wrote to Rand   Hilen 1993 (March 14, 1863).

one of the great comic moments   Hilen, "Charley Longfellow Goes to War," No. 1, 80–81.

Little Merrythought   MS Am 1340 (165), Houghton Library. The Peter Quince drawings are deftly handled in Irmscher, "Longfellow Redux."

Its Revolutionary War details are fictionalized   See Fischer, "The Union in Crisis: Longfellow's Myth of the Lone Rider," *Paul Revere's Ride*, 331–35.

As Matthew Gartner points out   "Longfellow and Paul Revere's Ride: A Study in American Literary Reputation," lecture, Old South Meeting House, Boston, Sept. 20, 2000.

the children's book market   A particularly striking example is Christopher Bing's three-dimensional *The Midnight Ride of Paul Revere* (New York: Handprint Books, 2001).

a solid ground in biographical fact   For the models, see Van Schaick, *Characters in Tales of a Wayside Inn.*

Luigi Monti   His unpublished, very lively memoir detailing his escape is in the Gulotta Collection, Houghton Library.

an environmentalist before his time   Longfellow and his children, for example, bought the Brighton Meadows in 1869, when the land was threatened with industrial development, to preserve the view from the Craigie House. The family later gave the land to Harvard.

a tragic poem on the Puritans   The complicated publishing history of *The New England Tragedies* is told, in part, in Tucker, *The Shaping of Longfellow's John Endicott.*

unstageable as drama   Yet a recent staged reading of *Giles Corey*, which took about ninety minutes, proved successful. The play is much terser than Arthur Miller's widely taught *The Crucible* but incorporates much of the same historical material.

the famous Dante Club   For details, including who attended, see J. Chesley Mathews, "Mr. Longfellow's Dante Club," *76th Annual Report of the Dante Society* (1958), 23–35. For a critique of his ability as a Dante translator, see Gilbert F. Cunningham, *The Divine Comedy in English, A Critical Bibliography, 1782–1900* (Edinburgh: Oliver and Boyd, 1965), 65–71.

the poet's fabled cellar   Most proper Bostonians drank very old madeira; Longfellow was unusual in his expert knowledge of European wine, his cellar containing not only burgundies, hock, and champagne but a variety of Italian wines (a taste acquired in 1828), purchased through the Italian consul. See his Cellarbook, LP.

When Longfellow read verse   Howells, "The White Mr. Longfellow," Literary Friends and Acquaintance, 155–56.

a visit with the Queen   A courtier said the queen told him afterwards, "The American poet Longfellow has just been here. I noticed an unusual interest among the attendants and servants.... When he took leave, they concealed themselves in places from which they could get a good look at him as he passed. I have since inquired among them, and am surprised and pleased to find that many of his poems are familiar to them." Kennedy, *Longfellow*, 183.

He breakfasted with Mr. Gladstone   Samuel Longfellow, *Life* III, 113.

several memorable portraits   On Healy's "Arch of Titus," see *The Lure of Italy*, 244–46; on Lewis's bust of Longfellow, 242–43. In Rome Longfellow also met Franz Liszt, who was in 1874 to write a cantata in which, in the first part, he did a repeated setting of the word "Excelsior!" (Wagner borrowed the theme for the opening of *Parsifal*); in the second, he set "The Bells of Strasburg Cathedral" from *The Golden Legend*.

Tennyson at Farringford   The two poets treated each other with wary respect; Tennyson did not particularly like Longfellow's work but greeted him cordially. Longfellow sold better than the Poet Laureate in Britain because in the absence of international copyright, British publishers could pirate American books and sell them more cheaply, in the absence of any royalties. (U.S. publishers returned the favor.) Longfellow allowed several of his later works to be published first in London, to guarantee that he would own the copyright.

the formidable Julia Margaret Cameron   Far more in fashion today than her neighbor Tennyson, Cameron presided over a circle immortalized in her great-niece Virginia Woolf's 1923 comedy *Freshwater*. See Colin Ford, "Geniuses, Poets, and Painters: The World of Julia Margaret Cameron," in Cox and Ford, *Julia Margaret Cameron: The Complete Photographs*, 40–79.

Morituri Salutamus

President Joshua Chamberlain's invitation He passed up the invitation to stay with the Chamberlains, however: The general had moved the house in which Henry and Mary had lived in 1831–32 to Maine Street, elevating it, with a new first floor underneath. The house, today a Chamberlain museum, retains the Longfellow's front door and front rooms.

he could stand at the pulpit Longfellow's influence as a medieval revivalist has been underestimated; he could take satisfaction in being in Richard Upjohn's Carpenter Gothic church, not far from the Upjohn's Romanesque college chapel, a chateauesque alumni hall, and Gervase Wheeler's much-copied Gothic Revival "cottage-villa."

Five more volumes In addition to his own work, he had begun in 1876 his *Poems of Places*, which eventually ran to thirty-one volumes, covering all of Europe and parts of Asia, translated by many hands, including his own.

the massacre at Little Big Horn In Evan S. Connell's *Son of the Morning Star* (a 1984 biography of Gen. George Custer), Longfellow is criticized for rushing the poem to the market and getting many details wrong. He in fact depended on such newspaper accounts as were available; the poem is notably pro-Sioux for its time and place.

Henry James's observation *William Wetmore Story and His Friends*, 311. James allows Mr. Verver to quote from "The Psalm of Life" in *The Golden Bowl* (1904).

steady flow of distinguished visitors Not all of these visitors were famous; Longfellow often greeted respectable-looking strangers at the door himself. For a particularly charming account of such a visit, see Bok, *The Americanization of Edward Bok*, 41–47. The poet was delighted to find someone to read a Dutch translation of his work to him.

perhaps one serious flutter of the heart Hilen suggests several romantic interests on the part of Longfellow and younger women in the 1870s, but the evidence is slim.

Priscilla Mullins's contribution to the antiques trade See, for example, Celia Betsky, "Inside the Past: The Interior and the Colonial Revival in American Art and Literature, 1860–1914" in Axelrod, *The Colonial Revival in America*, 241–77, and Condon and Shuckhart, *Inside SPNEA: Priscilla*, 5–21.

the deaths of close friends During Hawthorne's final illness, his son Julian read to him from *Evangeline*. *Nathaniel Hawthorne and His Wife*, II, 335.

Darwinism Perhaps because of his close friendship to Agassiz, the nation's leading anti-Darwinian scientist, Longfellow did not express a public opinion on a matter much discussed in advanced Boston-Cambridge circles, like the Radical Club (which the poet occasionally attended). In public he remained a conventional Unitarian, whose verse and drama were filled with biblical themes, but in his later years he grew more agnostic. Howells, 171, and R. H. Dana III Memoir, 14–16.

Annie Fields's literary salon   Mrs. Fields is now given as much credit as he is for the success of her husband's publishing house, Ticknor & Fields, at the Old Corner Book Store in Boston. See, for example, Gollin, *Annie Adams Fields.*

Uncle Tom Appleton   Fanny's beloved brother, Tom, was a noted wit, art collector, and yachtsman who is given credit for having said, "When good Americans die, they go to Paris." Having rejected a business career in America, he spent as much time as possible abroad, a kind of proto-Jamesian figure.

literally nursed him   Richard Henry Dana III wrote: "Mr. Longfellow had to act as valet and trained nurse in one," patiently helping his old friend day and night. Dana Family Papers, Box 44, Massachusetts Historical Society.

his photo album   Laidlaw (ed.), *Charles Appleton Longfellow: Twenty Months in Japan, 1871–1873.*

Ernest proved more conventional   He disinherited his nephews H. W. L. ("Harry") Dana and Allston Dana "for their socialistic and pacifistic views." Rosamond Wild Dana, "Privileged Radicals: The Rebellious Times of Six Dana Siblings in Cambridge and New York in the Early Twentieth Century." M.A. thesis, City University of New York, 1991, 25.

Perhaps their Brahminism gave them the confidence to go against the grain. Richard Henry Dana IV became a conscientious objector in World War I; Harry, an enthusiastic supporter of the Soviet Union in the 1920s and 1930s, was arrested (though acquitted) on a morals charge in 1935 and became a pioneer gay liberationist as well as the family's historian; Edward Dana was a socialist and civil rights activist; Delia Dana, a socialist and feminist; only Frances Appleton Dana de Rahm led a conventional social life, becoming a very close friend of Franklin Roosevelt, though she committed suicide in 1933.

I cannot recall the name of our friend   Kennedy, 278.

Aftermath

a stroll through Westminster Abbey   *The Sketch Book of Geoffrey Crayon, Gent.* in *Washington Irving: History, Tales & Sketches* (Library of America, 1983), 896.

reputation among the British reading public   Evidence of his fame is spread across Europe: I am grateful to Artine Artinian for telling me of the Longfellow bust in Menton, France, and to Brunhild Fischer for sending me photos of the Longfellow fountain in Geisenheim, Germany, with its quotation from *The Golden Legend.*

the Valhalla of the English-speaking race   Higginson, Longfellow, 252.

In Washington in 1909   Appropriately enough, the Mayflower Hotel is only a few steps away!

at the Music Hall in Woonsocket   The program is in the Gulotta Collection, Houghton Library.

the Afro-British composer   For an analysis, see Tortolano, "Hiawatha," *Samuel Coleridge-Taylor*, 39–71.

Antonin Dvorak   There is an extensive literature on the composer's American influences, including African American music. On the Hiawatha connection, see, for example, Michael Beckerman, "The Dance of Pau-Puk-Keewis, the Song of Chiabos, and the Story of Iagoo: Reflections on Dvorak's 'New World' Scherzo," in Tibbetts, *Dvorak in America, 1892–1895*, 210–27.

George Saintsbury   "Longfellow's Poems," *Prefaces and Essays*, 340.

As Carol Christ has suggested   Christ, 157.

his mother back in Idaho   Humphrey Carpenter, *A Serious Character: The Life of Ezra Pound* (Boston: Houghton Mifflin, 1988), 5–6, 22.

Longfellow's poetic practice   He pops up in unexpected places. In a 1977 television interview with William F. Buckley, Jr., Jorge Luis Borges said: "I don't know why people look down on Longfellow. Maybe he was too much of a literary man, no? He was the same kind of poet as Ezra Pound. I mean he took mostly from books and not from his own experience. But his translation of the Divine Comedy is a very fine translation. In fact, I read it in English before I read it in Italian." Transcript, PBS, Feb. 18, 1977. Copy at Maine Historical Society. On Longfellow's lingering influence in Latin America, see Kirsten Silva Gruesz, "*El Gran Poeta*: Longfellow and a Psalm of Exile," *American Literary History* 10:3 (Fall 1998), 395–427.

Who, except wretched schoolchildren   Lewisohn, *Expression in America*, 65–66.

the homophobic witch hunt   See Werth, *The Scarlet Professor*, passim.

Howard Nemerov   "Introduction," *Longfellow*, 7–27.

"greener" than we had thought   Buell, on Longfellow's "Aftermath," in *The Environmental Imagination*, 109–10.

the poet Dana Gioia   *The Columbia History of American Poetry*, 64–96.

more critical attention in Britain   Jay Parini, "Longfellow and American Optimism," *Times Literary Supplement*, May 25, 2001, 5–6.

as Gulotta explained   Basbanes, *Among the Gently Mad*, 194–97.

As Gioia notes   *The Columbia History of American Poetry*, 67.

"Acadian" eventually became "Cajun"   See Brasseux, *Acadian to Cajun: Transformation of a People, 1803–1877*, passim.

the Saturday Club's Parker House   The present hotel, which opened in 1927, replaced the original 1855 building in which the club met.

For further details of Longfellow's life and career, visit the Longfellow pages, www.mainememory.net, on the Maine Historical Society's Maine Memory Network.

᪣ SELECTED BIBLIOGRAPHY ᪣

Manuscript Sources

Houghton Library, Harvard University
Longfellow National Historic Site, Cambridge, Mass.
Maine Historical Society, Portland, Maine
Special Collections, Bowdoin College, Brunswick, Maine
Pejepscot Historical Society, Brunswick, Maine
Massachusetts Historical Society, Boston
Boston Athenaeum
Society for the Preservation of New England Antiquities, Boston
Bostonian Society
Francis A. Countway Library of Medicine, Harvard Medical School, Boston

First American Publication of Longfellow's Work in Book Form

(All were published in Boston, except as noted.)

Catalogue of the Library of the Peucinian Society, Bowdoin College (Hallowell, Maine: Goodale, Glazier & Co. Printers, 1823)

Manuel de Proverbes Dramatiques (Portland, Maine: Samuel Colman,1830)

Elements of French Grammar, by M. Lhomand (Portland, Maine: Samuel Colman, 1830)

Novelas Espanolas. El Serrano de las Alpujarras; y el Cuadro Misterioso (Portland, Maine: Samuel Colman, 1830)

Le Ministre de Wakefield (Gray and Bowden, 1831)

Syllabus de la Grammaire Italienne (Gray and Bowden, 1832)

Saggi de' Novellieri Italiani d'Ogni Secolo (Gray and Bowden, 1832)

Outre-Mer, A Pilgrimage Beyond the Sea (Hilliard, Gray, & Co.: No. I, 1833; No. II, 1834)

Hyperion, A Romance (New York: Samuel Colman, 1839)

Voices of the Night (Cambridge, Mass.: John Owen, 1839)

Poems on Slavery (Cambridge, Mass.: John Owen, 1842)

Ballads and Other Poems (Cambridge, Mass.: John Owen, 1842)

The Spanish Student: A Play, in Three Acts (Cambridge, Mass.: John Owen, 1843)

The Poets and Poetry of Europe (Philadelphia: Carey and Hart, 1845)

Poems (Philadelphia: Carey and Hart, 1845)

The Belfrey of Bruges and Other Poems (Cambridge, Mass.: John Owen, 1846)

The Estray: A Collection of Poems (William D. Ticknor & Co., 1847)

Evangeline, A Tale of Acadie (William D. Ticknor & Co., 1847)

Kavanagh, A Tale (Ticknor, Reed, and Fields, 1849)

The Seaside and the Fireside (Ticknor, Reed, and Fields, 1850)

The Golden Legend (Ticknor, Reed, and Fields, 1851)

The Song of Hiawatha (Ticknor and Fields, 1855)

Prose Works, 2 vols. (Ticknor and Fields, 1857)

The Courtship of Miles Standish, and Other Poems (Ticknor and Fields, 1858)

Tales of a Wayside Inn (Ticknor and Fields, 1863)

Flower-de-Luce (Ticknor and Fields, 1867)

The Divine Comedy of Dante, 3 vols. (Ticknor and Fields, 1867)

The New England Tragedies: I. *John Endicott*, II. *Giles Corey of the Salem Farms* (Ticknor and Fields, 1868)

The Divine Tragedy (James R. Osgood and Company, 1871)

Christus, 3 vols.: *The Divine Tragedy, The Golden Legend*, and *The New England Tragedies* (James R. Osgood and Company, 1871)

Three Books of Song (James R. Osgood and Company, 1872)

Aftermath (James R. Osgood and Company, 1873)

The Hanging of the Crane (James R. Osgood and Company, 1874)

The Masque of Pandora and Other Poems (James R. Osgood and Company, 1875)

Poems of Places, 32 vols. (James R. Osgood and Company, 1876–79)

Keramós and Other Poems (Houghton, Osgood & Company, 1878)

Ultima Thule (Houghton, Mifflin & Company, 1880)

In the Harbor (Houghton, Mifflin & Company, 1882)

Michael Angelo (Houghton, Mifflin & Company, 1884)

"Origin and Growth of the Languages of Southern Europe and of Their Literature: An Inaugural Address ..." September 2, 1830. (Bowdoin College, Brunswick, Maine, 1907)

Longfellow's Boyhood Poems (Saratoga Springs, N.Y.: R. W. Pettengill, 1925)

For first British publication, private printings, and first appearance of individual poems in gift book and other formats, see Jacob Blanck, *Bibliography of American Literature*. Vol. V (Oak Knoll Books).

Selected Editions of Longfellow's Works

The Complete Works of Henry Wadsworth Longfellow. 7 vols. Boston: Ticknor and Fields, 1866.

The Works of Henry Wadsworth Longfellow. The Riverside Edition. 11 vols. Horace E. Scudder, ed. Boston: Houghton, Mifflin & Company, 1886.

The Complete Works of Henry Wadsworth Longfellow. Standard Library Edition. 14 vols. Boston: Houghton, Mifflin & Company, 1891. [Includes the 3-volume *Life* by Samuel Longfellow.]

The Complete Poetical Works of Henry Wadsworth Longfellow. The Cambridge Edition. Horace E. Scudder, ed. Boston: Houghton, Mifflin & Company, 1894.

Henry Wadsworth Longfellow: Selected Poems. Lawrence Buell, ed. New York: Penguin Books, 1988.

Poems and Other Writings. J. D. McClatchy, ed. New York: The Library of America, 2000.

Books and Articles

Aaron, Daniel. "The Legacy of Henry Wadsworth Longfellow." *Maine Historical Society Quarterly* 27:4 (1987), 42–66.

———. *The Unwritten War: American Writers and the Civil War.* New York: Alfred A. Knopf, 1973.

[Abbott, Edward]. *Mrs. James Greenleaf, A Commemorative Discourse.* Cambridge, MA: The Powell Press, 1903.

Abrams, M. H. *The Mirror and the Lamp: Romantic Theory and the Critical Tradition.* New York: Oxford University Press, 1953.

Abse, Joan. *John Ruskin: The Passionate Moralist.* New York: Alfred A. Knopf, 1981.

Acadian Culture in Maine. Washington, DC: National Park Service, 1994.

Ackerman, Alan L., Jr. *The Portable Theater: American Literature & the Nineteenth-Century Stage.* Baltimore: Johns Hopkins Press, 1999.

Ahlstrom, Sydney E. *A Religious History of the American People.* New Haven: Yale University Press, 1972.

Allen, Gay Wilson. *American Prosody.* New York: American Book Company, 1935.

Allibone, S. Austin. *A Critical Dictionary of English Literature and British and American Authors.* 2 vols. Philadelphia: J. B. Lippincott & Co., 1870.

Anderson, Benedict. *Imagined Communities: Reflections on the Origin and Spread of Nationalism.* Revised edition. New York: Verso, 1991.

Anderson, Patricia McGraw. *The Architecture of Bowdoin College.* Brunswick, ME: Bowdoin College Museum of Art, 1988.

Appleton, Nathan. *Introduction of the Power Loom and Origin of Lowell.* Lowell, MA: Proprietors of the Locks and Canals on Merrimack River, 1858.

[Appleton, Thomas Gold]. *Faded Leaves.* Boston: Printed for the Author, Roberts Brothers, 1872.

Arms, George. *The Fields Were Green: A New View of Bryant, Whittier, Holmes, Lowell, and Longfellow, with a Selection of Their Poems.* Stanford, CA: Stanford University Press, 1953.

Armstrong, Isobel. *Victorian Poetry: Poetry, Poetics and Politics.* London: Routledge, 1993.

Arnold, Matthew. *Essays in Criticism,* 2nd. ser. London: Macmillan, 1894.

Arvin, Newton. *Longfellow: His Life and Work.* Boston: Little, Brown and Company, 1962.

Austin, George Lowell. *Henry Wadsworth Longfellow. His Life, His Works, His Friendships*. Boston: Lee and Shepard, Publishers, 1883.

Austin, James C. *Fields of "The Atlantic Monthly," Letters to an Editor 1861–1870*. San Marino, CA: The Huntington Library, 1953.

Axelrod, Alan, ed. *The Colonial Revival in America*. New York: W. W. Norton, 1985.

Baltzell, E. Digby. *Puritan Boston and Quaker Philadelphia*. Boston: Beacon Press, 1979.

Banks, Ronald F. *Maine Becomes a State: The Movement to Separate Maine from Massachusetts, 1785–1820*. Middletown, CT: Wesleyan University Press, 1970.

Banner, James M., Jr. *To the Hartford Convention: The Federalists and the Origins of Party Politics in Massachusetts, 1789–1815*. New York: Alfred A. Knopf, 1970.

Basbanes, Nicholas A. *Among the Gently Mad: Strategies and Perspectives for the Book Hunter in the Twenty-First Century*. New York: John Macrae, Henry Holt and Company, 2002.

Beckerman, Michael B. *New Worlds of Dvôrák: Searching for America in the Composer's Inner Life*. New York: W. W. Norton & Company, 2003.

Beecher, Catherine E., and Harriet Beecher Stowe. *The American Woman's Home*. 1869. Reprint, Hartford, CT: Stowe-Day Foundation, 1975.

Ben-Atar, Doron, and Barbara B. Oberg, eds. *Federalists Reconsidered*. Charlottesville: University Press of Virginia, 1998.

Berkhofer, Robert F., Jr. *The White Man's Indian: Images of the American Indian from Columbus to the Present*. New York: Alfred A. Knopf, 1978.

Berlin, Isaiah. *The Roots of Romanticism*. Princeton, NJ: Princeton University Press, 1998.

Betjeman, John. *Collected Poems*. Boston: Houghton, Mifflin Company, 1971.

Biswas, Robindra Kumar. *Arthur Hugh Clough: Towards a Reconsideration*. Oxford: At the Clarendon Press, 1972.

Blackett, R. J. M. *Divided Hearts: Britain and the American Civil War*. Baton Rouge: Louisiana State University Press, 2001.

Blanchard, Mary Warner. *Oscar Wilde's America: Counterculture in the Gilded Age*. New Haven: Yale University Press, 1998.

Bok, Edward. *The Americanization of Edward Bok*. New York: Charles Scribner's Sons, 1923.

Boudreau, Kristin. *Sympathy in American Literature: American Sentiments from Jefferson to the Jameses*. Gainesville: University Press of Florida, 2002.

Bourque, Bruce J. *Twelve Thousand Years: American Indians in Maine*. Lincoln: University of Nebraska Press, 2001.

Brasseux, Carl A. *Acadian to Cajun: Transformation of a People, 1803–1877*. Jackson: University Press of Mississippi, 1992.

———. *In Search of Evangeline: Birth and Evolution of the Evangeline Myth.* Thibodaux, LA: Blue Heron Press, 1988.

Brault, Gerard J. *The French-Canadian Heritage in New England.* Hanover, NH: University Press of New England, 1986.

Bremer, Fredrika. *The Homes of the New World: Impressions of America.* Translated by Mary Howitt. 2 vols. New York: Harper & Brothers, 1853.

Brewer, Priscilla J. *From Fireplace to Cookstove: Technology and the Domestic Ideal in America.* Syracuse, NY: Syracuse University Press, 2000.

Brodhead, Richard H. *Culture of Letters: Scenes of Reading and Writing in Nineteenth-Century America.* Chicago: University of Chicago Press, 1993.

Brooks, Van Wyck. *New England: Indian Summer, 1865–1915.* New York: E. P. Dutton & Co., 1940.

Brotherston, Gordon. *Book of the Fourth World: Reading the Native Americans Through Their Literature.* Cambridge: Cambridge University Press, 1992.

Brown, Gillian. *Domestic Individualism: Imaging Self in Nineteenth-Century America.* Berkeley: University of California Press, 1990.

Buell, Lawrence. *Emerson.* Cambridge, MA: Belknap Press of Harvard University Press, 2003.

———. *New England Literary Culture: From Revolution through Renaissance.* New York: Cambridge University Press, 1986.

———. "Introduction," *Henry Wadsworth Longfellow: Selected Poems.* New York: Viking-Penguin, 1988, vii–xxxv.

Burgett, Bruce. *Sentimental Bodies: Sex, Gender, and Citizenship in the Early Republic.* Princeton, NJ: Princeton University Press, 1998.

Burns, Sarah. *Inventing the Modern Artist: Art and Culture in Gilded Age America.* New Haven: Yale University Press, 1996.

Bushman, Richard L. *The Refinement of America: Persons, Houses, Cities.* New York: Alfred A. Knopf, 1992.

Butler, Joyce. "The Longfellows: Another Portland Family." *Maine Historical Society Quarterly* 27:4 (1987), 20–41.

———. "The Wadsworths: A Portland Family." *Maine Historical Society Quarterly* 27:4 (1987), 2–19.

Calhoun, Charles C. *A Small College in Maine: Two Hundred Years of Bowdoin.* Brunswick, ME: Bowdoin College, 1993.

Cameron, Kenneth Walker, ed. *Longfellow Among His Contemporaries.* Hartford, CT: Transcendental Books, 1978.

Carbone, Teresa A., and Patricia Hills. *Eastman Johnson: Painting America.* New York: Brooklyn Museum of Art, 1999.

Carlyle, Thomas. *On Heroes, Hero-Worship, and the Heroic in History.* New York: John Wiley & Son, 1869.

Carnes, Mark C., and Clyde Griffen, eds. *Meanings for Manhood: Constructions of Masculinity in Victorian America.* Chicago: University of Chicago Press, 1990.

Carr, Helen. *Inventing the American Primitive: Politics, Gender and the Representation of Native American Literary Traditions, 1789–1936.* New York: New York
University Press, 1996.

Chapman, Mary, and Glenn Hendler, eds. *Sentimental Men: Masculinity and the
Politics of Affect in American Culture.* Berkeley: University of California Press,
1999.

Charvat, William. "Longfellow's Income from his Writings, 1840–1852," *Papers
of the Bibliographical Society of America* 38:1st Quarter (1944), 9–21.

———. *The Profession of Authorship in America, 1800–1870.* Matthew J. Bruccoli,
ed. Columbia: Ohio State University Press, 1968.

Cheever, George B. *American Common-Place Book of Poetry.* Boston: Carter,
Hendee & Co., 1832.

Christ, Carol T. *Victorian and Modern Poetics.* Chicago: University of Chicago
Press, 1984.

Clark, Charles E., James S. Leamon, and Karen Bowden. *Maine in the Early Republic: From Revolution to Statehood.* Hanover, NH: University Press of New
England, 1988.

Clinton, Catherine. *Fanny Kemble's Civil Wars.* New York: Simon & Schuster,
2000.

Collins, Paul. *Banvard's Folly: Thirteen Tales of Renowned Obscurity, Famous
Anonymity, and Rotten Luck.* New York: Picador USA, 2001.

Condon, Lorna, and Lindsay Shuckhart, "Inside SPNEA: Priscilla." *Old-Time
New England* 78:269 (2000), 5–21.

Conforti, Joseph A. *Imagining New England: Explorations of Regional Identity from
the Pilgrims to the Mid-Twentieth Century.* Chapel Hill: University of North
Carolina Press, 2001.

Conrad, Glenn R., ed. *The Cajuns: Essays on Their History and Culture.* Lafayette:
Center for Louisiana Studies, 1983.

Cott, Nancy F. *The Bonds of Womanhood: "Woman's Sphere" in New England,
1780–1835.* New Haven: Yale University Press, 1977.

Coultrap-McQuin, Susan. *Doing Literary Business: American Women Writers in the
Nineteenth Century.* Chapel Hill: University of North Carolina Press, 1990.

Cox, F. Brett. "'What Need, Then, for Poetry?': The Genteel Tradition and the
Continuity of American Literature." *New England Quarterly* 67:2 (1994),
212–33.

Cox, Julian, and Colin Ford. *Julia Margaret Cameron: The Complete Photographs.*
Los Angeles: J. Paul Getty Museum, 2003.

Crain, Caleb. *American Sympathy: Men, Friendship, and Literature in the New
Nation.* New Haven: Yale University Press, 2001.

Crompton, Samuel. *A Report on the Treatment of Burns and Scalds, Drawn Up at
the Request of the Provincial Medical and Surgical Association.* Manchester, UK,
1851.

Crosby, R. R. *Longfellow as Dramatist.* Ph.D. dissertation, Indiana University, 1958.

Crowley, John E. *The Invention of Comfort: Sensibilities and Design in Early Modern Britain and Early America.* Baltimore: Johns Hopkins University Press, 2001.

Crowninshield, Clara. *Diary: A European Tour with Longfellow, 1835–1836.* Andrew Hilen, ed. Seattle: University of Washington Press, 1956.

Cunningham, Valentine. *The Victorians: An Anthology of Poetry & Poetics.* Oxford: Blackwell Publishers Ltd., 2000.

Dalzell, Robert F., Jr. *Enterprising Elite: The Boston Associates and the World They Made.* Cambridge, MA: Harvard University Press, 1987.

Damrosch, David. *What Is World Literature?* Princeton, NJ: Princeton University Press, 2003.

Dana, Henry Wadsworth Longfellow. *The Craigie House: The Coming of Longfellow (1837–1841).* Cambridge, MA: Cambridge Historical Society, 1939.

Davis, Philip. *The Victorians, 1830–1880.* Oxford English Literary History 8. Oxford: Oxford University Press, 2002.

Deloria, Philip J. *Playing Indian.* New Haven: Yale University Press, 1998.

Derbyshire, John, "Longfellow and the Fate of Modern Poetry." *The New Criterion* 19:4 (2000), 12–20.

Description of Banvard's Panorama of the Mississippi, Painted on Three Miles of Canvas. Boston: John Putnam, 1847.

Dickens, Charles. *American Notes and Pictures from Italy.* London: Macmillan and Co., 1893. Reprint of 1843 edition.

Diehl, Carl. *Americans and German Scholarship, 1770–1870.* New Haven: Yale University Press, 1978.

Dobson, Joanne. "Reclaiming Sentimental Literature." *American Literature* 69:2 (1997), 263–88.

Donald, David Herbert. *Charles Sumner.* New York: Da Capo Press, 1996. Reprint of *Charles Sumner and the Coming of the Civil War* (1960) and *Charles Sumner and the Rights of Man* (1970).

Douglas, Ann. *The Feminization of American Culture.* New York: Alfred A. Knopf, 1977.

Duberman, Martin. *James Russell Lowell.* Boston: Houghton Mifflin Company, 1966.

Dublin, Thomas. *Transforming Women's Work: New England Lives in the Industrial Revolution.* Ithaca, NY: Cornell University Press, 1994.

Dwight, Theodore. *History of the Hartford Convention.* New York: N. & J. White, 1833.

Dwight, Timothy. *Travels in New England and New York.* 1821. Reprinted in 2 vols., Barbara Miller Solomon, ed. Cambridge, MA: Harvard University Press, 1969.

Ebert, Monika M., ed. *Separate Spheres No More: Gender Convergence in American Literature, 1830–1930*. Tuscaloosa: University of Alabama Press, 2000.

Edwards, George Thornton. *The Youthful Haunts of Longfellow*. Portland, ME: Geo. T. Edwards, 1907.

Elkins, Stanley, and Eric McKitrick. *The Age of Federalism: The Early American Republic, 1788–1800*. New York: Oxford University Press, 1993.

Elliott, Maud Howe. *Uncle Sam Ward and His Circle*. New York: Macmillan, 1938.

Ellison, Julie. *Cato's Tears and the Making of Anglo-American Emotion*. Chicago: University of Chicago Press, 1999.

Ellmann, Richard. *Oscar Wilde*. New York: Alfred A. Knopf, 1988.

Emerson, Edward Waldo. *The Early Years of the Saturday Club, 1855–1870*. Boston: Houghton, Mifflin & Company, 1918.

Emerson, Ralph Waldo. *Essays and Lectures*. New York: The Library of America, 1983.

———. *The Journals and Miscellaneous Notebooks of Ralph Waldo Emerson*. Vol. XIII, 1852–1855. Ralph H. Orth and Alfred R. Ferguson, eds. Cambridge, MA: The Belknap Press of Harvard University Press, 1977.

Empson, William. *The Structure of Complex Words*. London: Chatto & Windus, 1951.

Faderman, Lillian. "Female Same-Sex Relationships in Novels by Longfellow, Holmes, and James." *New England Quarterly* 51:3 (1978), 309–32.

Farrell, Betty G. *Elite Families: Class and Power in Nineteenth-Century Boston*. Albany: State University of New York Press, 1993.

Fields, Annie. *Authors and Friends*. Boston: Houghton, Mifflin & Company, 1897.

Fields, James T. *Yesterdays With Authors*. Boston: James R. Osgood and Company, 1878.

Fischer, David Hackett. *Paul Revere's Ride*. New York: Oxford University Press, 1994.

Fischer, Hermann. *Romantic Verse Narrative: The History of a Genre*. Translated by Sue Bollans. Cambridge, UK: Cambridge University Press, 1991.

Fiske, Christabel F. "Mercerized Folklore." *Poet-Lore* 31 (1920), 538–75.

Fletcher, Angus. "Whitman and Longfellow: Two Types of the American Poet." *Raritan* 1:4 (1991), 131–45.

Flint, Kate. *The Victorians and the Visual Imagination*. Cambridge, UK: Cambridge University Press, 2000.

Ford, Colin. *Julia Margaret Cameron: Nineteenth-Century Photographer of Genius*. London: National Portrait Gallery, 2003.

Fowler, L. N. *The Illustrated Phrenological Almanac*. New York: Fowler and Wells, 1859.

Fox, Finis. *The Romance of Evangeline*. New York: A. L. Burt Co., 1929.

Franchot, Jenny. *Roads to Rome: The Antebellum Protestant Encounter with Catholicism*. Berkeley: University of California Press, 1994.

Frederickson, George M. *The Inner Civil War: Northern Intellectuals and the Crisis of the Union*. New York: Harper & Row, 1965.

Fuller, S. Margaret [Marchesa Ossoli]. *Papers on Literature and Art*. New York: Wiley and Putnam, 1846.

Gannett, W. C. *Studies in Longfellow. Outlines for Schools, Conversation Classes, and Home Study*. Boston: Houghton, Mifflin & Company, 1884.

Gartner, Matthew. "Becoming Longfellow: Work, Manhood, and Poetry." *American Literature* 72:1 (2000), 59–85.

———. "Longfellow's Place: The Poet and Poetry of Craigie House." *New England Quarterly* 73:1 (2000), 32–57.

———. "Public Obligation and Poetic Vocation in the Poetry of Henry Wadsworth Longfellow." Unpublished Ph.D. dissertation, The City University of New York, 1999.

Gay, Peter. *Schnitzler's Century: The Making of Middle-Class Culture, 1815–1914*. New York: W. W. Norton, 2002.

Gerdts, William H., and Theodore E. Stebbins, Jr. *"A Man of Genius": The Art of Washington Allston (1779–1843)*. Boston: Museum of Fine Arts, 1979.

Gernsheim, Helmut. *Lewis Carroll, Photographer*. Reprint. New York: Dover Publications, Inc., 1969.

Gienapp, William E. *The Origins of the Republican Party, 1852–1856*. New York: Oxford University Press, 1987.

Gifra-Adroher, Pere. *Between History and Romance: Travel Writing on Spain in the Early Nineteenth-Century United States*. Madison, NJ: Fairleigh Dickinson University Press, 2000.

Gilmore, Michael T. *American Romanticism and the Marketplace*. Chicago: University of Chicago Press, 1985.

Gilmore, William J. *Reading Becomes a Necessity of Life: Material and Cultural Life in Rural New England, 1780–1835*. Knoxville: University of Tennessee Press, 1989.

Gitter, Elisabeth. *The Imprisoned Guest: Samuel Howe and Laura Bridgman, the Original Deaf-Blind Girl*. New York: Farrar, Straus and Giroux, 2001.

Gohdes, Clarence. *American Literature in Nineteenth-Century England*. New York: Columbia University Press, 1944.

———. "Longfellow and His Authorized British Publishers." *PMLA*, LV (1940), 1165–79.

Gollin, Rita K. *Annie Adams Fields: Woman of Letters*. Amherst: University of Massachusetts Press, 2002.

Gooch, Robert. *An Account of Some of the Most Important Diseases Peculiar to Women*. Philadelphia: E. L. Carey & A. Hart, n.d.

Goold, Nathan. *The Wadsworth-Longfellow House: Its History and Occupants.* Portland: Maine Historical Society, 1908. Reprint, 1973.

Gorman, Herbert S. *A Victorian American: Henry Wadsworth Longfellow.* New York: George H. Doran Company, 1926.

Gould, Philip. *Covenant and Republic: Historical Romance and the Politics of Puritanism.* Cambridge, UK: Cambridge University Press, 1996.

Gould, William. *Portland in the Past with Historical Notes of Old Falmouth.* 1886. Reprint, Bowie, MD: Heritage Books, 1997.

Greenleaf, Moses. *A Survey of the State of Maine.* 1829. Reprint, Augusta: Maine State Museum, 1970.

Grier, Katherine C. *Culture & Comfort: Parlor Making and Middle Class Identity, 1850–1930.* Washington, DC: Smithsonian Institution Press, 1988.

Griffiths, Naomi. "Longfellow's Evangeline: The Birth and Acceptance of a Legend." *Acadiensis* 11:2 (1982), 28–41.

Griswold, Rufus Willmot. *The Poets and Poetry of America. With an Historical Introduction.* Philadelphia: Carey and Hart, 1842.

Hale, Susan. *Life and Letters of Thomas Gold Appleton.* New York: Appleton, 1885.

Halttunen, Karen. *Confidence Men and Painted Women: A Study of Middle-Class Culture in America, 1830–1870.* New Haven: Yale University Press, 1982.

Hammer, Carl, Jr. *Longfellow's "Golden Legend" and Goethe's "Faust."* Baton Rouge: Louisiana State University Press, 1952.

Handlin, Oscar. *Boston's Immigrants 1790–1880: A Study in Acculturation.* Cambridge, MA: Belknap Press of Harvard University Press, 1941, 1991.

Hansen, Karen V. *A Very Social Time: Crafting Community in Antebellum New England.* Berkeley: University of California Press, 1994.

Haralson, Eric L. "Mars in Petticoats: Longfellow and Sentimental Masculinity." *Nineteenth-Century Literature* 51:3 (1996), 327–55.

Harap, Louis. *The Image of the Jew in American Literature: From Early Republic to Mass Immigration.* Philadelphia: Jewish Publication Society of America, 1974.

Harris, Susan K. *The Cultural Work of the Late Nineteenth-Century Hostess: Annie Adams Fields and Mary Gladstone Drew.* New York: Palgrave Macmillan, 2002.

Harwell, Richard. *Hawthorne and Longfellow: A Guide to an Exhibit.* Brunswick, ME: Bowdoin College, 1966.

Hatfield, James Taft. *New Light on Longfellow: With Special Reference to His Relations to Germany.* Boston: Houghton, Mifflin & Company, 1933.

Hawkins, Peter S., and Rachel Jacoff. *The Poets' Dante.* New York: Farrar, Straus and Giroux, 2001.

Hawthorne, Julian. *Nathaniel Hawthorne and His Wife. A Biography.* 2 vols. Boston: James R. Osgood and Company, 1885.

Hawthorne, Manning, and Henry Wadsworth Longfellow Dana. *The Origin and Development of Longfellow's "Evangeline."* Portland, ME: The Anthoensen Press, 1947.

Hawthorne, Nathaniel. *The American Notebooks.* Claude M. Simpson, ed. The Centenary Edition of the Works of Nathaniel Hawthorne VIII. Columbus: Ohio State University Press, 1972.

———. "Chiefly About War Matters. By a Peaceable Man." *Atlantic Monthly*, July 1862, 43–61.

———. *Tales and Sketches.* New York: The Library of America, 1982.

Heald, Sarah H. " 'In the Japanese Style': Charley Longfellow's Sitting Room." *Old-Time New England* 78:269 (2000), 22–41.

Hedrick, Joan D. *Harriet Beecher Stowe: A Life.* New York: Oxford University Press, 1994.

Hendler, Glenn. *Public Sentiments: Structures of Feeling in Nineteenth-Century American Literature.* Chapel Hill: University of North Carolina Press, 2001.

Hewett-Thayer, Harvey W. *American Literature as Viewed in Germany, 1818–1861.* Chapel Hill: University of North Carolina Press, 1958.

Higginson, Thomas Wentworth. *Henry Wadsworth Longfellow.* Boston: Houghton, Mifflin & Company, 1902.

———. *Old Cambridge.* New York, 1899.

Hilen, Andrew. "Charley Longfellow Goes to War." *Harvard Library Bulletin* 14:1,2 (1960), 59–81, 283–303.

———. *The Letters of Henry Wadsworth Longfellow.* 6 vols. Cambridge, MA: The Belknap Press of Harvard University Press, 1966–1982.

———. *Longfellow and Scandinavia.* New Haven: Yale University Press, 1947.

Hillard, George S. *The Relation of the Poet to His Age, A Discourse Delivered Before the Phi Beta Kappa Society of Harvard University.* Boston: Charles C. Little and James Brown, 1843.

Hirsch, Edward L. *Henry Wadsworth Longfellow.* Minneapolis: University of Minnesota Press, 1964.

Hoeltje, Hubert H. "Hawthorne's Review of Evangeline." *New England Quarterly* 23:2 (1950), 232–35.

Holifield, E. Brooks. *Theology in America: Christian Thought from the Age of the Puritans to the Civil War.* New Haven: Yale University Press, 2003.

Holland, Merlin, and Rupert Hart-Davis, eds. *The Complete Letters of Oscar Wilde.* New York: Henry Holt and Company, 2000.

Hollander, John, ed. *American Poetry: The Nineteenth Century.* 2 vols. New York: The Library of America, 1993.

Holt, Michael F. *The Rise and Fall of the American Whig Party.* New York: Oxford University Press, 1999.

House, Madeline, Graham Storey, and Kathleen Tillotson, eds. *The Letters of*

Charles Dickens. Vol. III: 1842–1843. Oxford: Clarendon Press, 1974. Vol. XI: 1865–1867. Oxford: Clarendon Press, 1999.

Howe, Daniel Walker. *The Political Culture of the American Whigs.* Chicago: University of Chicago Press, 1979.

———. *The Unitarian Conscience: Harvard Moral Philosophy, 1805–1861.* Middletown, CT: Wesleyan University Press, 1988.

Howe, Julia Ward. *Reminiscences, 1819–1899.* Boston: Houghton, 1900.

Howells, W. D. *Literary Friends and Acquaintances: A Personal Retrospect of American Authorship.* 1900. Reprint, Bloomington: Indiana University Press, 1968.

Hymes, Dell. *"In Vain I Tried to Tell You": Essays in Native American Ethnopoetics.* Philadelphia: University of Pennsylvania Press, 1981.

Irmscher, Christoph. "Longfellow Redux." *Raritan* 21:3 (Winter 2002), 100–129.

———. *The Poetics of Natural History: From John Bartram to William James.* New Brunswick, NJ: Rutgers University Press, 1999.

Isenberg, Nancy. *Sex and Citizenship in Antebellum America.* Chapel Hill: University of North Carolina Press, 1998.

Isenberg, Nancy, and Andrew Burstein, eds. *Mortal Remains: Death in Early America.* Philadelphia: University of Pennsylvania Press, 2003.

James, Henry. *The Golden Bowl* (1904). New York: Alfred A. Knopf, 1992.

———. "Hawthorne" (1905). Reprinted in *Essays on Literature, American Writers, English Writers.* New York: The Library of America, 1984.

———. *William Wetmore Story and His Friends.* Boston: Houghton, Mifflin & Company, 1903. Reprint, New York: Da Capo Press, 1969.

Jellison, Charles A. *Fessenden of Maine, Civil War Senator.* Syracuse, NY: Syracuse University Press, 1962.

Johns, Elizabeth. *American Genre Painting: The Politics of Everyday Life.* New Haven: Yale University Press, 1991.

Johnson, Carl L. *Professor Longfellow of Harvard.* Eugene: University of Oregon Press, 1944.

Jordan, William B., Jr. *Index to Portland Newspapers, 1785–1835.* Bowie, MD: Heritage Books, 1994.

Kaplan, Fred. *Sacred Tears: Sentimentality in Victorian Literature.* Princeton, NJ: Princeton University Press, 1987.

Kaplin, Justin. *Walt Whitman: A Life.* New York: Simon & Schuster, 1980.

Kass, Amalie M. *Midwifery and Medicine in Boston: Walter Channing, M.D., 1786–1876.* Boston: Northeastern University Press, 2002.

Kennedy, W. Sloane. *Henry W. Longfellow. Biography, Anecdote, Letters, Criticism.* Cambridge, MA, 1882. Reprint, New York: Haskell House Publishers, Ltd., 1972.

Kerber, Linda K. *Women of the Republic: Intellect and Ideology in Revolutionary America.* New York: W. W. Norton, 1986.

Kete, Mary Louise. *Sentimental Collaborations: Mourning and Middle-Class Identity in Nineteenth-Century America*. Durham, NC: Duke University Press, 2000.

Kett, Joseph. *Rites of Passage: Adolescence in America, 1790 to the Present*. New York: Basic Books, Inc., 1977.

Kucich, John, and Dianne F. Sadoff, eds. *Victorian Afterlife: Postmodern Culture Rewrites the Nineteenth Century*. Minneapolis: University of Minnesota Press, 2000.

Kuklick, Bruce. *The Rise of American Philosophy: Cambridge, Massachusetts, 1860–1930*. New Haven: Yale University Press, 1977.

Laidlaw, Christine Wallace, ed. *Charles Appleton Longfellow: Twenty Months in Japan, 1871–1873*. Cambridge, MA: Friends of the Longfellow House, 1998.

Larcom, Lucy. *A New England Girlhood, Outlined from Memory*. 1889. Reprint, Boston: Houghton Mifflin Company, 1986.

Lawson, Melinda. *Patriot Fires: Forging a New American Nationalism in the Civil War North*. Lawrence: University Press of Kansas, 2002.

Leamon, James S. *Revolution Downeast: The War for American Independence in Maine*. Amherst: University of Massachusetts Press, 1993.

Lee, Robert. *Researches on the Pathology and Treatment of Some of the Most Important Diseases of Women*. London: S. Highley, 1833.

The Legacy of James Bowdoin III. Brunswick, ME: Bowdoin College Museum of Art, 1994.

Leithauser, Brad. " 'Sweep on, O River…' " *New York Review of Books* (Dec. 16, 1993), 20–24.

Lerner, Laurence. *Angels and Absences: Child Deaths in the Nineteenth Century*. Nashville, TN: Vanderbilt University Press, 1997.

Leverenz, David. *Manhood and the American Renaissance*. Ithaca, NY: Cornell University Press, 1989.

Levine, Lawrence W. *Highbrow/Lowbrow: The Emergence of Cultural Hierarchy in America*. Cambridge, MA: Harvard University Press, 1988.

Lewis, R. W. B. *The Jameses: A Family Narrative*. London: Andre Deutsch, 1991.

Little, George Thomas. *Longfellow's Boyhood Poems*. Saratoga Springs, NY: R. W. Pettengill, 1925.

Logan, Thad. *The Victorian Parlour*. Cambridge, UK: Cambridge University Press, 2001.

Long, Orie C. *American Literary Pioneers: Early American Explorers of European Culture*. Cambridge, MA: Harvard University Press, 1935.

Longfellow, Ernest Wadsworth. *Random Memories*. Boston: Houghton, Mifflin Company, 1922.

Longfellow, Samuel. *Life of Henry Wadsworth Longfellow, with Extracts from His Journals and Correspondence*. 2 vols. Boston: Ticknor and Company, 1886.

————, ed. *Final Memorials of Henry Wadsworth Longfellow*. Boston: Ticknor and Company, 1887. Printed as Volume 3 of the *Life* in 1891 and after.

Lönnrot, Elias, compiler. *The Kalevala, or Poems of the Kaleva District*. Translated by Francis Peabody Magoun, Jr. Cambridge, MA: Harvard University Press, 1963.

Lystra, Karen. *Searching the Heart: Women, Men, and Romantic Love in Nineteenth-Century America*. New York: Oxford University Press, 1989.

[Mackenzie, Alexander Slidell]. *A Year in Spain, by a Young American*. Boston: Hilliard, Gray, Little, and Wilkens, 1829.

Maillet, Antonine. *Pelagie-la-Charette*. Montreal: Lemeac, 1979.

Mantz, Harold Elmer. *French Criticism of American Literature Before 1850*. New York: Columbia University Press, 1917.

Martin, Robert Bernard. *Tennyson: The Unquiet Heart*. Oxford: Clarendon Press, 1980.

Matthiessen, F. O. *American Renaissance: Art and Expression in the Age of Emerson and Whitman*. New York: Oxford University Press, 1941.

May, Joseph, ed. *Samuel Longfellow. Memoir and Letters*. Boston: Houghton, Mifflin & Company, 1894.

Mayer, Henry. *All on Fire: William Lloyd Garrison and the Abolition of Slavery*. New York: St. Martin's Griffin, 1998.

McCarthy, Kathleen D. *American Creed: Philanthropy and the Rise of Civil Society*. Chicago: University of Chicago Press, 2003.

McClatchy, J. D. "Return to Gitchee Gumee." *New York Times Book Review*, (October 22, 2000), 39.

McDonald, John J. "Longfellow in Hawthorne's 'The Antique Ring.'" *New England Quarterly* 46:4 (1973), 622–26.

McGill, Meredith L. *American Literature and the Culture of Reprinting, 1834–1853*. Philadelphia: University of Pennsylvania Press, 2003.

McKee, Christopher. *Edward Preble: A Naval Biography, 1761–1807*. Annapolis, MD: Naval Institute Press, 1972.

Menand, Louis. *The Metaphysical Club: A Story of Ideas in America*. New York: Farrar, Straus and Giroux, 2001.

Merish, Lori. *Sentimental Materialism: Gender, Commodity Culture, and Nineteenth-Century American Literature*. Durham, NC: Duke University Press, 2000.

Michener, Roger. "Henry Wadsworth Longfellow: Librarian of Bowdoin College, 1829–35." *Library Quarterly* (1972–73), 42–43.

Miller, Angela. *Empire of the Eye: Landscape Representation and American Cultural Politics, 1825–1875*. Ithaca, NY: Cornell University Press, 1993.

Miller, David C., ed. *American Iconology: New Approaches to Nineteenth-Century Art and Literature*. New Haven: Yale University Press, 1995.

Miller, Edwin Haviland. *Salem Is My Dwelling Place: A Life of Nathaniel Hawthorne*. Iowa City: University of Iowa Press, 1991.

Miller, Perry. *The Raven and the Whale: Poe, Melville, and the New York Literary Scene*. Baltimore: Johns Hopkins University Press, 1997. Reprint of 1956 edition.

Morison, Samuel Eliot. *Three Centuries of Harvard, 1636–1936*. Cambridge, MA: The Belknap Press of Harvard University Press, 1936.

Moss, Sidney P. *Poe's Literary Battles: The Critic in the Context of His Literary Milieu*. Durham, NC: Duke University Press, 1963.

Mott, Frank Luther. *A History of Magazines in the United States, 1741–1850*. New York: D. Appleton and Company, 1930.

———. *A History of American Magazines, 1850–1865*. Cambridge, MA: Harvard University Press, 1938.

Moulton, John K. *Captain Moody and His Observatory*. Falmouth, ME: Mount Joy Publishing, 2000.

Moyne, Ernest J. "Parodies of Longfellow's *Song of Hiawatha*." *Delaware Notes* 30 (1957), 93–108.

Mulvey, Christopher. *Anglo-American Landscapes: A Study of Nineteenth-Century Anglo-American Travel Literature*. Cambridge, UK: Cambridge University Press, 1998.

Nemerov, Howard. "Introduction," *Longfellow*. Richard Wilbur, ed. The Laurel Poetry Series. New York: Dell Publishing, 1959, 7–27.

Newbury, Michael. *Figuring Authorship in Antebellum America*. Stanford, CA: Stanford University Press, 1997.

Norton, Charles Eliot. *Henry Wadsworth Longfellow. A Sketch of His Life, Together with Longfellow's Chief Autobiographical Poems*. Boston: Houghton, Mifflin & Company, 1906.

Novick, Sheldon M. *Henry James: The Young Master*. New York: Random House, 1996.

O'Connor, Thomas H. *Civil War Boston: Home Front and Battlefield*. Boston: Northeastern University Press, 1997.

Papers Presented at the Longfellow Memorial Conference, April 1–3, 1982. Cambridge, MA: Longfellow National Historic Site, 1982.

Parini, Jay, ed. *Columbia History of American Poetry*. New York: Columbia University Press, 1993.

Parini, Jay. "Longfellow and American Optimism." *Times Literary Supplement* (May 25, 2001), 5–6.

Payne, Edward F. *Dickens Days in Boston, A Record of Daily Events*. 2 vols. Boston: Houghton, Mifflin & Company, 1927.

Pearce, Charlotte A. "Longfellow and Spanish America." *Hispania* 58 (December 1975), 921–26.

Perry, Bliss. *Park-Street Papers*. Boston: Houghton, Mifflin & Company, 1908.

———. *Richard Henry Dana 1851–1931*. Boston: Houghton, Mifflin & Company, 1933.

Phelps, Elizabeth Stuart. *Chapters from a Life*. Boston: Houghton, Mifflin & Company, 1897.

Pinch, Adela. *Strange Fits of Passion: Epistemologies of Emotion, Hume to Austen*. Stanford, CA: Stanford University Press, 1996.

Pittinger, Charles B. "The Anesthetization of Fanny Longfellow for Childbirth on April 7, 1847," *Anesthesia and Analgesia* 66 (1987), 368–69.

Poe, Edgar Allan. *Essays and Reviews*. New York: The Library of America, 1984.

Proceedings of the Maine Historical Society. Henry Wadsworth Longfellow. Seventy-Fifth Birthday. February 27, 1882. Portland, ME: Hoyt, Fogg and Donham, 1882.

Radden, Jennifer, ed. *The Nature of Melancholy: From Aristotle to Kristeva*. New York: Oxford University Press, 2000.

Reynolds, David S. *Beneath the American Renaissance: The Subversive Imagination in the Age of Emerson and Melville*. Cambridge, MA: Harvard University Press, 1988.

———. *Walt Whitman's America: A Cultural Biography*. New York: Alfred A. Knopf, 1995.

Rice, Grantland S. *The Transformation of Authorship in America*. Chicago: University of Chicago Press, 1997.

Richardson, Robert D., Jr. *Emerson: The Mind on Fire*. Berkeley: University of California Press, 1995.

Rivard, Paul E. *A New Order of Things: How the Textile Industry Transformed New England*. Hanover, NH: University Press of New England, 2002.

Rockland, Michael Aaron, ed. *Sarmiento's "Travels in the United States in 1847."* Princeton, NJ: Princeton University Press, 1970.

Rose, Anne C. *Victorian America and the Civil War*. Cambridge, UK: Cambridge University Press, 1992.

Rose, Jonathan. *The Intellectual Life of the British Working Class*. New Haven: Yale University Press, 2001.

Rotundo, E. Anthony. *American Manhood: Transformations in Masculinity from the Revolution to the Modern Era*. New York: Basic Books, 1993.

Royal, Mrs. Anne. *The Black Book, or a Continuation of Travels in the United States*. 2 vols. Washington, DC: Printed for the Author, 1828.

Ryden, Kent C. *Landscape with Figures: Nature & Culture in New England*. Iowa City: University of Iowa Press, 2001.

Saintsbury, George. *Prefaces and Essays*. London: Macmillan and Co. Ltd., 1933.

Samuels, Shirley, ed. *The Culture of Sentiment: Race, Gender, and Sentimentality in Nineteenth-Century America*. New York: Oxford University Press, 1992.

Sandweiss, Martha. *Photography in Nineteenth-Century America*. New York: Abrams, 1991.

Sargent, Mrs. John T. *Sketches and Reminiscences of the Radical Club of Chestnut Street, Boston*. Boston: James R. Osgood and Company, 1880.

Sattelmeyer, Robert. *Thoreau's Reading: A Study in Intellectual History*. Princeton, NJ: Princeton University Press, 1988.

Schoolcraft, Henry Rowe. *Algic Researches. Indian Tales and Legends*. Vols. I and II. 1839. Reprint, Baltimore: Clearfield Company, 1992.

Schramm, Wilbur L. "Hiawatha and Its Predecessors." *Philological Quarterly* XI (1932), 321–43.

Schulz, Hans-Joachim, and Phillip H. Rhein, eds. *Comparative Literature: The Early Years*. Chapel Hill: University of North Carolina Press, 1973.

Sedgwick, Eve Kosofsky. *Epistemology of the Closet*. Berkeley: University of California Press, 1990.

Seelye, John. "Attic Shape: Dusting Off Evangeline." *Virginia Quarterly Review* 60:1 (1984), 21–44.

———. *Memory's Nation: The Place of Plymouth Rock*. Chapel Hill: University of North Carolina Press, 1998.

Sellers, Charles. *The Market Revolution: Jacksonian America, 1815–1846*. Oxford: Oxford University Press, 1991.

Sentilles, Renee M. *Performing Menken: Adah Isaacs Menken and the Birth of American Celebrity*. New York: Cambridge University Press, 2003.

Siegel, Jonathan. *Desire and Excess: The Nineteenth-Century Culture of Art*. Princeton, NJ: Princeton University Press, 2000.

Skinner, Henrietta Dana. *An Echo from Parnassus, Being Girlhood Memories of Longfellow and His Friends*. New York: J. H. Sears & Company, 1928.

Smeed, J. W. *Faust in Literature*. London: Oxford University Press, 1975.

Smith, H. Augustine. *The Romance of Immortal Hymns*. New York: Fleming H. Revell Company, 1931.

Smith, Seba. *'Way Down East: or, Portraits of Yankee Life*. Philadelphia: John E. Potter and Company, 1832.

Spengemann, William C. *A Mirror for Americanists: Reflections on the Idea of American Literature*. Hanover, NH: University Press of New England, 1989.

Sprague, Laura Fecych, ed. *Agreeable Situations: Society, Commerce, and Art in Southern Maine, 1780–1830*. Kennebunk, ME: Brick Store Museum, 1987.

Stearns, Frank Preston. *Cambridge Sketches*. Philadelphia: J. B. Lippincott Company, 1905.

Stedman, Edmund Clarence. *Poets of America*. Boston: Houghton, Mifflin & Company, 1896.

Stevenson, Louise L. *The Victorian Homefront: American Thought and Culture, 1860–1880*. Ithaca, NY: Cornell University Press, 1991.

Story, Ronald. *Harvard and the Boston Upper Class: The Forging of an Aristocracy, 1800–1870*. Middletown, CT: Wesleyan University Press, 1980.

Stowe, William W. *Going Abroad: European Travel in Nineteenth-Century American Culture*. Princeton, NJ: Princeton University Press, 1994.

Struck, Wolf-Heino. *Geschichte der Stadt Geisenheim*. Frankfurt: Verlag Waldemar Kramer, 1972.

Sullivan, Jack. *New World Symphonies: How American Culture Changed European Music*. New Haven: Yale University Press, 1999.

Sullivan, James. *History of the District of Maine*. 1795. Reprint, Augusta: Maine State Museum, 1970.

Sussman, Herbert. *Victorian Masculinities: Manhood and Masculine Poetics in Early Victorian Literature and Art*. Cambridge, UK: Cambridge University Press, 1995.

Taylor, Alan. *Liberty Men and Great Proprietors: The Revolutionary Settlement on the Maine Frontier, 1760–1820*. Chapel Hill: University of North Carolina Press, 1990.

Taylor, Anne-Marie. *Young Charles Sumner and the Legacy of the American Enlightenment, 1811–1851*. Amherst: University of Massachusetts Press, 2001.

Tennyson, Hallam. *Alfred Lord Tennyson, A Memoir by His Son*. 2 vols. New York: Macmillan Company, 1897.

Tharp, Louise Hall. *The Appletons of Beacon Hill*. Boston: Little, Brown and Company, 1973.

Thomas, Julia. *Victorian Narrative Painting*. London: Tate Publishing, 2000.

Thompson, Lawrance. *Young Longfellow (1807–1843)*. New York: Macmillan Company, 1938.

Thompson, Ralph. *American Literary Annuals & Gift Books*. New York: H. W. Wilson Company, 1936.

Tibbetts, John C., ed. *Dvořák in America, 1892–1895*. Portland, OR: Amadeus Press, 1993.

Timpe, Eugene F. *American Literature in Germany, 1861–1872*. Chapel Hill: University of North Carolina Press, 1964.

Todd, Janet. *Sensibility: An Introduction*. London: Methuen, 1986.

Tompkins, Jane. *Sensational Designs: The Cultural Work of American Fiction, 1760–1860*. New York: Oxford University Press, 1985.

Tortolano, William. *Samuel Coleridge-Taylor: Anglo-Black Composer, 1875–1912*. Metuchen, NJ: The Scarecrow Press, 1977.

Townsend, Kim. *Manhood at Harvard: William James and Others*. Cambridge, MA: Harvard University Press, 1996.

Trachtenberg, Alan. "Singing Hiawatha: Longfellow's Hybrid Myth of America." *Yale Review* 90:1 (2002), 1–19.

Traister, Bruce. "The Wandering Bachelor: Irving, Masculinity, and Authorship." *American Literature* 74:1 (2002), 111–37.

Truettner, William H., and Roger B. Stein, eds. *Picturing Old New England: Image and Memory*. New Haven: Yale University Press, 1999.

Trumpener, Katie. *Bardic Nationalism: The Romantic Novel and the British Empire*. Princeton, NJ: Princeton University Press, 1997.

Tucker, Edward L. *The Shaping of Longfellow's John Endicott: A Textual History Including Two Early Versions.* Charlottesville: University Press of Virginia, 1985.

Tucker, Herbert F. *A Companion to Victorian Literature & Culture.* Oxford, UK: Blackwell Publishers, 1999.

Turner, James. *The Liberal Education of Charles Eliot Norton.* Baltimore: Johns Hopkins University Press, 1999.

Turner, Michael R., ed. *Victorian Parlor Poetry: An Annotated Anthology.* 1969. Reprint, New York: Dover Books, 1992.

Tyack, David B. *George Ticknor and the Boston Brahmins.* Cambridge, MA: Harvard University Press, 1967.

Underwood, Francis H. *Henry Wadsworth Longfellow: A Biographical Sketch.* Boston: James R. Osgood and Company, 1882.

U.S. Department of the Interior/National Park Service. *The Longfellow House: Historic Furnishings Report,* Vol. I: "Administrative and Historical Information, Illustrations, and Bibliography." Harpers Ferry, MD: National Park Service, 1999.

Van Schaick, John, Jr. *Characters in "Tales of a Wayside Inn."* Boston: Universalist Publishing House, 1939.

Vendler, Helen. *Coming of Age as a Poet.* Cambridge, MA: Harvard University Press, 2003.

Von Frank, Albert J. *The Trials of Anthony Burns: Freedom and Slavery in Emerson's Boston.* Cambridge, MA: Harvard University Press, 1998.

Voorhies, Felix. *Acadian Reminiscences, with the True Story of Evangeline.* 1907. Reprint, Lafayette: University of Southwestern Louisiana Press, 1977.

Wadsworth, Peleg. *Letters of General Peleg Wadsworth to His Son John, Student at Harvard College, 1796–1798.* Portland: Maine Historical Society, 1961.

Wagenknecht, Edward. *Henry Wadsworth Longfellow: His Poetry and Prose.* New York: Ungar, 1986.

———, ed. *Mrs. Longfellow. Selected Journals and Letters of Fanny Appleton Longfellow.* New York: Longmans, Green and Co., 1956.

Walker, Cheryl. *Indian Nation: Native American Literature and Nineteenth-Century Nationalisms.* Durham, NC: Duke University Press, 1997.

———. *The Nightingale's Burden: Women Poets and American Culture Before 1900.* Bloomington: Indiana University Press, 1982.

Ward, Gerald W. R., ed. *The American Illustrated Book in the Nineteenth Century.* Winterthur, DE: Henry Francis DuPont Winterthur Museum, 1987.

Ward, Robert Stafford. "Longfellow's Roots in Yankee Soil." *New England Quarterly* 41:2 (1968), 180–92.

Warner, Michael. *Letters of the Republic: Publication and the Public Sphere in Eighteenth-Century America.* Cambridge, MA: Harvard University Press, 1990.

Wawn, Andrew. *The Vikings and the Victorians: Inventing the Old North in Nineteenth-Century Britain.* Cambridge, UK: D. S. Brewer, 2000.

Werth, Barry. *The Scarlet Professor. Newton Arvin: A Literary Life Shattered by Scandal.* New York: Nan A. Talese, Doubleday, 2001.

Wheeler, George Augustus, and Henry Warren Wheeler. *History of Brunswick, Topsham, and Harpswell, Maine.* 2 vols. Boston: Alfred Mudge & Son, 1878.

Whipple, John Adams, ed. *Homes of American Statesmen with Anecdotal, Personal, and Descriptive Sketches, by Various Writers.* New York: G. P. Putnam & Co., 1854.

Whitehill, Walter Muir, and Lawrence W. Kennedy. *Boston: A Topographical History.* 3rd ed. Cambridge, MA: The Belknap Press of Harvard University Press, 2000.

Whitman, Iris Lilian. *Longfellow and Spain.* New York: Instituto de las Españas en los Estados Unidos, 1927.

Williams, Cecil B. *Henry Wadsworth Longfellow.* New York: Twayne Publishers, Inc., 1964.

Williams, Stanley T. *The Spanish Background of American Literature.* 2 vols. New Haven: Yale University Press, 1955.

Williamson, William D. *The History of the State of Maine; from Its First Discovery, A.D. 1602, to the Separation, A.D. 1820, Inclusive.* 2 vols. Hallowell, ME: Glazier, Masters & Co., 1832.

Willis, William. *A History of the Law, the Courts, and the Lawyers of Maine from its First Colonization to the Early Part of the Present Century.* Portland, ME: Bailey & Noyes, 1863.

———. "Introductory Remarks." Collections of the Maine Historical Society, Vol. I (1831), 7–10.

Wilson, A. N. *The Victorians.* New York: W. W. Norton, 2003.

Wilton, Andrew, and Tim Barringer. *American Sublime: Landscape Painting in the United States 1820–1880.* London: Tate Publishing, 2002.

Winship, Michael. *American Literary Publishing in the Mid-Nineteenth Century: The Business of Ticknor and Fields.* Cambridge, UK: Cambridge University Press, 1995.

Winter, William. *Old Friends, Being Literary Recollections of Other Days.* New York: Moffat, Yard and Company, 1909.

Winterer, Caroline. *The Culture of Classicism: Ancient Greece and Rome in American Intellectual Life, 1780–1910.* Baltimore: Johns Hopkins University Press, 2002.

Winthrop, Robert C. "Memoir of the Hon. Nathan Appleton." *Proceedings of the Massachusetts Historical Society, 1860–1862.* Boston: Massachusetts Historical Society, 1862.

Wood, Joseph S. *The New England Village.* Baltimore: Johns Hopkins University Press, 1997.

Woodward, E. L. *The Age of Reform, 1815–1870*. Oxford, UK: At the Clarendon Press, 1938.

Wright, Conrad, ed. *American Unitarianism, 1805–1865*. Boston: Massachusetts Historical Society and Northeastern University Press, 1989.

Wright, Conrad Edick, and Katheryn P. Viens, eds. *Entrepreneurs: The Boston Business Community, 1700–1850*. Boston: Massachusetts Historical Society, 1997.

Zbory, Ronald S., and Mary Saracino Zbory. " 'Have You Read . . . ?' Real Readers and Their Responses in Antebellum Boston and Its Region." *Representations* (1997), 139–70.

Zimmerman, Michael. "War and Peace: Longfellow's 'The Occultation of Orion.'" *American Literature* 38:1 (1967), 540–46.

⚓ ACKNOWLEDGMENTS ⚓

One of the pleasures of writing about Longfellow has been the frequency with which friends and strangers alike have offered evidence of his survival in American culture, whether a fond memory of having to memorize "The Wreck of the Hesperus" in eighth grade or the mention of a Lake Minnehaha in their home town. Sharing a cab to the airport in Indianapolis not long ago, to take only one example, I learned from my fellow passenger Carol Bosserman that the Cross of Snow in Longfellow's great sonnet still exists: on Colorado's Holy Cross Mountain. I cannot begin to express my thanks to all these contributors to this project.

But the role played by several friends, colleagues, and librarians has been so central to the task, I am happy to have this opportunity to salute them. They form a kind of virtual Dante Club, meeting in the pages of this book—if only I could offer them the oysters, the game pie, the Chambertin afterward!

First, Deanne Urmy, my original editor at Beacon and a gallant champion of this book, and her successor, Amy Caldwell, a paragon of patience, insight, and thoughtful enthusiasm. They brought to our meetings over six years the intellectual zest of the ideal tutorial (we took turns as tutor and pupil). Anyone who thinks modern American publishing is a grim, soulless, mechanical business has not dealt with Beacon Press, at the corner of Mount Vernon and the aptly named Joy Street in Boston. My thanks to publisher Helene Atwan for bringing such a staff together.

For help during the very earliest, preconscious stages of this book, I am grateful to Malcolm David Eckel and Mark W. Cutler, who each in his own way turned me into a New Englander. This transformation was enhanced by the hospitality and friendship of the late Donald Colton Esty Jr., at whose last party on Greening Island, Maine, in 1992 I met Frances Appleton Wetherell, Longfellow's great-granddaughter through the Thorp line. She and Brad Wetherell have become both valued friends and the tutelary genii of this project.

The book would not have been possible without the generous support of loyal friends who made the research trips possible. I deeply thank David Ober (who introduced me to Nova Scotia), Waltrud Lampé, John A. Herring, and my late uncle Charles H. Calhoun, of Baton Rouge, Louisiana, who funded one year of the archival research. A second year was made possible by the National Endowment for the Humanities, by way of a Research Fellowship in 2000 in their admirable category of "independent scholar."

Support both practical and inspirational also came from my colleagues at the Maine Humanities Council, especially its legendary director Dorothy Schwartz. At the Council both Erik Jorgensen and Victoria Bonebakker (the first person to urge this project on) have contributed more than they realize.

Some of my happiest moments of the past six years have been spent in the rare books and manuscripts departments of several great libraries. The Platonic ideal of such places is the Houghton Library at Harvard, whose staff (especially Susan Halpern and Tom Ford) were invariably welcoming, helpful, and dauntingly efficient. (And at how many other libraries in the world will you be offered coffee and cake as a pick-me-up every Friday morning?) Closer to home, the Maine Historical Society has played a central role in my work, both as custodian of the Longfellow-Wadsworth House and as sponsor of the annual Longfellow Forum, held in Portland each September. My warm thanks to its director, Richard D'Abate; its librarian, Nicholas Noyes; its registrar, Holly Hurd-Forsythe; and the entire staff. And, if there is any institution for which I feel unqualified love, it is the Hawthorne-Longfellow Library at Bowdoin College. Such education as I have, I got there. My deepest thanks to librarian Sherrie Bergman, special collections librarian Richard H. F. Lindemann and his staff, Patricia Mishrall and Phyllis McQuaide in circulation, and most especially associate director Judith Montgomery.

I am also grateful to the Boston Athenaeum (where early chapters of this book were written), especially James Feeney in circulation, the Bostonian Society, the Society for the Preservation of New England Antiquities, the Massachusetts Historical Society, the Maine State Library, the Bodleian Library and Oxford University Archives, the Pejepscot Historical Society (Brunswick, Maine), the Bowdoin College Museum of Art, Greater Portland Landmarks, the Portland Museum of Art, the Portland Public Library, the libraries of the University of Maine and the University of Southern Maine, and the Countway Medical Library of the Harvard Medical School.

Warren Davis of the National Trust, Great Britain, was, as always, hospitable and eager to help, and I am especially grateful to John Whitton for getting me into the Carlyle House out of season.

The Longfellow National Historic Site—the Craigie House—in Cambridge, Massachusetts, is proving perhaps the most effective agency of all in keeping Longfellow's name before the public. It has been my privilege not only to use its archives (and wander its rooms) but to become friends with its enthusiastic and scholarly staff, including site manager James Shea, archivist Anita Israel, director of visitor services Nancy Jones, and senior guide Paul Blanchard.

My understanding of Longfellow's region (and his role in creating it) grows out of my collaboration in teacher professional development programs with the scholars of the American and New England Studies Program at the University of Southern Maine. I am grateful to Joseph Conforti, who introduced me to the concept of regional studies, and his colleagues Donna Cassidy, Kent Ryden, and Ardis Cameron. Portland is also blessed in having a cluster of superb local historians ("local" in the sense of their topographical focus, not in the range of their expertise): I have in mind Joyce Butler (the first to explore the Wadsworth and Longfellow families), Laura F. Sprague (consultant for the recent Wadsworth-Longfellow House restoration), William David Barry, and State Representative Herbert Adams.

Among academic specialists on Longfellow's work, I don't think there is anyone the poet-professor would have more enjoyed meeting than my friend Christoph Irmscher, now at the University of Maryland, Baltimore County. And since Longfellow loved books as physical objects as well, let me hasten to include in this circle the bibliophile Victor Gulotta, who kindly let me explore his collection before its recent transferal to the Houghton Library.

A number of other friends offered much appreciated support throughout the project, notably Sarah and Neil Gallagher, Jay Selberg, Stephen Hall, Ruth Peck, Linda Docherty, John Woodhead (who made it possible for me to live on Casco Bay, not far from the site of Longfellow's Verandah Hotel), Donna Gulotta, Gordon and Molly Dean, and my friends on the annual "Leaves and Literature" tours. The ever-inquisitive members of the Longfellow Seminar, an NEH-funded teacher institute of the Maine Humanities Council, deserve special recognition, too.

And, finally, my thanks to Michael, without whom none of this would have happened.